MUSEUM PIECE

A recent portrait of the author

MUSEUM PIECE

or the Education of an Iconographer

JAMES LAVER

ANDRE DEUTSCH

FIRST PUBLISHED 1963 BY
ANDRE DEUTSCH LIMITED
105 GREAT RUSSELL STREET
LONDON WC1
COPYRIGHT © 1963 BY JAMES LAVER
ALL RIGHTS RESERVED
PRINTED IN GREAT BRITAIN BY
EBENEZER BAYLIS AND SON LTD
WORCESTER AND LONDON

IN GRATEFUL MEMORY
OF
L. D. H.

To the true philosopher there
are no trivialities

FOURIER

CONTENTS

1	My Grandmother's House	*page* 11
2	Growing Up	30
3	Early 'Twenties	57
4	Victoria and Albert	86
5	Coast of Bohemia	112
6	In the Wings	131
7	Occupations: Various	153
8	*Nunc te, Bacche, canam*	164
9	Towards the Brink	179
10	Wandering Voice	198
11	Familiar Spirits	216
12	Taste and Fashion	234
	Index	252

ILLUSTRATIONS

A recent portrait of the author   Frontispiece

An early portrait of the author's maternal grandmother,
   Lucy Wilkinson (1858)   *facing page* 32

A portrait of the author as a young man (1918)   33

Tea with George Bernard Shaw at the Malvern Festival   48

Gertrude Lawrence
Anna May Wong
   (Photograph by Walter Frederick Seely, Los Angeles)   49

The author with Douglas Fairbanks Jr and Dolores del Rio
   (Photograph by Howard Coster, FRSA)   96

Veronica Turleigh
   (Photograph by Mostyn Lewis)   97

Pamela Brown and James Mason in *The Heart Was Not
   Burned*
   (Photograph by Angus McBean)   112

Authors versus Actresses – Mr Priestley's XI
   (Photography by London News Agency Photos Ltd)   113

Early days in television. The author with J. G. Leinks,
   the furrier. Alexandra Palace, 1939
   (Photograph by BBC)   160

Veronica Turleigh as the Goddess Hera in *The Rape of
   the Belt*
   (Photograph by Houston Rogers)   161

Veronica Turleigh as the Mother Superior in *Teresa
   of Avila*
   (Photograph by Anthony Buckley)   176

The author with Madame Schiaparelli   177
   (By courtesy of the *Sunday Times*)

CHAPTER 1

My Grandmother's House

When my mother died I was four years old and my sister was seven. My mother was ill for some months before the end and during such a period of domestic crisis two small children were terribly in the way in a small house. We were therefore transferred to the house of my paternal grandmother and stayed there for some years.

It was a much larger house than ours, old-fashioned, with a tall stucco front and iron balconies protruding from the first-floor windows. A small patch of lawn lay to the front with a hedge and railings to shield it from the street; and, at the back, french windows opened on to a garden with an ivied wall, a border of London Pride and a bare, untended rockery. Revisiting it after many years, I was astonished by its smallness. In my childish eyes it was as vast as a wilderness and as haunted as a forest.

The most striking feature about the house, and the one which I remember best, was a spiral staircase beginning in a dark flagged passage between the two cellar kitchens and climbing steeply, the full toll of its fifty stairs, to a top-landing between bathroom and box-room. Higher still was an oval skylight, very large when you were near it, but, from the bottom of the well, a tiny window divided, superfluously, into tinier panes.

The house formed part of a terrace in a street in the south end of Liverpool, called The Elms. It was not entirely a misnomer, for a few mighty trees still remained. The district was known as The Dingle and had once, no doubt, been a pleasantly wooded fold in the hill which sloped gently to the Mersey. But now The Dingle was a tram terminus. Just round the corner was the Ancient Chapel of Toxteth, which had existed as a place of worship since the seventeenth century. It had originally been a stronghold of the Independents but was now Unitarian. It was therefore regarded by my family with a certain distaste. It was outside this chapel that Matthew Arnold, on his way to visit his friends the Croppers (whose large house has long been a home for incurables), fell down and died of a heart attack. This tragic event took place in 1888.

It is an astonishing thing that, with the exception of a few proud-pedigreed families, few people know anything at all of their forbears beyond four or five generations back. How did one come to be born in Liverpool at all? What brought one's ancestors there in the first place? For something must have brought them. Liverpool was quite a small town in the eighteenth century; it could never have attained its present size without a huge influx of immigrants – from Ireland, Wales, and from other parts of England.

Like so many others, my own forbears arrived by sea. (I am not claiming that they came in with the Norse pirates who sailed up the Mersey and careened their long ships in the creek which is now called Water Street and who were so pleased with the place that they gave it its name – the Safe Harbour Pool they called it, finally corrupted to Liverpool.) Curiously enough, my own name seems to mean something similar, but it certainly did not originate in Liverpool; nor in Ireland, as is often assumed. Lavery, Laverty are Irish; Laver is an Essex name.

During the Second World War, anxious to get my children into the country, I answered a house-agent's advertisement and in due course found myself approaching for the first time what a more poetical age might have called the cradle of my race. 'The Moated Farm, Little Laver': those were the enticing words which had drawn me to this unfrequented part of Essex, had set me down at Harlow and had brought me up out of the valley to the higher, barer land. The country had few superficial attractions. It had none of the cosiness of Kent, nor the sweetness of Surrey, nor the broad, rolling sweep of Sussex. It was just a little bleak and uninviting. It was not here that I would have chosen to pitch my tent.

In fact, nothing but the name lured me on and that name I saw not so much as a place on a map as at the head of a sheet of writing paper: 'The Moated Farm, Little Laver'. Even for that I would have preferred the more euphonious name of the neighbouring village, Magdalen Laver, or the dignity of High Laver, for all these places lie within a few miles of one another, surrounded by the Rodings, just south of Matching Green. But when I came to them they were all equally disappointing, if something can be disappointing which can hardly be said to exist. All the Lavers together would hardly add up to one small village; and if the name Laver be really derived from them, I could understand why there are so few of us in the world. All I can suppose is that the Lavers started from here and spread thence to the neighbouring towns, especially to Colchester, which is the only place in England in which Laver is a comparatively common name. I like to think that the only other Laver in the British Museum Catalogue lived in Colchester and wrote a little book about oysters. Certainly the mere thought of oysters provokes in me a state of imaginative gourmandise which may be hereditary.

A whole succession of men called Laver were Royal Foresters, first at Epping and, later, at Windsor. Some of them spread further afield. The first solid fact is that my great-great-grandfather was a farmer at Creech, in Somerset. He seems to have been of sound yeoman stock (he was certainly not a gentleman-farmer), very English, and English perhaps most of all in this, that the younger sons showed a strong tendency to forsake the soil for the sea. My great-grandfather, Henry Laver, was a sailor, Master Mariner and the captain of a series of small coastal vessels.

He must, one thinks, since his family lived in Somerset, have started from Bristol. He ended his career in Liverpool. He was born soon after Trafalgar and his seafaring life extended from the middle eighteen-twenties to the late 'fifties or early 'sixties. During one of his early voyages he put in at a Welsh port, fell

13

in love with a Welsh girl named Anne Thomas and married her. My pen almost refused to write the word girl, for to me my great-grandmother as she appears, in a faded daguerrotype in the family album, is a formidable figure with an ample bust and a severe face framed in corkscrew curls, sitting bolt upright in a heavily upholstered chair.

Henry Laver had a brother who was also a seafaring man, and the two set up in business together in Liverpool, as owners of one small vessel. Unfortunately, George (for such was the brother's name) was a scallywag. While Henry, and Mrs Henry too, went to sea, he stayed in Liverpool to manage their joint affairs. He managed them very badly; so badly that when the good brother and his wife returned from one of their longer voyages they found that Brother George had dissipated their joint possessions in drink and women. Drink and women! I can still see the disgust on my father's face as he told the story. Henry started again, on his own, and George went to sea for another company. He seems to have been competent enough, for he rose to the command of a vessel. He had a tragic end. His ship was found adrift in mid-Atlantic. It was hailed, but there was no reply. The boarding party found only dead men. The entire crew, from the captain downwards, had died of yellow fever, picked up no doubt at New Orleans, the last port of call.

Henry Laver was more fortunate. He had a long and honourable career as a Master Mariner. The following details are taken from G. F. Honey's *Some Notes on the Early History of Britain's Premier Coastal Line*:

'The brig "Pearl", Captain Laver, was acquired in 1845 by Cram Powell & Co., and ran as a regular trader between Canning Dock, Liverpool and Redcliffe Backs, Bristol, until 1860, when she was sold. The firm owned at that period the barque "Eliza Ann", also a brig "Queen of the Avon". Both of these traded foreign.

'Steamers were by now ousting sailing vessels on all regular services, so the firm purchased a new steamer about 1860, and

named her "Athlete". She carried 300 tons of cargo and in-
augurated the fixed and regular sailings of the line, leaving Liverpool every Tuesday and returning from Bristol on Saturdays.
These sailings have been continued with wonderful regularity
from that time to the present. She was commanded by Captain
Laver at the outset of her career, who retained command until
1875, when he retired after 30 years' service in command. During
the whole of this period the vessel was navigated without accident
and owing to this good reputation merchant shippers did not find it
necessary to insure their goods when shipping by this vessel.

It may be interesting to note that during a period of illness,
Captain Laver, anxious to keep his reputation and the fixed
sailings, carried with him a daughter as a Stewardess, princi-
pally to nurse him when at sea; this girl eventually married one
of the ship's engineers. She lived to the ripe age of 90.'

I know nothing of this great-aunt. But Henry Laver retired
from the sea and settled down in a little house near Parliament
Street, Liverpool. His youngest son, Robert, took to the sea
also and was for many years pilot to the Port of Liverpool.
His eldest son, my grandfather, James Laver, had other notions.
He was apprenticed to a printer and some time in the early
'eighties set up for himself as a printer and stationer in South
Castle Street. The firm he founded is still in existence on the
same premises, although it has now passed into other hands.

James Laver was married twice, his second wife being an
Irishwoman, Jane Martin (but she was really of Scottish planter
stock, for she came from Carrickfergus) and their son, Arthur
James Laver, was my father. It is the history, with slight
variations, of almost any Liverpool family.

English, Welsh, Irish-Scottish! But it seems likely that there
was yet another strain in my ancestry. For the Martins of
Carrickfergus are supposed to have been French Protestant
refugees driven from their home by the *dragonnards* of Madame
de Maintenon, after the Revocation of the Edict of Nantes.
They settled in Ulster and helped to found the linen industry. I

would like to think so, anyway; for I have always been incurably Francophile. If what Arthur Koestler calls French 'flu is really a disease, I have suffered from it for the greater part of my life.

My father married, in 1895, Florence Mary Barker, whose family lived in Bootle, and they set up home in the south end of Liverpool, not far from The Elms. They had three children, my sister, myself, and a still-born baby boy. My mother died shortly after his birth. I search my mind in vain for any memory of the house in which we lived. Such memories as ever existed have been overlaid by the more vivid recollections of my grandmother's house. Here there lived, besides us two children, my grandmother, her unmarried sister, and a protective male who had no real existence, but whose dusty bowler hat hung permanently on the branched hat-stand in the hall for the terrifying of possible burglars. In the hall also hung two faded brown lithographs of 'The Emigrants' Departure' and 'The Emigrants' Return'; and on the first-floor landing an oleograph of Nelson being protected from the too enthusiastic crowd. The back bedroom where we slept had a picture of swans and reeds painted over mirror-glass, and on the chimney-piece a large wooden clock with a tick as loud and terrifying as the strokes of Fate.

The front parlour was never used, except by my grandmother when she beat upon the window in order to scare small boys from playing immediately outside our railings. She lived in terror that they might break the expensive plate-glass with balls or stones. The furniture had a stiff and formal look, due in part to its antique design and in part to the dust-covers which protected the loose-covers, which in turn protected the upholstery of the chairs. Scattered about were several small footstools, oddly known as 'buffets', covered with blue and white glass beads. There was a good deal of china about, including one magnificent Staffordshire jug. We children were not encouraged to play in the front parlour, or even to enter it.

The back parlour was the living-room and here my grandmother who, like so many old ladies of her generation, bore a marked resemblance to Queen Victoria in face and figure, sat in state on a high rocking-chair fastened by springs to an immovable base. She suffered from her heart and from her legs and, although neither of these ailments prevented her from sweeping through the house like a tornado armed with a duster – if one can admit so incongruous an image – she spent a considerable portion of her time in her accustomed seat. She was much addicted to the use of homoeopathic medicines and kept an array of microscopic bottles of pillules always at her right hand. *Nux vomica* and *Carbo veg.* are two names that have lodged in my memory. Someday, when the social anthropologists really get down to business they will explain why Homoeopathy, Nonconformity, Free Trade and Teetotalism always went together.

There was also a mahogany box containing an electrical machine. By grasping a small brass cylinder in either hand and getting someone else to turn a handle, a slight electric current could be sent through the body. This was supposed to be good for rheumatism. I delighted to turn the handle and sometimes, out of mischief, I would step up the current by moving a little lever in order to see my grandmother jump. In spite of the severity of her manner, she was very indulgent to this and other minor misdemeanours.

The medicine bottles, the electrical machine, a large Bible and, oddly enough, an illustrated edition of *The Ingoldsby Legends*, all rested on the corner of a huge dining-room table (it was never used for meals) covered with a thick chenille cloth edged with ball-fringe. There was a great deal of ball-fringe about the house, or so it seems to me in retrospect. It was attached to the draperies of windows and chimney-piece (for chimney-pieces were always draped) and even to the looped curtain which hung over the door to exclude draughts.

Most people when they are grown up realize that they passed their childhood in an interior décor thirty years behind their mature taste. Owing to my mother's death, my décor of childhood was *sixty* years out of date. Nothing much had been changed since my grandmother's marriage in the middle 'sixties. The ball-fringe, the marble clock under a glass shade, wax fruit under another, the steel engravings on the wall: if all this Victoriana had not been sold for a song on my grandmother's death it would now realize substantial prices in the antique shops of modern Chelsea.

We children played with our toys at the great mahogany table or told one another stories in the low window seat looking out on the garden, although the view was somewhat obscured by the imitation stained glass pasted on to the lower panes. My sister, three years older, was already a great reader, but I spent most of my time with a pair of scissors cutting out figures from the illustrated papers. These figures represented, if my memory serves me, either Russian or Japanese soldiers, for that was the particular war then in progress; and I cut out so many of them that I had a permanent callosity on my second finger.

My great-aunt dwelt entirely in the basement, never emerging except to climb to her top-storey bedroom and that, of course, was long after we had been put to bed. On Sunday evenings, however, she put on a black cape embroidered with sequins and a little bonnet with a feather and went to church, for she was a staunch churchwoman of the Evangelical school. The rest of the family was Noncomformist, and my great-aunt's worship was always something of a mystery to our infant minds. I don't think I ever saw the inside of a 'church', as opposed to a 'chapel' until I had reached my teens.

She was very careful of her complexion, which was indeed remarkable for a woman of her age, and carried a sunshade which she would immediately put up if there was any chance of the sun's direct rays falling upon her face. She would even do this in a tram – there were no buses in Liverpool in those days – to the astonishment, and, no doubt, inconvenience of the other passengers. Of course, she never rode in a tram on a Sunday, and indeed our whole family eschewed the use of any wheeled thing on the Sabbath. The sunshade, rolled, was also used to shake at any rare passing motorist. My great-aunt strongly disapproved of motors – 'Nasty, stinking things' – and would stand on the pavement and admonish their owners as they puffed and chugged on their way.

If my grandmother was the Government in the house, my great-aunt was the Opposition. My grandmother was all aggressive energy, my great-aunt all passive resistance, and it was she who nearly always won. Disputes on questions of domestic management were conducted by shouts from parlour to kitchen and back again. Some noise, perhaps a crash of crockery, would be heard from the basement:

'Sarah, what are you trying to do?'

'I am not trying to do anything, Jane. I'm doing it.' When the interchange was over my grandmother would thump herself with her clenched fist to dissipate the wind which had gathered about her heart. We children were always half awed and half delighted by this performance and, with the unconscious cruelty of youth, would beg her to do it again.

I dreaded bedtime, for it meant climbing fearfully up the haunted stairs and passing through the horrible dark landing between the bedrooms. Even Nelson looked sinister after night-fall and the harmless aspidistra on the what-not was a nameless horror. Fortunately, I slept with my sister and, in her comforting company, even the Clock of Destiny gave a tolerable tick. I was entirely under her influence and my imaginative life therefore had a feminine bias which lasted until I went to school. In bed, before we went to sleep, we would play at being ladies, and sometimes, for a treat, we allowed ourselves to wear evening dress. This meant undoing the necks of our night-dresses and pushing them down over our shoulders – an idea borrowed, no doubt, from some chance picture in an illustrated magazine of the 'sixties. Real evening dress we had, of course, never seen.

Sometimes my sister would recite, in a low voice, the opening lines of *Marmion* or Longfellow's *The Children's Hour*, and these two poems have had a magical significance for me ever since. Even now I can raise a delicious shudder at the lines:

> Do you think, O blue-eyed *banditti*,
> Because you can scale the wall,
> Such an old moustache as I am
> Is not a match for you all?

Moustache and *banditti*! Potent and incomprehensible words! What wonder has been lost to me since you slipped into your proper perspective!

In the morning it was understood that my sister, whose name was Lucy, should help me to dress, and this she did, willingly enough, until my fifth birthday. Then she announced, with irritating calm, that she would do so no longer, and I was left with the apparently insoluble problem of inserting two small legs into one pair of knickerbockers. At last I had an inspiration and, placing the garment flat on the floor, lay down beside it and slowly wriggled myself into it. It was the end of my infancy.

At the local Church School I soon learned to read. The Victorian household often contained a surprising number of books and ours was no exception. Pride of place, in the great glass-fronted mahogany bookcase, was taken by the ten fat volumes of Dr Adam Clarke's *Commentary*. This, apart from the Bible itself, was my great-aunt's only reading, and very good reading it was, as I discovered at an early age. Adam Clarke was Methodism's most learned man, and his work, for the early nineteenth century anyway, was a monument of scholarship. It is true that many of his co-religionists regarded his views as dangerously sceptical, even tinged with heresy. Had he not suggested, albeit in a footnote, that Satan appeared to Eve in the Garden not in the shape of a serpent but in the form of an ape? A perilous flirting with a Darwinism which as yet had not been heard of. But he sprinkled his pages with Greek and Hebrew, showed diagrams of such mysteries as the Dial of Ahaz, and when he found a parallel to some Biblical story in one of the Hindu epics, printed the page in full. O admirable Adam! O learned Clarke! Not for you the pious chit-chat of ordinary commentators, the driving home of 'lessons', the elaboration of points of Protestant doctrine. The whole world of scholarship was your parish, and one infant mind at least came to you hungry and was not sent away unsatisfied.

What else was to be found on the bookshelves? There was Gibbon in a frightening number of volumes, there was Lloyd's *Encyclopaedic Dictionary*, there was Hooker's *Ecclesiastical Polity*. But the 'complicated fugue of Hooker', as Ruskin calls it, was beyond me, and I never did more than dip. There *had* been, I was informed, *Tom Jones* and *Tristram Shandy*, but my grandmother, becoming aware of the nature of their contents, had consigned them to the flames. There were several early numbers of *The Leisure Hour* and *The Sunday at Home*. The latter was a boon. It was so obviously a Sunday book that there could be no question about it. But was *The Leisure Hour* a 'Sunday book' also? The decision, to my infinite relief, was finally given in its favour. *The Skipper's Wooing*, which had unaccountably found a place in this austere congregation, was less fortunate. Six days shalt thou enjoy the nautical humour of W. W. Jacobs and the sprightly drawings of Will Owen.

As children will, I had built up a mental picture of these two heroes: bluff sailors, large and beefy. Later I came to know them both at the Omar Khayyám Club and found that the reality was very different. For Jacobs was a little retired-jockey of a man and Owen, although stouter, had nothing of the sailor about him. They were amused when I told them that their combined efforts had not succeeded in producing a book which was fit to be read on Sunday.

The Secret History of the Oxford Movement, that sinister story of a Catholic plot, fascinated me. I did not then know that there was another side to the picture, for it was not until Oxford days that I came across the *Apologia* and submitted to the incantation of Newman's prose. There were bound copies of old magazines like *Great Thoughts*, which combined high moral tone with a certain amount of literary information. It was in these pages that I first learned that there were such people as Goethe and Shelley. There was also an 'unclaimed binding job' consisting of half a dozen volumes of *The Review of Reviews*. I knew all about the Dreyfus Case at a very early age. And I retain a vivid picture of an extremely youthful H. G. Wells who had, I gathered, disgraced himself by publishing a book called *The Island of Dr Moreau*. But the greatest treasure to me in the whole library was a huge volume, so heavy that I was unable to lift it on to the table and had to look at it on the floor. This was *Don Quixote* illustrated by Gustave Doré. Later, when I came to read *Sinister Street*, I found that Compton Mackenzie, or his hero, had had this volume also in childhood. Would that all children could have it, for it is a priceless possession, a leading of the mind among strange peoples, far landscapes and fantastic skies. I know now of course exactly how these pictures were produced. Doré made a drawing, in pen and wash, the lights touched in afterwards with Chinese white, and then Pisan or another of the astonishing craftsmen who made cheap illustration possible, translated it into terms of wood-engraving, rendering tone by a system of parallel lines, each a miniature mountain ridge, and each high-light a crater in the boxwood block. Knowing nothing of all this as a child, the lines were a perpetual mystery to me. I tried to reproduce them and failed miserably. Perhaps it all added to the magic, for magic it was. Those rocks, those streams, those winding leafy dells, those sinister forests, those castles perched on cliffs, those cloud-heaped skies and infinite sierras composed for me a whole region of the imagination, a glimpsed but undiscovered country, a beckoning land. 'Onward, to the Kingdom of Micomicon.'

I did not, of course, spend all my time indoors, although I think I would willingly have done so if I had had an unlimited supply of books to read and look at. I have been an incurable book-worm all my life and the mere smell of books, the curious aroma of decayed leather, and of 'loaded' paper, can still excite me strangely.

We were not allowed to play in the street, but there were two parks not far away and, for a treat, we were sometimes taken on day-long expeditions 'across the water'. In Liverpool 'across the water' meant, and probably still means, the Cheshire side of the Mersey. One crossed the river by ferry-boat to New Brighton, which was practically the seaside and had a Tower like the one at Blackpool, or to New Ferry or Rock Ferry, or, higher up the estuary, at the beginning of the Manchester Ship Canal, to Eastham.

The fare was trifling or else we wouldn't have gone, for my grandmother was an economist of the old school. In her younger days she had been known to walk to the other end of Liverpool in order to buy two nutmegs for three-ha'pence instead of the penny each demanded by the local grocer. In my grandmother the Scottish, or Northern Irish, strain was very strong. Apart from the fare the total cost of an expedition to Eastham was sixpence. This was paid for hot water and the use of a room. We took our own bread and butter and our own tea and sugar. I do not think we ever bought ice-cream or lollipops and we were certainly not encouraged to waste our pennies on the automatic machines which lined the landing stage.

Occasionally we took the ferry-boat to Birkenhead in order to have tea with Mrs Carey, who lived at a farm on the slope of Bidston Hill in what was then open country. The farmhouse was an old grey-stone building, with a pair of quite enormous stone balls flanking its gate, and a flagged kitchen the floor of which was decorated with a pattern of green lines still produced in the traditional manner by scraping dock-leaves against the newly washed stones. The remarkable thing about Mrs Carey was that she was, or had been, a Mormon, had indeed, as a little girl, travelled across the great American plains in a covered waggon and been attacked by Indians on the long road to the West; until at last they had come to a great salt lake and decided to stop there and found a city.

I knew nothing of Mormons except that they were half a joke and half a horror, but the Indians were another story and I regarded the heroine of so many adventures with suitable awe. But how recent a thing is history, especially American history! I think Mrs Carey helped me to realize that *history is happening now*. Children are often supposed to regard fairy tales as reality.

But they also regard reality as a fairy tale and the stories in history books as belonging to some elf-land in which they only half believe. They are rather like the old lady in the story who, when told that Jericho and Jerusalem were in Palestine, exclaimed in surprise: 'In Palestine! I thought they were in the Bible.' So Julius Caesar and Caractacus and Henry VIII and Napoleon share a country of the mind with Jack-the-Giant-Killer and Little Bo-Peep.

After my grandfather's death in the early years of the century, the business in South Castle Street was run by my father and his younger brother. As a child I was sometimes taken to see the works in College Lane and was amazed at the dexterity of the type-setters – in those days everything was done by hand – and by the appalling noise and vibration of the gas-engine which made the wheels go round. The firm printed most of the Customs forms and other documents for the Port of Liverpool, and the business was, in general, thriving enough.

Yet my father was a strange businessman in many ways. Like the Quakers, he had convinced himself that while God approved of a profit of five per cent, He did not approve of anything larger: and when his assistant proudly showed him on one occasion that a certain transaction had brought in a profit of ten per cent my father was much perturbed. He finally solved the problem by presenting the assistant with the difference and telling him not to do it again.

He was a man of great austerity of life, and perhaps the most completely unselfish person I have ever known. He neither drank nor smoked. For his personal expenses he allowed himself ten shillings a week. Whenever he attended a religious service he put half-a-crown on the plate, and as he attended such services three times every Sunday, he was left with one half-crown for himself.

He liked to have a rule for everything. Once, when some domestic upheaval prevented him for a month from having his midday meal at home, he went to a neighbouring restaurant and ordered that the same fare should be served to him every day: roast lamb, boiled potatoes, and rice pudding.

He took an annual fortnight's holiday and, if he had had his way, would have gone to the same place and the same lodging every year. The place, for the first six years of my existence, was Blackpool. I loved it, of course, chiefly because of the unlimited expanse of sand. I remember very little else, except that the boarding house where we stayed had a conservatory, that is, a narrow passage glazed on one side, and with drooping plants on shelves. I have one mental picture, vivid as a snapshot, of my mother, in a blouse and skirt and with a gent's boater perched forward over her forehead, walking along the promenade.

I was not yet seven when my father married again. The care of two young children was too much for him, and too much for my grandmother, and he wanted an establishment of his own. Unfortunately, he chose to live next-door-but-one to my grandmother's house, and this was certainly a mistake. For my stepmother resented the old lady's domineering ways and my father was torn between two loyalties. My stepmother was a good woman who did more than her duty by us. She loved me deeply and I owed her a great deal. But she was considerably older than my father, already too old to have children of her own, and the cares of the household lay heavy upon her. She suffered from a perpetual sick-headache; and even today I close a door with unnatural carefulness.

Between my grandmother's house and ours was the house of 'the Minister' or, as my father insisted on calling him, 'the Itinerant'. In Wesley's day this had meant the wandering preacher, but it now signified a regular minister who moved to another town every five years or so. A popular minister might be asked to stay for ten years.

There were in our street several ministers of various denominations. Higher up was the Anglican parson, but he was as Evangelical as his Nonconformist confrère, and like him wore a turned-down collar and a white tie. He would have regarded the clerical collar as Popish or, at least, Puseyite. Lower down the street was the Congregational minister, the Rev. Mark Simon, one of four brothers named, respectively, Matthew, Mark,

Luke and John. John was the father of Sir John, later Lord Simon.

We very rarely had visitors, but, occasionally, for Sunday midday dinner we entertained 'the Supply'. This was the minister or layman who had preached at the morning service when the regular minister was on holiday or preaching elsewhere. If I could remember the text I was given a penny, which was immediately put into the 'missionary box'. There was no question of my keeping it for myself.

The sermons preached by these visitors ranged from the old-fashioned blood-and-thunder to a dangerous trifling (on the part of some of the younger men) with R. J. Campbell's *New Theology*. Perhaps the name of R. J. Campbell evokes no response in the modern mind, but in the first decade of the century he was a very controversial figure in Nonconformist circles. He was the minister of the City Temple in London and attracted large congregations. His book *The New Theology* was a Modernist manifesto. I have just re-read it and find it sensible enough; but as he denied the Virgin Birth, most of the miracles, and the literal inspiration of the Bible, and was disgusted by hymns extolling 'the fountain filled with blood, drawn from Emanuel's veins', he was regarded by the old school of Nonconformists as little better than an atheist.

I was something of a connoisseur of preaching in those days. Sometimes we were taken to the Central Hall in Liverpool to hear famous preachers like Gipsy Smith and Campbell Morgan, even if they did not belong to our own denomination. Yet my father did not really approve of men so much (at that time) in the public eye. They smacked too much of 'the World'. When the Nonconformist journals boasted of 'Methodist Mayors' and the like he was frankly disgusted. ' "Come out from among them, and be ye separate," saith the Lord,' was his favourite text. Until the First World War we never even took in a daily paper, on the ground that the affairs of the world were no concern of Christian people.

My father sometimes preached himself and his behaviour in

the pulpit was marked by the innocent eccentricity of so many of his actions. He did not attempt to drive home any moral lessons or expound points of doctrine. He gave his audience *facts*, fragments of Biblical learning culled, no doubt, from Adam Clarke's *Commentary*. If any member of the congregation turned round to look at the clock (it was fixed in the middle of the gallery facing the pulpit), he would stop in the middle of a sentence and, with the remark, 'I see I have gone on long enough,' would close the Book. On one occasion, finding that his new set of false teeth impeded his utterance, he said, 'Confound these teeth!', took them out, laid them on the velvet cushion of the pulpit and continued his discourse. Once, while praying for those in peril on the sea, he broke down and wept. The news had just been received of the sinking of the *Titanic*.

Of course we had Family Prayers. Every evening as the clock struck ten my father would reach for the Bible, and I am certainly grateful to him for a knowledge of the Scriptures which is becoming increasingly rare in the modern world. Quite recently, a parson friend of mine, after helping himself to another glass of his own excellent port, passed the decanter to me saying, 'Take a little wine for thy stomach's sake.'

'You don't know where that comes from,' he added, and was quite astonished when I answered, 'Of course I do. It comes from the First Epistle to Timothy.'

My father did not read selected passages from the Bible. He worked his way steadily, a chapter a night, through the whole book. Parts of the Old Testament, as may well be imagined, were pretty heavy going. But the proceedings were occasionally enlivened by an unexpected incident. My father was peacefully traversing yet another stage of his journey through Exodus when he came to the strange business of the circumcision of the son of Moses. Zipporah, having performed the act, says to Moses, 'Surely a bloody husband art thou to me'. My father choked on the last word and, as we looked at him in astonishment, he suddenly began to laugh. And he laughed and laughed until the tears ran down his cheeks.

27

Family prayers that night had to be abandoned. We children were hustled off to bed.

I suppose that we were behind the times even then. Pious, Puritan households such as that in which I spent my childhood were plentiful enough in the nineteenth century. They have been described for all time by Edmund Gosse and Logan Pearsall Smith; but by 1900 they must already have been growing rarer. Now they seem to have vanished altogether. That they were limited in their outlook and claustrophobic in their effect is plain enough. Yet they had a certain strange poetry of their own. When in later life, I read André Gide's *La Porte Etroite*, it had a feel, an atmosphere that I understood quite well. But by then I had come to regard Puritanism as a pathological state of mind, as some kind of alibi. I felt no temptation to return to it.

My first rebellion was, I think, an aesthetic one. Long before I had begun to have 'doubts', I was conscious of the quite extraordinary ugliness of our particular place of worship. It had been built about 1880 in strata of differently coloured bricks: and the interior was painted in two shades of chocolate – milk and bitter – with a frieze of what looked like flat-irons. The upright box-pews were of varnished pitch-pine and in me they evoke nothing of the Betjeman nostalgia. Naked butterfly gas-jets flared in round glass globes. When in winter one entered the chapel for the evening service one was almost knocked down by the smell of gas. For the janitor, after the last service, had simply put out the lights by turning off the gas at the main. He was too lazy to turn off the individual taps, so that when he came to light up again he simply turned the gas on at its source and rushed round putting a taper to the fizzing spouts.

The result of this was that fainting was quite a common occurrence. Sooner or later one of the ladies would flop down and be carried out into the vestry. My father's first-aid remedies were simple and drastic. He would pull out a penknife and slit the high-boned collar which was then the mode. Perhaps it is not surprising that some of the victims transferred their worship to another chapel, or even to another sect.

This was not quite so simple a process as might be supposed, owing to the strange social stratification of religious belief in England. Doubts, for example, of the validity of infant baptism never rose higher than the middle of the middle class. Even in Methodism (not yet re-united in one church) there were social differences. The Wesleyans were a cut above the United Methodists. Then came the Baptists, the Plymouth Brethren and the Peculiar People, with the Salvation Army, rather splendidly, bringing up the rear. Congregationalists were, in general, one better than Methodists, and Unitarians better still, with Quakers on about the same level. The Church of England fell outside my purview and I was hardly, as yet, aware of Catholicism. I don't think I ever met a Catholic until I was grown up.

What united all these Nonconformist bodies (with the exception, of course, of the Unitarians) was their Evangelicalism. Alan Pryce-Jones once remarked that almost all English autobiographies were concerned with sensitive boys brought up in Evangelical surroundings, and perhaps this is, for a few more years, inevitable. Most writers are of middle-class origin and, fifty years ago, the middle class in England was incurably Evangelical. No – not incurably, for it has, in fact, been cured.

Perhaps the only class which is ever religious *as a class*, is the middle-middle class. Paganism, touched with ancestor-worship, is the prerogative of aristocracy. Upper middle classes tend to be agnostic; proletarians are heathen. But one of the most startling social facts of our time is that the middle- and lower-middle classes have ceased to be religious, at least in any definite, doctrinal way their ancestors would have recognized.

If Catholicism is a stable liquid which can be kept in an open vessel (a chalice, for instance), Protestantism seems to be an unstable liquid which can only be preserved in the closed chamber of some fanatical sect. Open it to the air and it simply evaporates, leaving behind it an off-white deposit known as Ethics. Such, at least, are the reflections which are forced upon me as I look back on my childhood of more than half a century ago.

CHAPTER 2

Growing Up

In Liverpool on July 20, 1835, Lord Brougham laid the foundation stone of a Mechanics' Institution. The list of gentlemen who had 'subscribed the Munificient Sum of £500 each' included such well-known Liverpool names as Cropper, Roscoe, Leyland, Booth and Rathbone. 'The building,' says a contemporary chronicler, 'is in the Ionic style of architecture, and has an imposing appearance . . . The basement contains the classrooms for the children of mechanics exclusively. The upper portion is occupied by the sons of the more opulent, for the purpose of diffusing education amongst all classes.'

That it was a school at all was something of an afterthought. The original intention had been to provide lectures and evening classes for 'mechanics'. These continued for some years, but by the time I had any acquaintance with the Liverpool Institute, as it is now called, it was a school and nothing but a school. None the less, a hint of its democratic origins still clung about it. Unlike the Liverpool College, it never sought admission to the Headmasters' Conference which would have made it, in the technical sense, a public school. It did not even claim the title of grammar school, but this, of course, was the kind of establishment it most nearly resembled. Its chief difference was in its complete religious toleration, one of the earliest resolutions of the Directors laying it down that 'This institution being supported by various sects, nothing shall be done or said in it to violate the consciences or wound the religious feelings of any of its members'.

It was to this school that I came in 1911, having won a City

Scholarship, which I held for seven years, the formative years of my life. I am – as I should be – extremely grateful. I was fortunate in my epoch. The value of a school depends almost entirely upon the personality of its headmaster. Our Headmaster was Henry Victor Weisse, and that he was a Personality there was never any shadow of doubt. He came from Rugby and while there had had his left hand blown off in some laboratory experiment. All that remained was the thumb and first finger and when he plucked with this claw at his beard small boys have been known to die of fright.

He was of German descent, his father having been a refugee from Germany in '48, and he had a passion for music. He was a personal friend of musicians, among them Fanny Davies, the singer, Donald Tovey, and Adrian Boult, and all of them gave concerts in the school hall. Like many of my contemporaries I attended these, at first, with restless boredom, but gradually they began to make sense, and I certainly owe to H.V.W. the foundations of my musical education.

In spite of his own scientific bent he was a passionate believer in the classics, and saw that they were well taught. He gradually increased the number of Oxford men on his staff, and one of the most remarkable of these was Edward Hickinbotham, who taught English and History. He was a slight, shy, untidy man with greying hair worn *en brosse*. He was a born teacher who had the gift of being able to suggest the right book at the right moment. He opened to me the world of literature, especially the world of poetry.

I had, in my adolescence, a passion for poetry, good, bad and indifferent. I loved Longfellow, was moved by the pious verses of Adelaide Anne Proctor and did not entirely despise Ella Wheeler Wilcox. In 1914, at the moment when the German hordes were sweeping over Belgium, I discovered Omar Khayyám. I have never had the slightest difficulty in learning verse (except, oddly enough, the verse of Yeats, which simply refuses to lodge in the memory) and very soon I had Omar by heart.

To the astonishment of Edward Hickinbotham I had a passion for Pope – he thought this very odd in a schoolboy – and it was Pope who inspired me to write mock-heroic couplets for the school magazine. But my real loves were Byron, Wordsworth and Browning: in that order, chronologically. Had I begun to read Byron later in life I might well have been put off by the rhetoric and the tinsel. Not so at the age of sixteen. I devoured his works, including the plays.

Perhaps it is a mistake to despise the rhetorical element in poetry. It is a way of warming up the engine, like the racing of the propellers before an aeroplane takes off. Many a modern poet seems to despise the 'run'. He insists on being a helicopter, with the result that very often he doesn't rise off the ground at all.

Wordsworth was another matter. My interest in his poetry (and I read it all, including *The Prelude* and *The Excursion*) was stimulated by the discovery of the Lake District, which was one of the most important things that ever happened to me.

As a child of six or seven I was once taken to a farm on the banks of Ullswater, my stepmother's sister being the farmer's wife. In the year of the War we spent a fortnight at Penrith and made a few excursions in the neighbourhood. But the mountains: these were a backcloth, no one ever thought of climbing them.

It was in the autumn of 1915 that there came into my life a man who was, in many ways, to transform it. Anonymity being one of his passions I shall call him L.D.H. He was then in his middle thirties but already had a record of public service behind him. He was cultivated, idealistic, wealthy. He had a passion for mountains and an almost equal passion for infecting others with it. He was a governor of the School and just before Christmas he decided to take a party of schoolboys to Patterdale. I was invited to join the party. We took the train to Penrith on December 23, drove in some kind of horse vehicle to Pooley Bridge and along the whole length of Ullswater under a threatening sky. How unimportant it sounds! How ordinary! But for me it was the glimpse of a new world.

The hotel seemed to me to be incredibly luxurious, but

An early portrait of the author's maternal grandmother,
Lucy Wilkinson (1858)

A portrait of the author as a young man (1918)

L.D.H. had no intention of allowing us to loll about in cushioned ease. Early next morning we set out for Helvellyn. I have climbed many mountains since in Alps, and Pyrenees, and Dolomites, but Helvellyn remains, for me, *the* mountain, for all that it is a mere three thousand feet high.

Not that climbing it in the depths of winter was a picnic. It would have been easy to lose one's foothold on the icy knife-blade of Striding Edge. The wind was bitter and the final scramble on to the summit breathless. The Red Tarn, now black and frozen over, lay menacing below us, and all around, range after range of the bare hills capped with snow.

I sometimes think that the Lake District was designed by God to be exactly the right size. You can set out after breakfast, climb your peak, eat your sandwiches in the shelter of the cairn at the top, descend to a farmhouse for tea and be back in your hotel in time for a steaming bath before dinner. Oh, the luxury of real physical fatigue! 'Strenuous' was L.D.H.'s favourite word. We boys staggered back, worn out and soaked to the skin, feet numb and faces tingling with the cold. I thought it was all wonderful. When I got back to Liverpool I still tried to pretend that the holiday wasn't over. I would close my eyes in my bedroom and think myself back in the Ullswater Hotel. I couldn't understand at first why I was able to do this so vividly: it was because the faint aroma of L.D.H.'s cigar still lingered in my clothes. When, I wondered, would I ever have such a holiday again.

Then, at Easter there came another invitation, this time to spend a few days following Wordworth's tracks: Hawkeshead, Coniston, Grasmere, Wordsworth was for me not only a great poet but the interpreter of a new language. 'The sounding cataract haunted me like a passion.' We stayed at Grasmere and piously visited his grave. We also called on Canon Rawnsley the Grand Old Man of Grasmere, upon whom a (very small) portion of his mantle was supposed to have fallen. And then, having made me responsive to one of Wordsworth's 'Two Voices', L.D.H. resolved that I should listen to the other.

His enthusiasm for mountains was only equalled by his love of the sea, which was perhaps natural enough, as he was a ship-owner. He did not at that time have a yacht of his own, but he hired one based on Bangor, North Wales, and in it we explored the coast of Anglesey and sailed round Puffin Island. A watching destroyer did not altogether approve of our being so far out to sea and signalled to us to return to the Straits. For, of course, there was a war on.

My attitude to the war was, I suppose, typical enough of youths of my age. A schoolboy's life is a busy one; he does not pay much attention to the outside world. But now the outside world was forcing itself on my notice. What a year before had been the sixth form had disappeared into the Army. One by one their names appeared in the casualty lists. Three of the masters had joined the Forces; two of them were already dead. Yet it never occurred to me that I might be in the War too.

I was in the Officers Training Corps like everybody else, and in the summer of 1916 we went into camp at Ilkley in York-shire. I remember causing some surprise by asking to be put on an extra guard duty in order that I might see the dawn. My schoolboy-sergeant thought I was mad, but I was merely curious. I had never seen a dawn before. My solitary vigil was a little frightening and rather melancholy, for one of the boys had been drowned the previous day while bathing. I kept saying to myself: 'People do die.' Even the deaths of so many of the older boys at the Front were somehow less real. I had seen the pitiable little muddy body dragged from the stream.

Then in October there was another climbing holiday, this time at Buttermere and L.D.H. introduced me to the sport of scree-running. We climbed Great Gable, one side of which is a mass of loose stones. As we descended, running and jumping, the whole mountain seemed to move with us. We reached the slopes above Wastwater in an avalanche of rolling pebbles, and in as many minutes as we had taken hours to climb up. All that is needed for scree-running is a fair sense of balance, strong ankles and stout boots. We enjoyed it so much that we did it again; and it was on the top of Great Gable, while we were eating our sandwiches, that L.D.H. suddenly said: 'Jimmie, I'm going to give you a thousand pounds – on condition that you use it to go to Oxford.'

To say that I hero-worshipped L.D.H. is to say the obvious. I thought he was the most wonderful man I had ever met. He was tall with a fine head and a quick smile. He was in excellent condition and in walking and climbing seemed completely tireless. I think he sometimes deliberately pushed me to the end of my tether: I would have died sooner than give up. I copied his mannerisms, his way of jutting out his lower lip; I caught his tricks of speech. I never succeeded in emulating his *phlegme britannique.*

Once when we were leaving an hotel in the Lake District to go to the station, he stood aside in the rather dark hall to let some people come in. When we were outside he said, 'That was my brother.' On another occasion he was driving his car round a hair-pin bend in the mountains. The surface of the road was icy and as we came round the corner the car began to skid. Immediately in front of us was a lorry loaded with girders sticking out at the back. It looked as if we would inevitably be impaled. The men on the lorry were shouting and gesticulating. At the last moment the Rolls gripped the road and, with an apologetic murmur, glided past. There was silence for a moment and then L.D.H. said, 'Foreigners, weren't they?'

Oddly enough I never adopted his opinions: his Fabianism, his instinctive anti-Establishment bias. This for him was not a pose; it was a part of the Great Radical Tradition. But I couldn't help being just a little conscious of the paradox of the rich Socialist: the man who, if he fancied a cruise, chartered a yacht. He would travel third-class on a crowded train, in case I should 'get the wrong ideas'; and then order a magnificent dinner to make up for it. There was a strain in his character which I have since come to recognize as typically Wykehamist.

He had been at Winchester himself, although not at New College, like his brothers: he had preferred to go round the world. There was no question in his mind that New College was where he wanted me to go, and in the spring of 1917 I duly presented myself for the preliminary examinations. The College was then almost entirely occupied by cadets of the Royal Flying Corps. The civilian students numbered six, and of these five were Indians. The odd man was a sandy-haired youth who was making his eighth attempt (he proudly told me) to pass 'Divvers'. I wondered why he didn't give it up and try some less intellectually exacting career. We discovered that we both came from Liverpool. 'But I hate the place,' he said, 'and nothing but the clamour of importunate relatives would induce me to go there.' This was my first acquaintance with the Oxford Manner.

What immediately struck me in Oxford was the beauty of the flowering trees. Certainly in my native Liverpool I had never seen the like. I explored the colleges and smelt for the first time that curious odour of boiled mutton which seems to emanate from all college kitchens. I had a few introductions: to Maurice Jacks (who gave me a copy of *The Shropshire Lad*) and to his father Dr L. P. Jacks, Principal of Manchester College. The latter invited me to tea and there were two other guests who, if I had not been an ignorant provincial, I would have regarded with awe. They were Dr Estlin Carpenter and Baron von Hügel. I did not know that Carpenter was the greatest 'comparative religionist' of his day and Baron von Hügel the famous 'Catholic Modernist', the intimate friend of Father Tyrell and Alfred Loisy but who, unlike them, had remained inside the Church. It is odd to reflect that this man of European reputation with his fine figure and magnificent head, his air of a Major Prophet, should have been the first Catholic I had ever knowingly spoken to in my life.

I suppose it was a sign of von Hügel's continuing 'Modernism' that he was there at all. For Manchester College was a Unitarian foundation: its object was to train candidates for the Unitarian ministry. But as it refused to impose any doctrinal test whatever, its students could be Anglicans, or Buddhists, or anything they liked. I made friends with one of them. He took me to his rooms where, to my astonishment, I saw a crucifix. He is now the well-known Anglican, Canon Demant.

L.D.H. himself came to Oxford on my last day there and carried me off to London, which I was seeing for the first time. He always put up at Brown's Hotel, but I, not understanding its impeccable *comme il faut*, would really have preferred some livelier establishment like the Regent Palace. When I woke next morning the newsboys were crying 'Piper! Piper!' in Albemarle Street. At first I didn't understand what they meant. We made a rapid tour of the city and, at tea-time, called on old, Lady Courtenay in Chelsea. She was, I gathered, L.D.H.'s aunt, and it further transpired that he had another aunt called Mrs Sydney Webb, and a cousin called Stafford Cripps. I was a little shocked by these Left-Wing connections.

While our sleeper to Liverpool was still waiting at Euston there were a few distant explosions. An air-raid had begun. But almost immediately the train started and, as it gathered speed, the bangs grew fainter and fainter. 'O God,' I prayed, 'don't let me miss *all* the air-raids' – a prayer which was to be abundantly answered some twenty-five years later.

Soon after my return I learned that I had been accepted by New College as a Commoner; but, of course, there was no question of going into residence yet. The war still dragged on. By rights I should have been called up when I was eighteen and a half, and that this did not happen was due to a gesture of my headmaster's. It was one of his weaknesses (being such a very large fish in his own pool) to think that he had more influence in high places than in fact he possessed. He wrote to the War Office and suggested that, as I was going to Oxford anyway when the war was over, it would be very suitable if I could be called up to the Officer Cadet Battalion which was actually in Oxford. I can easily imagine what happened. Some exasperated official pinned this letter to my calling-up papers and flung them to the bottom of his tray. By so doing he caused me much heart-burning at the time, but he probably saved my life. For I *ought* to have arrived in France early in 1918, just in time for the great German offensive, when the average 'life' of a second-lieutenant was rather less than a fortnight.

However, in the end, I *was* called up, and round about my nineteenth birthday left school and home and Liverpool for Romford in Essex, where my particular OCB was stationed. Army life had begun, and very strange I found it.

Men in the other three companies of the battalion I never met. Y Company consisted almost entirely of Australian and New Zealand rankers who had already had experience of the toughest fighting of the war. I was one of six schoolboys. The other men were very nice to us; they regarded us with tolerant amusement, and made only occasional efforts to 'bring us up'.

Even of the schoolboys I was probably the least mature in experience of the world. Incredible as it may seem, I had reached the age of eighteen before I knew what are so quaintly called 'the facts of life', and my first impression of my fellow-cadets was that they were all mad. I don't think I was a prig: I was merely an innocent, a child. As far as I could make out the entire company, the entire battalion for that matter, the moment parades were over, set off in search of girls. Not that they had very far to go. Just outside our billet at Gidea Park there was a golf course and once or twice, after nightfall, I went for a walk over it. I had to give this up; the walk was an obstacle race. *La bête à deux dos* was scattered too thickly over the ground. And every morning our doorstep and little garden path were littered with 'rubber goods'.

Some of the schoolboys joined, or pretended to join in the game. My room-mate issued invitations. 'You should come out with me,' he said, 'and see my curly girl. She has a sister who would just suit you.'

I don't think even L.D.H. quite realized how innocent I was. 'What a dip into life you must be having,' he wrote; 'I know you need no advice in making the most of it and, for the rest, avoid prostitutes, keep tight control of drink, and never gamble beyond your means or of those in whose company you are, and all will be well . . .'

Drink! Gambling!! Prostitutes!!! The only drink I had ever tasted was a swig of sweet vermouth L.D.H. himself had given me on top of a mountain; I had never gambled in my life for so much as a penny piece, and as for prostitutes, they were not only beyond my ken but beyond my imagination.

The other thing that astonished me about my fellows was their attitude to religion. But 'attitude' is wrong; they had no attitude, and certainly no religion. They attended Church Parade on Sundays. They had to unless they declared themselves atheists, and then they were given some particularly unpleasant fatigue instead. But when there was any kind of voluntary religious service it was a different story. I once attended Early Communion in the church hut. There were present (out of a thousand men): the officiating clergyman, the 'sanitary corporal' and myself. No doubt the Catholic services were better attended, but I did not see them. I had no right to attend the Anglican service at all. I had never been an Anglican. But like many, I surmise, who have been brought up in the bleak chapels of Nonconformity, I had a hunger for ritual, even such crumbs thereof as could be gathered in an Anglican army hut.

I even enjoyed the secular ritual of the Army. At the risk of disgusting all right-thinking people, I must confess that I rather liked the ceremonial parades, once the first awkwardness was over. I was not tall enough ever to find myself in the right of the line, but I was sometimes on the left, and then it fell to me to give the time for *un*fixing bayonets. The three machine-like paces forward, the thumped foot, the hand raised aloft, the click and rattle of the rifles: I got a lot of fun out of doing this – perhaps of over-doing it just a little.

All pleasure of this kind, however, soon vanished when our nice easy-going Colonel was replaced by a ferocious Scotsman with ginger moustaches, who had probably been sent specially to tighten up discipline. He used to charge about the parade ground on a huge black horse and terrify the life out of everybody.

We had to take it in turns to drill the Company and one

nervous youngster was doing this when suddenly the Colonel galloped towards us. The men were tired and peevish and disinclined to put any intelligence into their work. The temporary commander was weak-voiced and his slight frame did not inspire respect. An order, heard by only half the Company, had resulted in chaos. Terrible moment! The Colonel rode straight up to the trembling cadet and bellowed: 'Do you think you're fit to command men?'

'No, Sir,' quavered the unhappy wretch.

'Very good,' snapped the CO. 'Your papers will be sent to you tomorrow and you will be returned to your unit.' It might have happened to any of us. We all lived in terror of 'RTU', especially the schoolboys, for we had no unit to be returned to. We would be sent to some alien battalion and have to start all over again – as privates.

Still, we survived. We survived the Colonel, and the growing boredom, and the influenza epidemic of the summer of 1918. We even survived the final examination; indeed we schoolboys did rather well at it, having nimbler wits than the seasoned warriors. And the great day came at last when we were posted and put up our pips. I found myself a second-lieutenant in the King's Own Royal (Lancaster) Regiment. 'To Our Trusty and Well-Beloved James Laver, Greeting . . .' It is true that the Commission was stamped in one corner with the word 'Temporary', but who in his senses, I thought, would wish it to be anything else? And suddenly everybody became very nice. The ferocious Colonel beamed; the Sergeant-Major, of whom I had lived in terror for months, called me 'Sir'. The Adjutant made out our leave passes with a smile. 'Where do you want to go?'

I did not say Liverpool. I had had a letter from L.D.H. only two days before. 'My brother,' he wrote, 'has a little shooting box in the Grampians. Can you get away for a few days after your gazette and climb a mountain or two, and perhaps shoot a stag?'

He met me at Boat-of-Garten in the Grampians, about five o'clock in the morning and we walked together through the frosty air and the yellowing woods (for it was now early October), to the shooting box eight miles away. It proved to be quite a large house, or so it seemed to me. It was occupied by L.D.H.'s brother and his family as well as several guests. The ladies were quite indignant when they heard that L.D.H. proposed to start off again immediately after breakfast, but he only laughed and said that the stalker and the gillie with the pony were at the door.

'What about a gun licence and a game licence?' L.D.H. produced them both, made out in my name.

We set off, climbed a mountain, lay in the wet heather and scanned the horizon with telescopes. Even with the telescope I could see nothing, but the stalker said there were 'beasts' on the opposite slope. We climbed down into the valley and up again, but they had got our wind, and vanished. This went on all day, until at last even the stalker decided there was nothing more to be done.

Suddenly, almost beneath us as we lay in the deep hollow of of the Black Corrie, there came a sharp, bellowing roar. The stalker beckoned me forward to the edge of the corrie and I saw, unconscious of our presence, a magnificent stag followed by a large herd of hinds. A moment later the leader crossed our wind, tossed up his head and turned away in the opposite direction. The hinds followed.

The stalker thrust the rifle into my hands.

'Tak' your time,' he whispered, 'they're bound to swing round to the left to avoid the rocks. It's a long shot, but if ye tak' your time—.'

The sights of the Mauser bothered me; they were quite different from those on an army rifle; but I took my time. Up the slope went the herd, and the stag stopped for a moment to let the hinds go through. Then he was straight ahead, in full retreat, presenting only his buttocks and little white tail.

'Chance it,' whispered the stalker. I fired and, to my surprise, the stag stopped and swung round, presenting his broadside. The second shot went wide: I saw it chip a little white splinter off a rock a yard to the right. The third shot, as we afterwards found, struck the stag in the academically correct place, at the base of the neck. He toppled over and, after a convulsive heave, lay still.

This was my first stag – and my last. He was a splendid specimen, a ten-pointer, the best of the season. L.D.H. had the head mounted for me, and it was a white elephant for the greater part of my life. A ten-pointer stag can take up a great deal of room in a small flat. Forty years later I gave it to a young Surrealist friend as a wedding present.

At the time I think what impressed me most was that scarcely had the stalker thrown the entrails of the stag into the heather than two birds of prey appeared from nowhere and hovered overhead. The signal fire was lit and soon the gillie arrived with the pony and we loaded the seventeen-stone beast on his back. And then, the long walk home.

Next day we climbed Cairn Gorm and, following the ridge, tried to climb Ben Mac Dhui. But a snow blizzard came down and we had to turn back. Our fingers were too cold even to untie our packets of sanwiches, but L.D.H. broke the ice in a stream, mixed the water with whisky and gave it to me. It was the first whisky I had ever tasted: the water of life indeed.

I spent a few days at home before joining the garrison of Harwich where one of the battalions of my regiment was stationed. Everything seemed unchanged, but I knew that I was already a stranger. Under the disapproving eyes of my sister I smoked a cigarette. In what we still called the parlour I was sitting on the sofa (another Victorian relic of language) and I moved a cushion from one end of it to the other to make myself more comfortable. A moment later I realized that this was the first time I had ever done such a thing. In my father's house one did not move cushions; one adapted oneself to the cushions as they were.

It was not as anxious a parting as it might have been a few months earlier. The war had taken a turn for the better, and my chief anxiety was that I might be too late for it. How long would they keep me at Harwich? I wanted to get to France as quickly as possible. This was not patriotism but curiosity, a thirst for experience. I was unaware as yet that experience has to be purchased, sometimes at too stiff a price.

We were not actually stationed at Harwich but at Dovercourt and under canvas in spite of the rain and cold. The belltents seemed to be pitched on a quagmire: to leave the duckboards was to be up to the ankles in mud. When one went to be inoculated one stood in the rain outside the MO's tent and thrust an arm into the opening. I did not think this a disgraceful state of affairs at the time, even if I do now.

The way in which everything was conducted was a bit of a shock. At the Officer Cadet Battalion the authorities seemed to be in complete control, but here everything was casual, sometimes to the point of farce.

I was instructed to lecture to my platoon on the history of the regiment. Unfortunately, I had no idea that I was going to be posted to the King's Own; I had learned up the history of the King's Liverpool Regiment. However, I reflected that one battle is very much the same as another. It was all one to the troops, and the major who came to listen to my discourse was no wiser; so all was well. Then I was told to give the men a talk on venereal disease, about which I knew very little and the raw boys in my platoon even less. This was my first inkling of the strangeness of the military mind.

There were about a dozen junior officers in the mess and on Sunday their main idea was to get away from Harwich and go up to London – all, that is, except for myself and another very young second-lieutenant. There was a roll-call just before lunch, by which time they had already departed. We two survivors answered solemnly for all of them and the man taking the names didn't seem to notice anything. Perhaps he couldn't count. A cold meal had, of course, been prepared for the full company and the joke is that we two hungry youths used to eat it!

Sometimes the Navy – that is, the destroyers anchored in the harbour – would blow its sirens. The Navy then sat down to its dinner, but the Army ashore had to abandon everything and hurry off to man the trenches on the beach. This was supposed to be part of our training, and that, alas! was all it ever was.

Squatting in a dilapidated trench in the sand dunes I gazed mournfully out to sea, hoping against hope that the Germans, as a last desperate throw, would try a landing. 'Nothing ever happens to me,' I said, plaintively, and a gruff voice beside me in the darkness growled: 'You bloody little fool! What do you want to happen to you? Have your head blown off?'

Then, when the Navy had finished its dinner, the sirens would blow again and we were allowed to return to our quarters.

So it went on for a month until, at last, the despaired-of 'papers' came through. A medical check, a gas-test, and I was free to go. As I crossed London in the early dawn, Trafalgar Square was littered with enemy guns, the first fruits of victory, rushed over to boost London's morale. The Germans were in full retreat. I crossed the Channel on November 9, 1918 and as, so far as I know, I was the only junior officer aboard, I am probably the only soldier in the First World War to have received a medal for *every day* of active service: one for the 10th and one for the 11th. I was at the Base Camp at Étaples when we heard the news of the Armistice, and, sitting down on a box of ammunition, I wept with disappointment.

Going up the line proved to be a more complicated task than I had imagined. The Germans were retreating across the Rhine, the whole situation was fluid, and no one seemed to know exactly where my battalion was. A harassed transport officer thrust a warrant into my hand as the train was moving out of the siding at Étaples, and I tried to decipher the pencil scrawl across it. I could just make out that my destination was Porte d'Arras. I discovered as the train gathered speed that the warrant was not for myself alone but for a party, of which I was presumably in charge, and which consisted of twelve men of the Cheshires, six of the Gloucesters, seven of the South Wales Borderers, and two of the Loyal North Lancs. These unhappy troops are probably travelling still. Certainly I never set eyes on any of them.

I had got it into my head that I was going to Arras. 'Porte d'Arras' seemed to indicate as much; I had no means of knowing that it was the name of the railway station at Lille. And so I spent the best part of a week dashing about the Western Front by train and by lorry, trying to report for duty, and being misdirected by the RTO of every town I came to.

As a conscientious officer I was consumed with guilt; as a tourist I rather enjoyed it. Arras was the first devastated town I had ever seen. I arrived after dark and explored it by moonlight. It was strangely beautiful with some grotesque touches, like the pair of trousers hanging from a bedroom door in a house which had been sliced in two. I found only two civilians in the town: one was a smart-looking girl who kept a little shop among the ruins. She sold lace – and dirty postcards.

The other I found in the cathedral. I had climbed over the rubble into what had been the nave, raised high above its original level by the debris of the roof, which formed a long mound in the centre of the church, a mound already smoothed and hardened by the weather. As I advanced the moon appeared in the open patch of sky above the shattered roof and, to my surprise, shone upon a dark figure apparently seated over the spot where the high altar had stood. It rose and came towards me and I saw that it was a woman. Even the blanching moon could not obscure the rouge upon cheeks and mouth, and her eyes were immense under the unnatural whiteness of her forehead.

My astonishment grew when she addressed me in English, a curious English coloured by all the accents – Cockney, American, Negro even – that she had heard in the last four years. I could only stammer:

'But I thought no one lived in Arras. When did you come back?'

'I do not come back,' she answered. 'I 'ave been 'ere all ze time.'

I found my battalion at last, in one of the industrial suburbs of

Lille, and soon settled down into rather a cosy life. There was no battalion mess; one had one's meals in the billet with the other young officers of the same company, a captain and three full-lieutenants. The captain was twenty-three, the other younger. I was the baby and was treated as something of a joke, arriving when the war was over. How I envied them! It was only a couple of weeks since they had marched into Lille in triumph. The battalion office still had *Kommandantur* inscribed above it in large letters: the German duty-rosters were still pinned to the doors.

Early in December we left these comfortable billets and marched twenty-five miles across the old battlefields to the little village of Agnez-les-Duisons, a few miles from Arras. Here we found some rather dilapidated Nissen huts which we made as comfortable as possible and settled down for a rather boring and unprofitable winter. There was no more going up the line, and elaborate tactical exercises seemed rather a waste of effort. Everybody was waiting to be demobilized and the authorities were hard put to it to find the men something to do. We erected goal-posts in a neighbouring field; but the peasant-farmer wasn't having any of that, and when we woke next morning it was all ploughed up.

'The next war will be with the French, and the sooner the better,' was the general sentiment of the troops.

I went for long walks, sometimes with a companion, sometimes alone. I borrowed the Company horse and rode over to the neighbouring villages. To me the flat Picardy landscape distilled a curious poetry. Even today the first sight, from the Calais–Paris train, of the straight roads and the tall poplars sets my heart pounding. I have always been in love with France. But as yet my knowledge of the French tongue was far from perfect, and now, once more, L.D.H. intervened. He sent me a small sum of money, and told me to go to the local *curé* and ask him to give me lessons.

It was my first acquaintance with the French clergy or, indeed, with Catholic clergy of any kind. I had never in my life met a priest. I knocked timidly on the door of the *curé* of Agnez-les-Duisons and made my request. He received me kindly and said he would give me a lesson twice a week. But he wouldn't take any money.

I was astonished at the austerity of his life. Certainly no Anglican, or even Nonconformist, minister I had ever known lived quite so simply. In his sparsely furnished room lit by one oil-lamp ('*Misère de misère*,' the poor man ejaculated when the glass shade cracked one evening) he would eat his supper while correcting my French: a bowl of rather thin soup. But he had wine and bread. He was thin to the point of emaciation and was certainly not in the habit of shaving every day. A real *curé de village* and, withal, a good and cultivated man.

I had brought with me a copy of George Sand's *Consuelo*, which made the *curé* raise his eyebrows.

'*C'est bien écrit*,' he said, '*mais pas moral*'.

He went to his tiny bookcase and took down a work by Joseph de Maistre, and this became our textbook. He asked me about my background. Did Protestants believe in God? I was able to reassure him on this point and our religious discussion went no farther. He touched on politics and when the Dreyfus Affair crept in he undertook to give me a plain unvarnished account of the whole matter. He explained that in France there were two parties.

'Only two?' I asked.

'Two parties,' he repeated. On the one hand was the good, right-thinking patriotic party which had attacked Dreyfus, and on the other a gang of atheists and traitors who had finally persuaded or bribed the courts to find him innocent.

But the *curé* was not really interested in politics; he was more interested in me, as a biologist might be interested in some strange fish. I had refused his invitation to smoke, and confessed that I did not drink.

'Perhaps you gamble?' I did not gamble.

I could see him watching me with a curious expression; he couldn't make me out at all.

'*Mais quels sont vos plaisirs?*' he would ask me, and I hardly knew how to reply. After all, what were my pleasures?

The *curé* was right to be astonished at my innocence; I find it astonishing enough myself, in retrospect. On one of my long walks I came at nightfall to a cottage on the outskirts of a small village. There was a light in the window. I knocked and asked if I could have a meal. I was met with surprise, and a kind of scurrying which I found it difficult to understand. But if *Monsieur l'Officier* would be content with *pommes frites* they would be happy to oblige me.

There was an old woman and a young woman in the rather elaborately furnished room. There were chairs, a table, a wardrobe and an enormous bed with a quilt like balloon. The old woman was a crone, the young one quite handsome. The simple meal was soon put before me and I sat down to eat. Before I had finished there was a knock at the door and in came a smart staff captain who regarded me, quietly eating my chips, with surprise and unconcealed dislike. He began pacing up and down the room and was plainly anxious for me to go. Puzzled and rather hurt I finished my meal and went. People did not usually call at that particular cottage for *pommes frites*.

The days dragged on until, a week before Christmas, a chit was brought to the Company Office, that is to say, the Captain's bed.

'All officers,' it ran, 'who would be interested to see a demonstration of steam-ploughing near Amiens on December 22nd will send in their names not later than 8 a.m. tomorrow morning'. I sent in my name, and so did every other junior officer in the battalion, except the only real agriculturalist among them, who happened to be 'Orderly Dog' on that day.

However, when a second chit came round saying that the starting hour would be 5 a.m. the enthusiasm cooled and all but three subalterns, including myself, withdrew.

I had, I fear, no interest whatever in steam-ploughing. It was the magic word 'Amiens' that had inspired my early rising. So it had for the others, but their motives were perhaps rather

Tea with George Bernard Shaw at the Malvern Festival
(The party includes Mrs Shaw, Professor Allardyce Nicol and Sir
Barry Jackson)

Gertrude Lawrence

Anna May Wong

different. The great cathedral, miraculously preserved although the fighting had raged all round it: that was *my* objective. Would there be time to see it – perhaps on the way back?

I found myself with some dozen others from the Division climbing into a lorry in the darkness and bumping over the road to Amiens. Gradually it grew light and I could see the faces of my fellow-passengers: all junior officers, fired with enthusiasm for scientific farming.

The morning was well advanced before the lorry began to come near the field where the demonstration was to be held. Amiens was visible a couple of miles to the right, its towers and tiny *flêche* black against the wintry sky.

Then the lorry broke down. An acting-captain who seemed, as senior, to be vaguely in command of the party, climbed out to consult with the driver. The engine started again, but, after a few yards, there was another stoppage. Two more halts convinced the entire company that the field, in spite of every effort, could not be reached in time. The nose of the lorry was turned towards Amiens. Whatever mechanical fault it had suffered from seemed to have been miraculously repaired. It went like the wind, and soon we were threading the narrow streets.

A small subscription was raised to 'defray the expenses' of the driver – whatever that might mean – and we were free to spend the rest of the day in Amiens. I lunched with the two men from my battalion. I said I wanted to see the cathedral; they announced that they were going 'hunting'. We agreed to meet for dinner.

Amiens was the first great French cathedral I had seen and, even sand-bagged as it was and the glass removed, it seemed a miracle. How had that delicate fretwork escaped when the houses all about had been blown to pieces? When I was tired of exploring it was still an hour or so too early to meet my friends. I entered a barber's shop and had everything done to me, finishing up with my first (and last) manicure in a little room upstairs. When I left, the entire staff bowed me off the premises and wished me *'Bonne chance avec la dame!'*

I found my friends in high spirits having found, they declared, just what they wanted. They had arranged to spend the evening with 'two very nice girls'. We dined hilariously, after which they went off on their mysterious errand, and I explored once more the now dark streets. A narrow lane ran down towards the river and I followed it a trifle nervously, flashing my torch from side to side. Muttered curses followed me as I went and I realized what an unwelcome visitor I was with my steady solitary march and my flashing lamp. In every doorway stood a man and woman locked in each other's arms. I spent the night at the officers' club and, with my friends, returned next day to duty. A week later they were both posted sick – 'with hospital stoppages'. Sufferers from venereal disease got no pay when they were off duty.

Shortly after Christmas I discovered that I had earned a week's leave. My Company Commander, the twenty-three-year-old veteran, had just come back from Paris with a knowing look in his eye. I had a little accumulated pay; why should I not go too? This suggestion seemed to evoke the greatest interest in everybody. I was given the name of a cheap hotel near the Étoile and a great deal of bad advice. The MO looked in with a little cardboard packet which, when I had examined it, I dropped into the stove. The doctor shook his head gravely and went away saying something about young fools who needed nursemaids.

I was to jump a lorry to Arras and there take the train – if there was one. There was, although I had to wait a long time for it in the bare yard beyond the ruins of the station. While waiting I fell into conversation with a stout and genial Frenchman in a fur coat. He was amused that this was my first visit to Paris.

'*Ah! une bonne ville,*' he said, rubbing his hands.

'*Oui,*' I answered, '*il y a de jolies bâtiments, n'est ce pas?*'

My friend opened both his eyes wide and then closed one of them. Another example of *l'hypocrisie anglaise* to add to his collection.

'*Ah! oui, mon enfant,*' he replied, '*de jolies petites filles!*' But the joke was really on him, for he was quite wrong.

It was dark when the stumbling, halting train finally drew in at the Gare du Nord. I emerged from the struggling throng and, as I had all my baggage in a haversack, plunged into the Métro. The hotel, near the Étoile, was found without any difficulty but the door was shut. I pressed the bell and, to my surprise, the door opened silently and, when I had stepped inside, as silently closed. What I did not realize was that the hotel which had been recommended to me was a *maison de passe*. When, at last, by ringing a little handbell in the hall, I had succeeded in digging out the proprietor, he seemed surprised that I was alone. He explained that he had no single beds, but if monsieur would accept a double bed . . . ? Monsieur did not mind what kind of a bed it was. Any bed would be a luxury. I was soon asleep.

Next day I started to explore Paris: it was the beginning of a love affair which has lasted all my life. Many years later I tried to express something of this in my *Life of Huysmans*:

There are many people who say, and think, that they love Paris, but by Paris they mean the bright lights, the smart cafés, the theatres and the boulevards. What they love is the city of pleasure, the cosmopolitan rendezvous. The true lover of Paris is very different. On him the unfashionable quarters, the back streets exercise a perpetual fascination. For there are other boulevards beside the Boulevard des Italiens, other squares beside the Place de la Madeleine; by-streets and forgotten corners, alleys and *impasses*, dilapidated doorways and peeling façades, houses in abandoned *quartiers* where once the famous lived. What mere tourist explores the Rue d'Alésia, enters the backyard of the Rue du Paradis, or is brought to a halt, pensive, in the Impasse Floriment? . . . Paris reveals its secret only to pedestrians, with time on their hands.

I was a pedestrian and I had a whole week for my explorations. I wore out a pair of stout Army boots. Fortunately, the museums were still closed or I might well have been found dead on a bench in the Louvre, or huddled limply in some forgotten corner of the Luxembourg. I visited private galleries and penetrated narrow streets on the Rive Gauche where the dealers' shops were to be found.

On a hoarding I had seen an announcement of an exhibition of Cubist art, and I spent many hours trying to run this exhibition to earth. I could not find it, nor could I find again the hoarding which would have reminded me of the address. I gave up hope but, at the back of my mind still lurked the desire to see these elusive Cubist pictures before I left Paris.

My leave, indeed, was coming to an end. It was Sunday and I had just left the café where I had drunk my aperitif (for I had decided that in Paris it was absurd to be a teetotaller), and was strolling idly along the boulevard in the gathering winter dusk, when my eye was caught by a *colonne à affiches*, and I paused before it to examine the theatre programme pasted upon its surface. At the *Odéon* that very evening there was to be performance of *Hamlet*. How interesting it would be and how instructive to hear that great masterpiece performed in a foreign tongue!

I made a note of the time, and sought eagerly for a ticket agency in order to buy myself a seat. I found one at last, in the Avenue de l'Opéra, and entering, approached a functionary hidden behind two rows of little model theatres. Seeing my uniform, the man smiled ingratiatingly and asked what he could have the pleasure of doing for Monsieur. The name of *Hamlet* seemed to surprise him and he turned away to consult a colleague. He then rang someone up on the telephone, and replacing the receiver, announced with sorrow that all the tickets for the *Odéon* had been sold.

'What else can I go to?' I demanded, out of patience.

Without a word the man pushed a ticket towards me, and I saw printed upon it: Folies-Bergère. Oh, well! Why not?

I had heard of the place vaguely, and although I regretted

Hamlet, I was willing to accept another entertainment, perhaps as instructive, and probably more entertaining.

The immediate problem, however, was to dine, and chance led me to a little Italian restaurant in an arcade off the *Boulevard des Italiens*. Entering, I cast my eye down the unfamiliar menu. The fat bottles of red wine with their trimmings of plaited straw intrigued me. I had as yet scarcely touched the fringe of the Kingdom of Bacchus, and Chianti seemed to promise a new extension of landscape. I ordered a bottle, or rather a flask.

There is a great deal of wine in an Italian flask, and this happened to be very good. I had drunk half of it before I had even finished my macaroni, and when the veal came, curiously better than any veal I had ever tasted, my heart swelled with exultation and a genial warmth was creeping through my veins to the very tips of my fingers. An immense satisfaction possessed me. I lay back in my upholstered seat as if I were in a bath, a divine, intangible fluid lapping my limbs. The waiter who brought me some fruit had a chromatic edge, like that of an entomological specimen seen through an imperfectly adjusted microscope. He also seemed to be swaying slightly, like a tree in the wind. Glancing towards the door, I saw that it was open. No doubt there was a draught.

Having paid my bill I passed out of the restaurant into the street, and felt immediately as if I had stepped out of real life altogether. The gesticulations of the passers-by looked positively dangerous. With a conscious effort I refrained from imitating them, and hailed a taxi. It was growing late, and I was very punctilious about arriving at a theatre in time.

By this time, the ideas in my head had shifted strangely, so that I was firmly convinced that I was going to see a perfomance of *Hamlet – Hamlet*, that was it – at the Folies-Bergère. I knew it was the Folies-Bergère because it was printed on the ticket. The name of the play had apparently been omitted. 'Folies-Bergère,' I said to the taxi-man. The driver grunted, spat, and started his machine so violently that I was almost driven bodily through the back of the cab.

I paid him and walked warily into the theatre. The brilliance of the light was like a blow on the head. I staggered under it, but recovered myself sufficiently to allow an attendant to guide me to my seat. It was very odd; the red plush armchairs seemed to be arranged anyhow. Some of them even had their backs to the stage. Everybody was walking about, and paying very little attention to the rising curtain. Collecting my wits, I turned my attention to the stage, and sank back into my seat with a little sigh of satisfaction at being in time.

The illuminated square enclosed by the proscenium was hypnotic. The stage was full of whirling figures . . . all women . . . all in the same attitude, advancing, retiring, marching about with determination, borne forward on a great wave of tinkling sound. I almost expected them to march straight forward over the footlights and out through the front-door of the theatre into the streets beyond. An irresistible army . . . sweep the Germans over the Rhine . . . victory! victory! . . . hurrah!

My ears grew so accustomed to the torrent of syncopated melody that I ceased to hear it, forgot about it as one forgets the throb of the pulse. I could see the orchestra furiously agitated, yet no sound came from the instruments. I was, suddenly, far away, alone, and it was dark and very quiet. And then the darkness paled before the first rays of dawn, and the silence was broken by a thin bugle call, very far and faint.

'Show a leg! Show a leg!'

I became conscious of a weight lying across my knees, and looking down I saw – no! it could not be – a leg! It wore a tiny satin shoe and very thin hose. My eye rested on the ankle, and then moved upwards. Just below the knee I was surprised to find a skirt. This astonishing leg really belonged to somebody! With dignity I removed the offending member. The owner of the leg tittered, but I took no notice; and when, at last, I looked round, her seat was empty.

I found myself in the street, and turned, mechanically, westward, to walk back to my hotel. An agreeable melancholy made my pace slow, and I remembered, for the first time since I had come to Paris, that I was a lonely man. And here at every step somebody wanted to be nice to me. 'Come upstairs,' they said. Westward I walked, until I reached the Boulevard Haussmann and the crowd grew thinner. Westward ever, until I was alone in the wide street, my solitary footsteps waking the echoes as I went. But how strange that the echo should not keep time! I looked back and saw that a girl was following me at about twenty paces. The *grands boulevards* were already far; she must have tracked me for a long time. I was touched. Here was an opportunity. I stopped and waited for her.

'*Mam'selle,*' I said politely, '*J'ai une question à vous poser.*'

'*Eh bien?*'

'*Vous connaissez Paris, peût-être?*'

'*Mais oui! Si je connais Paris!*

'*Alors, mam'selle, ou se trouve l'Exposition de l'Art Cubiste?*'

By an instinct older than my Army training, I had taken off my hat, and I still stood with it in my lifted hand; but the lady, with a single *chut*, was walking rapidly in the opposite direction.

I gazed after her, motionless, all unconscious that I was standing under the statue of Shakespeare. I was tapped lightly on the shoulder, and turned to find a bearded Frenchman beside me.

'You do right,' said the newcomer, 'to pay homage to that great man. See, I also salute him.'

He did so, shook me warmly by the hand, and vanished into the night.

The rest of my military career can be briefly told. One of the battalions of the regiment had been sent to the Rhine, another to Archangel, but I did not succeed in getting myself posted to either. Instead, I was sent to a German prison camp in the suburbs of Rouen, and after a few weeks moved with my charges to the neighbourhood of Poperinghe. It was from here that I was at last demobilized in the middle of July, 1919, having been a soldier for eighteen not very glorious months.

L.D.H. had decided to celebrate the end of the War by renting a castle on the Island of Mull and filling it with guests for the whole of the summer. I was invited to join the party and stay as long as I liked. In my bedroom in a Scottish baronial turret looking out on the Sound of Mull I was able to reflect on my good fortune. The house was large, comfortable and beautifully situated. There were two cars, two yachts, a big one and a little one, and all the shooting. There was a crowd of young people and some very distinguished older ones including, rather surprisingly, Dean Inge.

He was already famous for his scholarly writings and was beginning to be known to the general public as the 'Gloomy Dean'. He certainly did not *look* very cheerful, and some of the guests found him rather intimidating. When I was the last down to breakfast, as I frequently was, I invariably found an empty place beside him. I did not even attempt conversation but left him to his thoughts. However, he preached an excellent sermon in the local Presbyterian Church.

One day a party set out to visit our neighbour, the Maclean of Duart, the party consisting of L.D.H., Dr L. P. Jacks, Dean Inge and my unimportant self. We found the Maclean, then a mere eighty years old (he lived to be a hundred) in his vast baronial hall, and he showed us his treasures, including the visitors' book signed by Johnson and Boswell. Embedded in the wall were the cannon balls fired at the castle by the ships of the Great Armada. For the rest we shot, fished, climbed the mountains and sailed among the islands as far as Iona and Staffa. One night the Sound was so calm that the moon was reflected in the sea unbroken, a thing I had never seen before and have never seen since. And another night, returning late from an expedition in two vessels, the sea was alive with phosphorescence, so that trailing a hand in the water sent up a shower of sparks.

The shooting was a bit of a joke. The younger members of the party, including myself, would be sent out to replenish the larder. All day, in the woods round the house, there would be a regular cannonade. And in the end we would return with one rabbit. So the golden days passed until it was time to sail away from Mull and return to Liverpool. And to Oxford, at last.

CHAPTER 3

Early 'Twenties

The Oxford I knew as an undergraduate was situated half way between the Oxford of Compton Mackenzie and the Oxford of Evelyn Waugh. I suppose it ought, in honesty, to be called the Oxford of Beverley Nichols. Certainly Nichols was the most famous undergraduate of my day. He has told us all about it in *Patchwork*, which, whatever its shortcomings as a novel, has a certain value as a period piece and as a manifesto.

The hero, Roy Sheldon, brilliant pianist, conversationalist and public speaker, goes up in January, 1919 and, disgusted with the returned officers who still speak of 'The Mess' and 'Church Parade', resolves to recreate the old Oxford. He devotes his life to 'proving the importance of being frivolous'. He founds clubs, starts a literary review, to which he contributes *priceless* articles, reads 'dear old Baudelaire', and wears suède shoes.

The first suède shoes I ever saw on the male foot were worn by Beverley Nichols. I saw them in the High in the summer of 1920 and was deeply shocked. (I now wear suède shoes myself, and have done so for a quarter of a century.)

By the time I arrived, in the autumn of 1919, the Nichols revolution, or counter-revolution, was in full swing. The military atmosphere had been dispersed, the only echo of the War being that veterans of twenty like myself were excused from Morning Chapel. I could never see the logic of this, but welcomed it none the less.

One noticeable result of the conflict was the disparity in the ages of undergraduates; some of my friends were in the late twenties, some just seventeen. It was an advantage in a way:

the cross-section was wider even than usual. I gazed about me, fascinated by the variety of the Oxford fauna.

First, there were the dons. Some of them, with flowing beards and flying gowns, still pedalled manfully along on tricycles. The present rule requiring retirement at seventy was not yet in operation. The Principal of Hertford died in my time, aged ninety-five. It was recorded of Warden Sewell, who had become Warden of New College in 1860 and died in office in 1903, that when he was asked if the bells should be rung for Mafeking, replied, 'We didn't ring them for Waterloo'.

The Warden of New College in my time was Spooner—the historic Spooner. Doubt has, quite rightly, been thrown on the authenticity of many Spoonerisms, but I can testify that the old man was still making them to the end of his life. I was present in Chapel when he announced that, 'Now we see through a dark glassly, but then face to face'.

Another picturesque figure was Ernest Barker, whom I was lucky enough to have for a tutor to guide my first faltering steps in the History Schools. Perhaps picturesque is the wrong word; there was nothing remarkable in Barker's appearance. But, with closed eyes, he would recite Latin chronicles with a broad Lancashire accent, or, recommending one of his own works on the origins of the English Parliamentary system, would feel constrained to add: 'Other scholars call my boo-ok sedooctive but erroneous'. He was a great inspirer and a most lovable man.

Then there was Horace William Brindley Joseph, who had been the senior philosophical tutor at New College for a generation and whose *Introduction to Logic* had made him famous on both sides of the Atlantic. He was much respected – and loved – but in his earlier days as a don his shyness and eccentricity had marked him down as the victim of many a rag. One elaborate jest was still vividly remembered. Just before Hall one evening he received an unsigned note with the ominous message: 'Tonight you will be ragged.' Terrified, he fled to his rooms and barricaded himself in. Shortly afterwards a wicked undergraduate, dressed as a girl, presented himself at the College gate and asked for Mr Joseph. He was directed to Joseph's rooms but went instead to his own and changed back into male attire.

Nine o'clock came and the College gate was closed. Ten o'clock, and eleven o'clock. And still Mr Joseph's lady visitor had not left the College. When midnight came the Porter thought it his duty to inform the Warden, and these two made their way to Joseph's rooms. They knocked, but there was no answer. They knocked again and a vague scuffling noise came from within. Finally they forced an entry and found the unfortunate man cowering under his bed crying, 'I won't be ragged!'.

'I am afraid, Mr Joseph,' said the Warden, 'you *have* been ragged'.

Joseph being a Greats tutor had no need to take any notice of men in the History Schools but he kindly asked me to breakfast one morning, as was the Oxford custom. Unfortunately, I forgot all about it. I breakfasted as usual in the Junior Common Room and had already devoured a plate of porridge, a piece of haddock, and eggs and bacon, and was helping myself to marmalade when I suddenly remembered. Hurrying off, I presented myself *chez* Joseph and found quite a large party already eating. I said I had overslept and was bidden to table. If I had kept my head all might yet have been well, but I was too shy to refuse the porridge, the haddock, the bacon and eggs . . . I spent the rest of the morning in the condition of a comatose boa constrictor.

Among the younger dons were J. B. S. Haldane and Julian Huxley, the former large and fleshy and belching audibly at intervals, as if to emphasize his liberation from bourgeois prejudices; the latter frail and sharp-featured and, as he had grown a red beard during some Arctic expedition, bearing a marked resemblance to Holman Hunt's 'Light of the World'.

'Who's that?' said I in astonishment, as he walked up the Hall on his way to High Table.

'Julian Huxley disguised as Our Lord.'

The speaker was Maurice Bowra. Bowra (now Warden of Wadham) and Cyril Radcliffe (now Lord of Appeal) were the two outstanding New College men of my day. They seemed to be perpetually engaged in a verbal fencing match. They coruscated wit. Most of us gazed at them with wonder touched with awe.

Not having been to one of the great public schools I found no ready-made set into which I could slip. I knew very few people at Oxford, and hardly any in my own College. The dominant flavour there, of course, was Wykhamist and I was astonished (I still am) how deeply Winchester stamps its products. Years afterwards, in the unlikely setting of a film-studio, I was able to say, as a man I had never seen before came in, 'That man is a Wykhamist'. And I was right. Certainly at Oxford one soon learned to distinguish the types: the earnest, carefully-courteous Wykhamists, the elegant Etonians, the noisy Carthusians and Rugbeians, the frank Philistines from Fettes and similar schools.

Feeling perhaps that I had some leeway to make up, I threw in my lot with the Philistines and even rowed in the (second) New College boat. As a Commoner I was not regarded with much interest by most of the dons, and at my twenty-first birthday party all my guests were hearties.

All that is, except R——. Not that he was an intellectual: far from it, but he was certainly not a hearty. He lived with six others, including myself, in a College house in Holywell Street known as 'The Cardinal's Hat'. His room (I quote from my diary) was 'fragrant with flowers and bright with a dozen candles'. The candles, I remember, were black, and framed reproductions of Bakst hung on his walls. Giving and attending lunch parties and dinner parties occupied his whole existence. He took no exercise and never even pretended to do any work. He would never have been admitted to the strenuous, earnest Oxford of today; he was the very type of the idle rich. Yet I think he exercised a civilizing influence. Certainly he was the first person to suggest to me that *perhaps* the Russian Ballet was more important than Gilbert and Sullivan, and for that I can still be grateful. It was not that I knew very much about either. The theatre was altogether taboo in my family. My father would refer to 'converted actresses', that is, those who had abandoned their abominable profession, and would quote with approval the story of the man who was about to go to the theatre when he heard the commissionaire shouting 'This way to the Pit'. 'Ah', he reflected, 'that is what indeed it is,' and resisted the dangerous temptation. However, the songs of Gilbert and Sullivan *had* reached my ears; in a friend's house, not in mine. The Russian Ballet was something too strange and exotic even to have been heard of.

Now, I fell an immediate victim to Bakst's singing blues and acid greens and passionate reds, and to the music of *Shéhérazade* that went with them. R—— had an excellent gramophone and I spent hours in his room listening to his records, eating his chocolate biscuits and drinking his liqueurs. At his luncheon and dinner parties I met all the aesthetes, including the one who was alleged to have fainted when his scout put out pink pyjamas with green sheets. When *he* had guests he would present each of them with a lemon and when asked 'What do we do with these?' replied: 'Just hold them. They're so decorative.' I was half amused and half fascinated by this last whiff of the 'nineties. A somewhat sinister note: at one of his dinner parties R—— declared that when his money was gone he would do himself in. And that is precisely what he did, about six years later.

For a year or more I pretended to be a hearty. I rowed, played hockey and ran with the beagles; but the incurable literary man soon began to show through. I contributed an article on undergraduate life to *The Liverpool Daily Post*. For this I received one guinea: the first money I ever earned with my pen. I sent a short story to *The Oxford Outlook* which, founded by Beverley Nichols, was now edited by L. P. Hartley, Alec Valentine and Basil Murray. Hartley is now a novelist of international fame; Valentine is Chairman of London Passenger Transport; Murray, Sir Gilbert Murray's brilliant son, died long ago. Christopher Hollis came in later.

The contributors included most of the undergraduates of the day with literary aspirations and some of them have since become well known. I note on the bright orange cover of one issue the names of Richard Hughes, V. de S. Pinto, and John Strachey. Charles Morgan was another contributor. With his fine features and his noble poise he struck me as almost alarmingly mature. I sent in some short stories and, of course, verse.

Like most young writers I still thought of myself as a poet. *The New Age* printed some of my verses, and although the newly-founded *London Mercury* rejected my first effort (returned with a kindly note from J. C. Squire) that journal published *The Sonnet* – a religious poem imbedded in a long satirical account of the process of its composition. 'Write some more, and send some more,' wrote Squire, 'and stop reading Browning'. But I kept all this dark from my hearty friends.

Even the intellectual climate of Oxford has never been thought particularly propitious for poets. What has it to show against the Cambridge galaxy of Milton, Gray, Wordsworth, Byron and Tennyson? Only Johnson, Matthew Arnold, Arthur Hugh Clough, and Oscar Wilde. Shelley also, of course, but he was sent down.

It is true that in the early 'twenties some formidable figures were still about. W. B. Yeats was living in Broad Street, John Masefield on Boar's Hill, Robert Bridges not far away. Aldous Huxley, Robert Nichols, Robert Graves and the Sitwells were in the neighbourhood. But all these, except the Sitwells, were of a previous generation. Among undergraduates the only nest of singing birds seemed to be Queen's. Here were Edmund Blunden, Alan Porter, Godfrey (later Lord) Elton and Louis Golding. It is sad that I never met any of them until years later, when several of them became my friends. It is strange how *capsulated* the Colleges were at that time.

My New College friends were completely unaware of my own poetic efforts and so there was considerable surprise among them when I won the Newdigate Prize.

It is easy to prove that the prestige which the Newdigate

still enjoys is out of all proportion to the merit of the winning poems. After all, the prize *is* awarded every year and there must be between forty and fifty Newdigate winners living today. Yet very few of them enjoy any fame as poets. In its long history of successful candidates, how few are remembered! All the world knows one line from one Newdigate poem:

> A rose-red city half as old as time,

but very few could give the name of the author (Dr Burgon) or even the subject of his poem (Petra). None the less a certain glamour attaches to this most famous of Oxford prizes, and it was therefore with both pleasure and incredulity that I learned from a casual acquaintance, while crossing the quad of New College after breakfast, that the winner for 1921, whose name was pinned up in traditional fashion on the door of the Divinity Schools, was myself. An hour later I had made sure that this was no error and had arranged with Basil Blackwell for the publication of my first book.

Many people from the Warden to my own scout offered congratulations, but my little success did not meet with universal approval. I ran into one of my rowing friends and the following dialogue ensued:

'You haven't congratulated me.'

'What the hell for?'

'I've just won the Newdigate.'

'What the hell's that?'

I explained, and a look of real horror came over his face.

'What a disgrace!' he said. He was genuinely shocked.

The Newdigate poem, like other prize-winning compositions, is traditionally read at the Encaenia. This takes place in the Sheldonian Theatre where the Vice-Chancellor, in full panoply, opens 'a Convocation of the University' and proposes 'to the House that Honorary Degrees be conferred on certain distinguished persons'.

The distinguished persons in 1921 included Clemenceau and

Sir Roger Keyes (later Lord Keyes of Zeebrugge), and when all the honorary degrees had been duly conferred and the Professor of Poetry had delivered the Creweian Oration, it was the turn of the prizemen. Mercifully for the public, there was only a token recitation of the Greek and Latin poems but the Newdigate in my day was always given in full. Nervous though I was, and conscious that I must have looked very peculiar in full evening dress with a short Commoner's gown on top of it, I got through it somehow. The Vice-Chancellor then 'dissolved the Convocation' and we all went off to lunch at All Souls. As I emerged into the bright June sunshine the policeman at the door congratulated me. 'It was the only thing I understood, sir,' which perhaps was not surprising. But appreciation was not limited to the constabulary, for on my way back to college to change my uncomfortable clothes I passed Blackwell's bookshop and, standing outside, were two figures I recognized as the Master of Balliol and Sir Roger Keyes.

'Ah!' said the Master, 'the shop is shut. We are too late to buy the poem. What a pity!'

What could I do but produce my own copy and present it to Sir Roger, signed with the 'Muggers' blue pencil? This incident, pleasant as it was, had passed from my memory until, some fourteen years later, browsing in a London bookshop, I opened the first volume of Sir Roger Keyes' *Naval Memoirs*. What was my astonishment, as I skimmed the preface, to find that it was almost entirely devoted to myself. I blushed as I read it. It seemed to me that the Admiral gave me an altogether disproportionate share of praise among the young writers of my age and country. Of course! the poem, the subject of which was *Cervantes*, had contained a description of the Battle of Lepanto. It must have been this that had caught the Admiral's imagination. But I couldn't help wondering, ungratefully, if the gallant sailor's appreciation of my poem were not due, perhaps, to its being the only poem he had ever read.

The Newdigate poem was still, by tradition, written in pentameter couplets, and I have always had rather a knack for this Popeian measure. I now began to exploit it in the field of light verse, and for the remainder of my time at Oxford I was a regular contributor to *The Isis*. The Editor, Alan Colling-ridge, even paid me a retaining fee of £5 a term.

I did not restrict myself to heroic couplets. I imitated Praed; I parodied Masefield:

> I must go down to the Turl again,
> To the lonely Turl and the High,
> And all I ask is a straight wall,
> And a lamp to steer me by.
> For my vision is really rather blurred,
> And the pavement's shaking.
> I hope I do not meet a Prog,
> When the grey dawn's breaking . . .

I composed *An Epic in Instalments* in the Spenserian stanza, and tried my hand at adapting Horace's *Non ebur neque aureum*:

> No waistcoats of yellow, no suiting
> By Adamson fashioned have I;
> No trunk worth the trouble of looting,
> No rooms overlooking the High;
> No cellar, of wine of the best full,
> No friends of exalted degree,
> No uncle, with wealth by the chestfull,
> And dying to leave it to me.

A certain facility in verse-writing is, I fear, no guarantee of the presence of the authentic Muse.

There was considerable political ferment in Oxford in the early 'twenties. There was a Conservative Club and a Labour Club and a Liberal Club and a National Liberal Club. Asquith and Haldane addressed us, as well as Lord Birkenhead and a rising young politician called Hore-Belisha. I did not find any of them very persuasive. Like most returned soldiers, I dis-trusted 'politicians'.

I never spoke at the Union as an undergraduate, although I have done so since, but I attended the debates from time to time, especially when there was a Distinguished Visitor. Certain visions remain in the memory: W. B. Yeats, a tall, impressive figure striding up and down the Debating Hall in his emotion and denouncing the activities of the Black and Tans ('I've seen ut! I've seen ut!'); Birkenhead, clutching the despatch box with both hands (not without reason) and pouring forth a stream of biting phrases; Horatio Bottomley, making one of the last of his public appearances, holding the lapels of his coat like some disreputable bishop and saying: 'I was educated in the University of Life'. I think it was Hore-Belisha who ended his speech in reply with the words. 'There are more things in Heaven and Earth, Horatio . . .'

I always tried to be present when Douglas Woodruff was speaking. Indeed he used to try out his witticisms on me beforehand, over tea at Buol's. On one occasion there was a visiting team of American undergraduates. They spoke well but their intense seriousness, not to say solemnity, was in striking contrast to the customary badinage of the Oxford Union.

One of them had just delivered an impressive speech. Woodruff, his opponent, lumbered to his feet – he was already massive as an undergraduate. He began by complimenting the speaker on his oratory.

'As I listened to him,' he said, 'I seemed to see, behind his shoulder, the ghost of Gladstone giving him ghostly advice, and the shade of Disraeli, giving him shady advice . . .'

Perhaps Oxford is too much taken with such sallies. Even today anyone who can bring them off is sure of a warm welcome at the Union. Father Christie, the famous Jesuit preacher, was once put up to oppose Dr Marie Stopes, on the question of birth control. Marie Stopes related her experience in Dublin when her meeting had been broken up, 'at the instigation of the priests' (which I doubt not). One of the rowdiest of the unruly was an old charwoman who was arrested and lodged in jail. With Christian forbearance Marie Stopes went to visit her.

'Ah!' said the old woman, 'here I am in jail. And they said if I did what I was told, nothing would happen to me!'

Marie Stopes sat down, having made an effective point, and Father Christie rose. He pointed a finger at his opponent and said:

'Dr Marie Stopes! Many a poor girl has said that about you!'

All poor Marie Stopes' arguments were swept away in a gale of laughter. When Father Christie told me this story he added: 'It was an inspiration of the Holy Ghost.'

'Well, Father,' I said, 'Let us call it an inspiration – and leave it at that.'

I fear that my religious beliefs at this period were as shaky as my political opinions. Having repudiated the Nonconformist Evangelicalism of my childhood I had found nothing to put in its place. In my diary I noted that 'my moral values suffer from a lack of organization', and that I was much concerned with 'the absorbing problem of whether the Absolute really has a kind heart' or not.

I was attracted by ritual and made the usual round of the 'High' Anglican churches, visited the Fathers of St John the Evangelist at Cowley, irreverently known as the 'Cowley Dads', and attended 'Mass' at St Barnabas', near the railway station. But what I really loved were the services in the College chapel. The language of the Liturgy, the singing of the excellent choir delighted me. New College, like Magdalen and the House, had its own choir school, at that time under Dr (later Sir Hugh) Allen. Bach's 'Spring Anthem' in which 'the words keep a due decorousness of pace while the music frolics round them—like an old man in the middle of a group of children'; Boyce's 'Where can Wisdom be found?' and *'Veni Sancte Spiritus'*; and the medieval quaintness of Abelard's:

> *Illic ex Sabbato succedit Sabbatum*
> *Perpes laetitia sabbatizantium,*
> *Nec ineffabilis cessabunt jubili,*
> *Quos decantabimus et nos et Angeli,*

moved me to ecstasy. Somehow, old Warden Spooner was part of the enchantment when, at the conclusion of the singing, he rose in his stall (he was such a little man that standing made no difference to his apparent height) and in a thin, quavering voice, pronounced the Blessing. Then, the great doors from the ante-Chapel into the Cloister were flung open and one emerged into the sunshine of a summer evening: these things gave me a pleasure I have never quite recaptured at any religious service since.

A pleasure, I fear, almost wholly aesthetic: proved perhaps by my indignation when the Evangelicals of the College tried to substitute for the exquisite motets of the choir a little 'hearty congregational singing'. I had had quite enough of that in childhood.

None the less, the Evangelicals had some hopes of me, for I found myself selected as a delegate to the Students' Christian Movement Conference in Glasgow. It was a strange experience for one who already considered himself an outsider. Bishop Temple (he was not yet an Archbishop) I listened to with respect, but most of the speakers were far too Fundamentalist for my acceptance. The neolithic notion of an angry God who can be propitiated by blood sacrifices made no appeal to me—nor does it now. I fear I returned from the conference more irritated than edified.

Another attempt to savour the varieties of religious experience made a deeper impression. I quote from the diary I was keeping at the time:

'Caught the bus to Headington, met Price [now Professor Price, of New College] and Chitty at the corner of Windmill Road as arranged and walked up Shotover Hill with them. A little higher up we met Brother G——,[1] the object of our meeting. He is a small man with a tonsured head, a red beard and kindly wrinkles round his eyes due to exposure to the glare of the sun. He wore a friar's dress, of coarse brown material

---

[1] I suppress his name, for I believe that he later fell into disgrace, which I find hard to believe, so vivid in my mind was the impression of his saintliness.

with a cowl and blanket of the same, and a thick rope knotted round his waist. We went into a field with him (there were six of us, including Brother G——), the field just above Dr Jacks' house, and sat in a semi-circle on the grass. The sky was all clear blue except where the sinking sun made it golden and a pallid half-moon showed almost overhead. The birds were singing and behind us the cattle munched grass. Brother G—— told us of his mission. He was given his Rule of poverty, chastity and obedience by Bishop Gore, and conducts a mission to tramps, living their life and trying to understand them and rescue them. He spoke of the miraculous effect of his prayers and gave us many instances where assistance had come to him just when he needed it most. He denied that the tramp's position was, in anything but the smallest degree, his fault, and also the idea that tramps do no work.

'I felt rather a hypocrite sitting there listening to him, being unable to understand such simple faith. Of his sincerity it is impossible to have the smallest doubt. He has been all over the country, sleeping in tramp-wards and barns and low lodging houses, forcing his religion on nobody but if challenged (as his dress makes probable) ready to talk as sweetly and as reasonably as he did to us. He is a 'varsity man, but has sunk his family, his prospects and everything to follow the example of St Francis. After a novitiate of three years in an English monastery, he took to the road, got a commission, was demobilised and is now at his old work. We walked back with him to the Cowley Road, then shook hands and said goodnight.'

Still I remained 'outside'. I attended Dean Inge's lectures at Manchester College (a Dean among the Unitarians!) and heard him speak of the Two Internationals: the Black and the Red. The Red, I gathered, was to be preferred, for it could not last for ever. 'But the Black International never lets you go.'

At the other extreme I listened to Baron von Hügel on 'Christianity and the Supernatural'. He had a quick, rather muffled voice. After speaking of natural and supernatural goodness he suddenly cried: 'I owe everything to Rome!' Was there something in Catholicism after all? I attended Father Martindale's talks at Bishop King's Palace and met him at lunch. He was then a most potent influence in Oxford. But I did not 'go over'.

Another great Catholic influence was 'Sligger' Urquhart, of Balliol, the first Catholic to hold a fellowship in any Oxford college since the Reformation. Evelyn Waugh tells us, in his *Life of the Right Reverend Ronald Knox* that 'Sligger owned a chalet which his father had built in 1864 in the valley of Chamonix. There every summer, except during the First World War, he took a reading party of his particular intimates. Ronald went once only, in 1908, and then not to *the* Chalet, for it had been burned down and was rebuilding, but to the neighbouring Chalet des Rochers . . . It was not at all a luxurious régime.'

In point of fact, neither chalet (and I have stayed in both) is actually in the valley of Chamonix. Both lie on the other side of the Col de Voza above St Gervais-les-Bains. L.D.H. rented the smaller chalet from 'Sligger' with the intention of making the ascent of Mont Blanc, and invited me to join him. It was not, as Waugh rightly says, a luxurious régime. The building itself was little more than a block-house, even the floors being made of unsquared timber, and the principal fuel was fir-cones. They make a bright fire but enormous quantities are necessary to keep it going. We needed a fire; the chalet stands at 5,000 feet.

We were looked after by a middle-aged couple who bore the delightful names of Achille and Césarine. Césarine asked on our arrival if we wanted an extravagant or an economical cuisine and L.D.H. replied, characteristically, that he would like it to be economical. But a Savoy peasant woman's notions of economy proved to be so rigidly austere that after a day or two he told her to be extravagant. The fare was extremely simple even then, but Césarine had all the vanity of a *cordon bleu*, and having set down a dish with a flourish would stand, arms akimbo, in the doorway, and say:

    'C'est bon, hein? C'est bien bon?'

Only when she had been assured repeatedly that it was the most exquisite food ever served to mortal man, would she retire to her kitchen.

In front the ground fell steeply to the valley in which St Gervais lies. Beyond, like a stupendous backcloth, was Mont Percé, a mountain which really has a hole near the top, for, as we were watching the sunset on the first evening the bright rays suddenly came through it. The only sounds were made by the rushing streams and an occasional cow-bell. Then far down in the valley, a nightingale began its song.

In the morning the whole panorama of the surrounding peaks was revealed. To the left lay the enormous Glacier de Bionassey which, a few years before, had taken a sudden leap forward and blotted out the village below. Beyond, hidden by the Dôme du Goûter, lay the great rounded summit of Mont Blanc. There were wild flowers everywhere: primulas and forget-me-nots, a symphony in blue.

During the first few days we climbed several of the lesser peaks to get into training. I was particularly keen to climb Mont Joly on the other side of the glacier and when L.D.H. decided he was too tired to attempt it, I determined to set out alone. This is never a very wise thing to do in the Alps, and L.D.H. tried to dissuade me, However, in the end he agreed that I should go.

I went straight down through the woods by a very precipitous route and reached the main road in the valley in a little less than an hour. I climbed up the opposite slope to the little village of St Nicolas de Veroce and there the rain began. I sheltered for a while in a chalet and was strongly advised not to persist. However, I pushed on and soon the rain turned to snow. The summit was shrouded in mist and when I reached it I could see nothing. The sensible thing to do would have been to retrace my steps, using my own footprints as a guide. Instead I broke through the snow cornice on the ridge (it stuck out two or three feet), glissaded for a hundred yards and found myself on a promising grass slope. Then my difficulties began. The grass gave way to schist and the slope became very steep. I was in a great cup of tiny stone fragments lying loosely on crags of brittle stone and divided down the middle by a stream. I could hear the water rushing over the edge of a precipice lower down.

It was impossible to climb back the way I had come; the loose stones provided no foothold. On steep schist it is equally impossible to stand or to walk. It is possible to run. I ran in short bursts, my hands black and sticky and cut with the sharp stones, and reached the edge of the hollow. Above me, at the level of my head, was the overhanging grass verge, and safety. A rock projected. I seized it and tried to swing up. It came away in my hands and both it and I were precipitated down the slope. I remember saying to myself, quite calmly: 'This is the end of you.'

I slid and bounced perhaps forty feet and then, spread-eagled and digging in my heels, almost on the edge of the precipice, suddenly stopped. I scrambled to my feet and ran, slithering over the schist. I managed to reach the grass verge lower down and then, and only then, was sick with terror.

My rücksack with a thick sweater inside had broken my fall, and except for a bruised shoulder and skinned hands and elbows I was physically none the worse. But I was shaking all over and for some time my legs refused to carry me. Slowly I crawled down to the village, went into a café and deliberately got drunk. This was the best thing I could have done. I walked the eight miles home singing; and the next day was climbing again.

A week later Achille, who would come from the neighbouring farm in the evening to discuss plans, decided we were fit enough to attempt Mont Blanc. I fall back on my diary:

'*Monday, 2 July*. Up early and caught the workmen's train on the *chemin de fer du Mont Blanc* at about 7.45. In the truck we found Broissat the guide and his son. Achille came with us as the other porter. The morning was fine and clear and we crawled slowly up the mountain side to the end of the track. We started up the snow slopes and arrived at Tête Rousse (10,390 ft.), the *cabane* of which was not yet open, soon after noon. Lunched on

72

the rocks outside and then slept in the sun until about two o'clock. Broissat's son Jean François drank too much snow-water and was violently sick in consequence.

'The ascent of the Aiguille du Goûter by the jagged rock face I thought a decidedly perilous business. Not the least danger is from falling stones. About a hundredweight of rock was sent hurtling at me about half way up, but it missed my head by a couple of inches bruising the arm which I instinctively flung up to save myself. We arrived at the *cabane* just below the summit of the Aiguille du Goûter (12,525 ft.) at about six o'clock. Hot tea and bread and meat restored my confidence and I slept for several hours under my four blankets. We arrived in a thick mist so saw nothing of the surrounding country.

'*Tuesday*, *3 July*. Broissat looked out of the *cabane* at 2 a.m. but decided that the weather was too bad. At three o'clock however, he (foolishly, as it turned out) got the party up, roped us to-gether, and we set out. We climbed laboriously to the top of the Dôme du Goûter (14,120 ft.) but the guide could not see his way in the *brouillard* and he seemed incapable of making use of L.D.H.'s compass. We stayed on the summit peering into the mist until I at least was sick and dizzy with cold and my fingers and toes felt as if they had been torn out by the roots. Finally we retreated to the *cabane*, heated some tea over candles (a lengthy and discouraging process) wrapped ourselves in blankets, for we had no more wood for a fire, and waited for the weather to improve. This first attempt occupied rather more than three hours.

'About eleven o'clock we were roused again – I had managed to snatch a little sleep – and after a hasty meal set out and toiled up the Dôme du Goûter once more in the blistering and blinding sunshine. How Jean François managed without sunglasses I do not know. The mist then began to surround us again and was quite thick when we reached the Refuge Vallot. This is the highest mountaineering hut in Europe, the observatory built upon the summit of Mont Blanc itself having sunk into the ice-cap and vanished without trace.

'We were looking forward to resting there but when we forced open the door we found that the interior was a solid block of ice. Snow had drifted in, melted and frozen again. We pushed on and when we were only 400 metres short of the summit L.D.H. said he couldn't go any further.

'I am aware of course that real mountaineers (the Everest men and the rock-face fanatics) despise Mont Blanc and call it merely a walk. All the same, the air at 15,000 ft. is rarefied enough to make breathing painful, and the heart beats twice as quickly as it should. Each foot seems to have a convict's ball and chain attached to it; the intense cold grips the throat, and anyone who is caught out in the open after nightfall is unlikely to survive. I wanted to divide the party and push on, but L.D.H. asked me not to. He said we would return in a year's time and finish the job [which we did].

'We returned to the *cabane* carrying some loose wood we had found outside the Refuge Vallot. We had intended to burn some of the replaceable furniture, but luckily this was now unnecessary. Achille made some excellent soup from snow, meat cubes and the remains of the mutton. I did not sleep much as I could not bear to touch the pillow (a folded sweater) with my blistered face. At six o'clock in the morning we made a hasty breakfast and began the descent.'

It took nearly all day and on the way down we had a sad disappointment. In the highest hut below the snowline we had secreted a bottle of champagne. We found it on our return and tried to open it – in vain. Perhaps owing to the difference of pressure the cork had jammed. We simply couldn't get it out, and neither of us, in our tired state, had the nerve to knock off the neck of the bottle. Pol Roger, 1911! Perhaps it is there still, hidden in the straw. Tired we certainly were. When we got back to the chalet soup was set before me, but I couldn't lift my hand to use the spoon. I had to be fed like a child.

There was one more adventure before the end of the holiday. Crossing a glacier, L.D.H. fell into a crevasse. Of course we were roped together but he was a big man and my ten stone couldn't hold him. Fortunately Achille and the anchor-man held us both. The green smooth sides of a crevasse make it almost impossible for a man who has fallen in to get out; and he has to get out quickly – or freeze to death. L.D.H. liked to recall this incident and often remarked that we would not have survived if it had not been for the 'anchor-man'.

I had taken my degree after two years, but L.D.H. thought I should have another year at Oxford, and it was decided that I should read for a B. Litt. In retrospect I regret this decision. I wish I had spent the year in France, Italy and Germany, for although I can read all three languages I am fluent only in French. This fluency was partly due, of course, to the wisdom of L.D.H. in getting me to take lessons from the *curé* of Agnez-les-Duisons. He himself, as a youth, had stayed with the *curé* of Loches, and in the summer of 1921 he tried to arrange for me to do the same. But the old man replied that he was now too feeble and excused himself. What should I do in the Long Vacation?

My tutor suggested that I should take a tutoring job for a few weeks, and so it was arranged. My pupil lived in a country house in the Cotswolds, and although he was always going off to play polo at Cheltenham, we did quite a lot of work together, mostly in a little summer-house on the slope of Bredon Hill. On a clear day we could see the spire of Gloucester Cathedral and the smoke of ships in the Bristol Channel. My pupil's parents were hospitable and kind; and, as he was the only pupil I ever had, and as he afterwards became a Governor of the Bank of England, I think I can claim 100 per cent success.

During this holiday (for my duties were by no means onerous and I was able to explore the lovely Cotswold country on a borrowed bicycle) I paid one visit to London. L.D.H.'s brother was a Liberal Member of Parliament (it was he who owned the shooting-box in Scotland), and he sent me an invitation to a party at his house in Lowndes Square, 'to meet the Asquiths'. It was my first experience of that kind of thing.

There were quite a number of people I knew: Henry

Andrews, of my own College, Arthur Rau, of Wadham, George Edinger, of Balliol, and the glamorous Sylvia Thompson, who, when she attended lectures with her fellow undergraduettes, was a phoenix among hens. She afterwards had considerable success as a novelist. Our host beamed in the background. Sir John Simon busied himself introducing people, and, at last, the Asquiths arrived.

What an astonishing contrast they were: the Old Roman with his white hair and flushed face, and Margot, pale and thin and hawk-like, with a quite astonishing décolletage, a row of miniature medals dangling from her corsage. She came and talked to me (little knowing how tepid was my Liberalism) and said – kindly if untruthfully – that she had met me at Oxford. To my unsophisticated eye she was extravagantly rouged. My only blunder of the evening was asking the formidable butler for 'cider cup'. 'White wine cup, sir!' he said, with justifiable contempt.

I quite enjoyed the party but could not help feeling that I was a fish out of water. I talked to a girl from the London School of Economics who thought that politics added 'such an interest to life'. I heard her introduced to Lady Simon as 'an ardent young Liberal', and shuddered. Talking to Arthur Rau I said that my plans for going abroad had fallen through. 'Meet me at the Carlton Hotel, Frankfurt, on August the 11th,' he said, and was carried away by the crowd. Well, why not?

That is how I came to spend the greater part of the summer of 1921 in Germany, mostly in Munich. I have not seen it since the devastation of the Second World War. After the First it was untouched; untouched, that is, by the War but the holes made in the façade of the Justiz-Palast by the machine-gun bullets which had scattered the Spartakists had not yet been plastered over. The theatres were booming and I had an orgy of opera and plays, from *Parsifal* and *Ariadne auf Naxos* to *Was Ihr Wohlt* and *Die Grosse Katherina* von Georg Bernard Shaw. Shaw seemed to be, after Shakespeare, the favourite dramatist. I sat half through the first act of *Der Arzt am Scheideweg* before I realized that I was watching *The Doctor's Dilemma.* All the picture galleries were open and there was a special exhibition of the *Secession.* This was my first acquaintance with the German Expressionist school. It has taken nearly forty years for its works to reach us in England.

Living was extraordinarily cheap, for the mark had already begun to slide down the slippery slope to the abyss of inflation. One could dine extremely well for half-a-crown. A good cigar cost twopence. I had a few letters of introduction, mostly from L.D.H., to the Norddeutscher Lloyd people: monarchists to a man, as indeed most of Munich seemed to be. The Wittelsbach family had lost the throne of Bavaria, but the fashionable shops had scarcely troubled to black out the arms of their royal patrons on their window fronts, and none of the names of the streets had been changed. There was still a Maximiliansplatz and a Wittelsbacher fountain. You could buy picture post-cards of all the members of the Royal family in any stationer's shop; and when I asked the shop-girl who one of them was she answered shortly: *Unser Prinz.* It was a little sinister, boding future conflict, that it was also possible to buy photographs of the assassin of the Left-Wing Eisner. One had the impression that the whole place was a pot about to boil over; and, one evening, while strolling along the streets, I saw a placard: '*Erzberger Gemordet*'. That night the hotel was barricaded and there was shooting outside.

I liked to spend my evenings in one of the beer-halls, particularly in the Hofbräuhaus, drinking the excellent *Münchener* from a *Stein,* and cutting up my own bread and sausage on the spotlessly scrubbed tables. Usually there was a concert but, one night, the music was interrupted by a little man with a falling lock and a toothbrush moustache who jumped on a table and began a speech denouncing the Jews. If I had only known – I would have stayed and listened.

Sometimes, with a young German Doktor ('Doktor' in the German sense) and the girl he called his *fiancée,* I would visit the cabarets. There was an excellent variety show at Boccaccio and at Serenissimus near the station, and a very good orchestra at the Odeon Casino in the Wittelsbacherplatz, where Maria Hagen used to dance, and the posters and menus were designed by Schnackenberg. In Schwabing, Munich's Chelsea, there were good cabarets too, of which the best was Benz. Our party of three would take the tram, past the Ministry of War, with a *feldgrau* sentry in a steel helmet in the doorway, past the State Library and the University, and so, under the Sieges Thor to Schwabing. And walking back along the Ludwigstrasse, with linked arms, we woke the echoes with the only song we all three knew: 'It's a long way to Tipperary.'

I returned to England via Münster, where I spent a few days with the man who had given me German lessons in Belgium when we were both in a prisoner-of-war camp – he on one side of the barbed wire and I on the other; and Hamburg, where I was entertained to lunch by the Directors of the Hamburg-Amerika Line. This was owing to a misapprehension. L.D.H. had written to Geheimrat Cuno, later German Chancellor, and asked him to be kind to me. Cuno obviously expected somebody much more important than the (just ex-) undergraduate who was shown into his palatial office. However, he received me with great courtesy and I solemnly sat down to table with a dozen shipping magnates. There was much *'Jawohl, Geheimrat!'* and clicking of heels.

I brought back from Germany a very confused impression. I wish now that I had gone on to Berlin. My monarchist friends in Munich, one of whom had been condemned to death during the short Communist ascendency and was only saved by the arrival of troops from Weimar, warned me against it. It was a horrible place, he said, dirty and disorganized and full of traitors and Jews. My friends were not Nazis yet, but they may have become so later. I shall never know.

Back in Oxford, I busied myself with my thesis. I had decided to write about John Newton, the friend of the poet Cowper, and this involved a close study of the whole Evangelical movement in the eighteenth century. Early in 1922 I realized that if I was to do the job properly, and to make a serious attempt on the Gladstone Prize (the theme of which, that year, was 'John Wesley') I would have to put in some work at the British Museum. I decided to spend a fortnight in London documenting myself on these related themes.

I took lodgings in Tavistock Square with a Greek family with whom I dined every evening. I don't know why they took lodgers at all, for the dinner was lavish and there was champagne every night. Among the other lodgers, for there were several, was a Greek boy who invited me to go with him to the Orthodox Church in Bayswater on Sunday. I was intrigued by the strangeness of it all and impressed by the hidden choir of deep male voices. But the real interest was that the service was conducted by no less a person than the Patriarch of Constantinople on his way from America to take up his appointment. He was an impressive figure, a huge man with a square iron-grey beard. Even he, however, seemed to find the massive gold mitre heavy, for he kept shifting it on his head. I kissed his hand and received from him a small cube of blessed (not consecrated) bread.

On weekdays I repaired to the great Reading Room of the British Museum and tasted there, for the first time, the *volupté* of research. To those who have never experienced it there is no more to be said. Those who have will understand what I mean. The very smell of the place entranced me; the echo of footsteps reverberating in the dome seemed like the beating of my own heart. I would go to the Library as soon as it opened and find my place at one of the desks. Strange characters sat on either side, bearded patriarchs, munching sandwiches at intervals. A pile of books was brought to me; before I knew it the morning had passed.

I explored the neighbourhood for cheap eating places, resolved to spend on my lunch no more than a shilling. I was looking forward to the life of a scholarly recluse, preferably in London. I would have a small book-lined room in Bloomsbury and would walk out at night into the fascinating garishness of

Tottenham Court Road. Could I live entirely by my pen? I wondered if that would be possible, even with lunches at a shilling. A job of some sort would be necessary. But what kind of a job? I pushed the problem from me and returned to the Reading Room. And there my cup of contentment was filled when, as the light faded, the huge electric arc suspended from the dome spluttered into life. I have worked in many libraries since but never with greater joy.

There were some advantages in being up for another year at Oxford, indeed if I had not been I would never have made the acquaintance of the College intellectuals at all. Now – I suppose on the strength of the Newdigate – I was admitted to the New College Essay Society, a club with a long history and some splendid plate from which mulled claret was dispensed during the meetings. Once a year a distinguished guest was invited to dinner. I noted in my diary:

'Annual dinner of the Essay Society with Galsworthy as guest. We assembled in Upper Junior Common Room and I was placed between Woodward and Jacob – good company. They have both "arrived" (Jacob is lecturing under Barker at King's College, London) and so can afford to be gracious. The dinner was excellent, and the speeches good. Woodruff and Radcliffe in particular surpassed themselves.

'We adjourned to Mr Smith's room and listened to a paper by Galsworthy, chiefly about Turgenev and Maupassant. I recall the scene very vividly: Galsworthy himself with a clean-cut strong face and hair going white reading his paper in a somewhat sing-song voice, Harrod in the corner keeping guard over the punch-bowl, Woodruff with his huge face and long, untidy hands, Trapper-Lomax pale and looking fatigued as if with the weight of a topheavy forehead, Steel with his bitter mouth and enormous tortoise-shell glasses, Strauss, up from King's Hospital, looking as sinister as ever, Bowra, a more philosophical and less charitable Pickwick, Livingstone, the don from Corpus, looking in the eightyishness of his heavy moustache and his white tie and black waistcoat spanned by a gold chain like one of Du Maurier's drawings in *Punch*. Woodward, of All Saints, incredibly babyish-looking and jerking his lower lip sideways . . .'

A flash-light photograph of a rather remarkable collection of able young men, for all except Livingstone were young. Forty years later we find Ernest Fraser Jacob as Chichele Professor of Modern History, Cyril Radcliffe a Viscount and a Lord of Appeal, Anthony Steel, Principal of University College, Cardiff, Sir Roy Harrod, an economist of world repute, Sir Maurice Bowra, Warden of Wadham College, Oxford, Douglas Woodruff, a leading Catholic publicist and editor of *The Tablet*, and Michael Trappes-Lomax, Somerset Herald. Eric Strauss was one of the pioneers of psychological medicine in this country and before his recent death was acknowledged as its leading authority. 'Mr Smith', then a young don, was for many years the well-loved Warden of New College.

As I had chosen a clergyman for the subject of my postgraduate thesis, I found myself, somewhat to my astonishment, in the School of Theology. I learned that there was a Theological Post-Graduate Group and attended one of its meetings, to find that the only other members were an American Methodist and a negro. 'We decided to bury the Society,' and I saw them no more.

It was the human side of Wesley and Newton that interested me, especially the contradictions in their character: the fact that Wesley was so very nearly a Newman and that Newton had gone on commanding a slaving vessel *after* his conversion, and yet had been conscientious enough to refrain from meat during his voyages lest he should be tempted by the charms of the young negresses aboard his ship. Then too this bluff extrovert had been the intimate friend of the shy and shrinking Cowper and had probably driven him mad. Surely there was a mystery here that needed to be unravelled.

I decided to go to Olney and see the place where Cowper had lived for so long. I was put up at the Vicarage, the house which had once been Newton's, and where Cowper himself had stayed. There was a pleasant garden at the back of the house with apple-trees in blossom and a great cluster of blue-bells. The door into Cowper's 'Guinea Field' had vanished but it was possible to see his summer-house over the wall. This is still just as it was in the eighteenth century with the little trap in the floor where

> smoke-consuming Bull,
> Even filling, never full,

kept his clay pipes. The Rev. William Bull (Cowper's *'Charissime Taurorum'*) spent much time there with the poet.

Bull, of course, like Newton and Cowper, was an Evangelical. My host, the present Vicar, was not and had gradually restored to the church some of the furniture it had lost at the Reformation. Newton's gallery had been taken down; his pulpit had been saved but moved to the side. His tomb is a massive affair – 'offering some little obstacle to the resurrection of the body', as the Vicar remarked with a rather acid smile.

The real continuers of the Newton tradition had been so much offended by the Vicar's idolatrous innovations that they had set up a Mission of their own where they could get 'Gospel preaching'. Of their way of thinking was the famous Thomas Wright of Olney, known for his *Life of Cowper* and his work on Blake and, much later, for letting the cat out of the bag about Dickens' affair with Ellen Ternan.

I was taken to see him and found a patriarch in a much-worn frock-coat, with a low collar and white tie like an old-fashioned dissenting minister. He received me in a small room entirely lined with books, and in the centre a table with more books piled up to the ceiling. It was some time before I realized that his wife was also in the room – on the other side of the pile. He showed me one of the few coloured copies in existence of Blake's 'Jerusalem'. I left him with respect.

I felt, however, more at home with the Vicar. He admired Cowper and shared my view that it had been his misfortune to fall among Evangelicals, at least among those of the Calvinist persuasion. The Arminian Wesley would have done him no harm.

How remote these bitter controversies seem today! On a recent visit to Canada I was astonished to learn that the Presbyterians and the Methodists had combined to form the United Church. When I said it was *impossible*, I was met with blank astonishment: the services, it was pointed out, were really very similar. No doubt, but doctrinally they are poles apart. John Wesley spent his life fighting the Predestinarians and is probably turning in his grave. So is John Knox.

With the Vicar I walked up the hill from Olney to Clifton Reynes and saw the church and the vicarage where Lady Austen stayed at the beginning of her friendship with the poet. We walked back in the growing dusk with the Ouse gleaming among the dark fields and a single star in the greenish sky.

Next morning we set out on a pious pilgrimage (or a sentimental journey) to many of the places mentioned in *The Task*, walking along the road to Weston Underwood, then striking up through the spinneys to the chestnut avenue, now in full bloom, and so to the 'Alcove', the little Georgian temple, somewhat decayed. It commands a splendid view over the plain, beyond Olney spire: park-like, undulating country with the river meandering through the middle of it. Directly in front is a long avenue of limes clothed at this time of year in a luminous green haze of budding leaves. We walked along it till we came to 'the Wilderness', and so to the hot dusty road. Weston is a pretty village and Cowper must have delighted in the drive from Olney to visit the Throckmortons. In any biographical task it is essential, I think, to follow the man's footsteps. It is also one of the greatest pleasure of life, as I was to find later with Whistler and Huysmans.

But occupied as I was with Newton and Wesley and the rest, I was becoming increasingly conscious that the time was not far off when I would have to earn a living. Fortunately, I had no private income. I say 'fortunately' because I have known several people who had a small private income in the early 'twenties, and who resolved to live on it until Fame brought them Fortune. Fame, alas! did nothing of the kind, and the private income which was adequate forty years ago is now scarcely sufficient to buy them cigarettes. It was plain to me from the beginning that if I intended to be a writer I had better take another job.

But what job? I was firmly resolved not to be a school-master, and no-one had asked me to be a don. I applied to the University Appointments Board, filled in a form, and waited. The first job I was offered was as secretary to the Literary and Philosophic Society in a northern industrial town. I applied for it but, by the mercy of God, was turned down. More than thirty years later, I was asked to give a lecture to that Literary and Philosophic Society – and the successful candidate was still there!

Then I was told that there would be a competition for the administrative grade at the Victoria and Albert Museum. I decided to apply and, after a series of interviews, first at the Museum and then before the Civil Service Commission, I learned that three candidates had been successful: Leigh Ashton,[1] Kenneth Codrington,[2] and myself.

My last term at Oxford was drawing to a close. I sent my final contribution to *The Isis*:

> For three swift-flying seasons I
>   (But now 'tis ended! Ah, well!)
> Have paced the Corn, the Turl, the High,
> And watched the waters hurry by,
>   Of Isis and of Cherwell.
>
> In hearing distance of the chime
>   Of thy sweet bells, St Mary,
> I've played, and worked and babbled rhyme;
> I've had a very decent time
>   *In statu pupillari*

---

[1] Later Sir Leigh Ashton, Director of the Victoria and Albert Museum.
[2] Later Professor of Oriental Archaeology in London University.

I've seen my scholarship grow ripe,
   In spite of wind and weather;
I've copied lectures into type,
And watched my tutor smoke his pipe
   For many hours together.

I've gained – of Restoration plays –
   A reasonable knowledge;
I've slept in punts for days and days,
And found out several devious ways
   Of getting into college.

Once in the middle of the quad
   A Dean of Arts embraced me;
It was his way of praising God
For many bumps – I thought it odd;
   And once a Buller chased me.

I've been a member of a 'crew',
   I've hunted hares at Radley;
I once had breakfast with a Blue,
And once a Peer said 'How d'you do?' –
   I haven't done so badly.

We all must vanish – by Degrees,
   And in the world grow busy;
And I, too, go, but on my knees
Let me implore – remember please,
   De mortuis nil nisi . . .

The Victoria and Albert Museum required my services immediately. So, early in August 1922, I passed through the Edwardian-baroque portals beneath the 'Imperial crown surmounted by the figure of Fame', and made my way, as instructed, to the Department of Engraving, Illustration and Design. I was to remain there for thirty-seven years.

CHAPTER 4

Victoria and Albert

My immediate chief in the Department of Engraving, Illustration and Design was Martin Hardie, a distinguished etcher and water-colour painter in his own right. In my ignorance I had assumed that the RE after his name meant Royal Engineers; I now learned that it stood for Royal Society of Painter-Etchers and Engravers – the Engraving equivalent of the Royal Academy. Hardie ruled (as I was myself to do later) not only over the Department of Engraving, Illustration and Design, but over the Department of Paintings, which included an enormous number of water-colours and probably the best collection of miniatures in the world. The miniature expert was Basil Long, and I rather envied him his chance of specializing in a reasonably small field. The scope of EID was prodigious. I was supposed to have, or to acquire as rapidly as possible, a working knowledge not only of the technique of engraving, etching, wood-engraving, mezzotint, aquatint, stipple and lithography, and the history of these processes, but of Old Master drawings, posters, playing cards, fashion plates, trade labels, Persian miniatures, brass rubbings, Japanese prints, Christmas cards, caricatures, and of every kind of design from architecture to embroidered waistcoats. To have a detailed knowledge of all these was plainly impossible. To learn 'something of everything and everything of something' was the best that could be hoped for; and this I set myself to do.

The first six weeks was a severe test of adaptability and, perhaps I ought to add, bluff. For Martin Hardie was awaiting my arrival to go away for a holiday, and as soon as I was in-

stalled, off he went and left me to sink or swim. This was probably the best thing he could have done. One of my duties was
to be available for consultation by the public, and throughout
the day a whole succession of visitors would arrive. Some wanted
to give things to the Museum, some to sell things, some
wanted valuations (which we were not allowed to give), some
merely wanted advice. 'Is this a genuine Rembrandt?'

I soon found that every known state of Rembrandt's etchings
had been classified and photographed and that it was only
necessary to know where to look. Helped by kindly colleagues
I picked my way among works of reference, and by dint of
turning over our own prints I gradually came to distinguish good
from bad. When Hardie came back from his holiday I had almost
forgotten that I had ever been ignorant of the difference between
an etching and a drypoint. I had learned to produce the little
magnifying glass from my pocket with a flourish and to say,
with the finality of conviction, 'No; it is a late impression from
a very worn plate'.

The Rosenheim collection of engraved ornament was just
coming into the market, indeed Hardie was cataloguing it
for Sotheby's. I helped him in this and later sat beside him in
the saleroom while he struggled to acquire as much as possible
of it for the Museum. Our collection of engraved ornament
('the key to the history of design') was already extensive,
rivalled only by the Kunstgewerbemuseum in Berlin. Fortunately for us the German museums (it was the period of inflation)
were unable to compete and, as the giant American museums
had not yet awakened to the importance of engraved ornament,
we secured almost everything we wanted at fairly low prices.
It was my first introduction to the excitements of the saleroom.

No-one could have desired a better chief than Hardie. He
was always genial, never fussed and yet ran his large, and complicated, departments with great efficiency. In addition he had
the rare quality of generosity to his juniors, and was one of the
first to insist that Museum handbooks and catalogues should

go out under the name of the man who had actually written them and not under that of the head of the Department.

The Director of the Museum was Sir Cecil Harcourt-Smith, a somewhat remote figure with whom, as a new boy, I had very little to do. He had a noble appearance; he was tall and straight-backed and elegant: in his youth he had been known as 'The Light Dragoon'. There is an amusing caricature by Max showing him, commanding and immaculate, receiving a group of round, lumpy men in shapeless garments who are supposed to represent a delegation of provincial museum curators. He was soon to be succeeded by Eric Maclagan, who, when I arrived, was Keeper of the Department of Architecture and Sculpture. He too was a striking figure, in his different way. He was tall, thin and cadaverous and he wore a black double-stock. He had a great reputation as a scholar and had ventured to differ with the great Dr Bohde, of Berlin, over the Kaiserfriedrich Museum's bust of *Flora* supposed to be the work of Leonardo. The Kaiser, called in to support the German professor, had gazed for a few moments at the bust and then pronounced the solemn words: 'It *is* by Leonardo.' But when the Kaiser had fled to Holland the authorities of the Kaiserfriedrich examined the bust more closely and found inside it a fragment of a nineteenth-century waistcoat . . . Maclagan's stock in the international art world was therefore high.

The only other Keeper I saw much of was 'Georgie' Palmer, a most kindly old gentleman who had been in charge of the Library since before I was born. The younger men were an interesting lot: Herbert Read, recently transferred from the Treasury (of all places), William King, the expert on Chelsea porcelain, soon to leave us for the British Museum, and Leigh Ashton.

We were soon joined by men still slightly younger, for during the War there had been no new appointments and there were now several gaps to be filled. Montague Weekly came from Trinity, Oxford. He was known as an athlete, and if we had been told that he was the son of Frieda von Richthofen it wouldn't have meant anything to us at all. The D. H. Lawrence saga was not yet public property. From my own College came Arthur Wheen and Charles Oman.

Herbert Read already had a reputation as a writer. He had published poems and was known to be in touch with 'the Movement'. A little group of us lunched about once a week in a public house in Beauchamp Place, and these gatherings were sometimes graced by the presence of T. S. Eliot. He was charming with his thin-lipped but benevolent smile. My only regret was that he never seemed to *say* anything.

The huge palazzo in Cromwell Road had originally been designed for the 'Science and Art Department'. Science had moved over the way, but the building now housed not only the Victoria and Albert Museum but also the Royal College of Art, of which the Principal was Will (not yet Sir William) Rothenstein. I knew his name, of course, and was already acquainted with his admirable lithographs, 'Oxford Portraits'. I met him at the staff table in the restaurant.

In those days the Museum restaurant was still located in the rooms which had been built for the purpose and which are now used for an exhibition of Pre-Raphaelite applied art. William Morris had been responsible for the decoration of one of the rooms (it was his first non-ecclesiastical commission) and Burne-Jones had painted the panels. Glazed earthenware tiles by Godfrey Sykes adorned the other two rooms ('We fell in love with the tiles in the South Kensington Museum', as Wyndham Lewis remarks in his pamphlet *Architects, where is your Vortex?*), and in one of these there had in former days been a grill so good that it was quite fashionable to dine there.

These glories had departed, but the staff table in the Morris Room was used not only by the officials of the Museum but by the staff of the Royal College of Art. There was nothing luxurious, or even civilized, about the fare, but Rothenstein often brought his friends to lunch, and these friends included some of the most distinguished men of the day. He was making a series of sanguine portraits, and, when he published them, got his literary

friends to write appreciations of the sitters. He asked me to
contribute the piece on J. C. Squire. He also introduced me to
Edmund Gosse, but my closer acquaintance with Gosse was due
not to Rothenstein, but to Mary Hogarth.

She was an artist, the favourite pupil, it was said, of Sickert,
and she ran a kind of non-profit-making hostel for girl students
in a house in Queensberry Place, the site of which is now occupied by the *Institut Français*. One of her greatest friends was
Duncan Grant, whose designs she reproduced in *petit point*.
She offered one day to take me to see Gosse in Regent's Park.

The Times obituary notice referred to her as 'a woman of
striking appearance'. She was certainly that. She was very tall
and thin, her features very pronounced, and adorned with a
white moustache. Her outdoor garb consisted of a series of
superimposed cloaks of dun-coloured cloth, and on her head was
a kind of Arab burnous, a sort of floating cloud of grey material
attached in some mysterious way to a close-fitting pork-pie
hat. She had a very loud voice, and she kept up a continual flow
of intimate conversation about her friends, especially Sickert.
This did not matter so long as her remarks were drowned by the
noise of the tube, but suddenly the train stopped at a station,
the doors opened and in the moment's silence which ensued the
voice of Mary Hogarth rang through the compartment like
the voice of the recording angel 'And Sickert, of course, was
a *Devil* with women!'

I was looking forward to meeting Edmund Gosse. To young
literary men today he is probably no more than a name, but in
the early 'twenties by means of 'those weekly exercises in
urbane journalism' he loomed large in the world of letters.
'His readers', says John Freeman, the critic, writing in 1924,
'have come to regard him as an institution, set up for the illumination of contemporary literature'. I had, of course, read
Father and Son with its evocation of a childhood not unlike my
own. I knew that he had been the friend of Henry James and
Coventry Patmore, of Swinburne and Stevenson, that he had
seen George Eliot driving in the Park with George Henry

Lewes and had noted the contrast between 'the solemnity of the face and the frivolity of the headgear'. He seemed to me the very embodiment of the literary tradition, and I was rather pained that his acquaintances, almost without exception, were so catty about him behind his back.

Once, at Rothenstein's, I found a bitter-faced little man, with tiny feet and hands. He was asked to recite his satire on Gosse. I can only remember two lines:

> Play lackey to the flattery of the Great,
> And still, like Fido, feed off silver plate.

Even the tolerant Rothenstein joined in the applause, and then described a dinner in honour of Samuel Butler's memory at which Gosse had been present. He couldn't bear having had nothing to do with the discovery of Butler and had made a far from complimentary speech. 'But Gosse,' said Rothenstein, 'had one virtue at least – the genius of survival. Everything comes to him who lives long enough. When I think of the wicked things that old scoundrel John Lane did, I am surprised I could bear to meet the man. And yet, when I sat next to him at dinner, and found him a white-bearded patriarch, I treated him with the utmost respect.'

At the house in Regent's Park we were welcomed by Mrs Gosse (her husband had not yet received his knighthood) with quick bird-like movements, and after a few moments Gosse himself appeared. He talked about Italy in a high, squeaking voice. Then, to my astonishment, the Sitwell brothers entered. I say to my astonishment because in my incredible naïvety I thought of them as revolutionaries and our host as a pillar of the literary Establishment. I did not yet realize that social loyalties are more potent than aesthetic opinions. I was fascinated by Osbert's check trousers. He and Sacheverell had just 'returned from Syracuse', where they had been to bury an aunt and catalogue her furniture. They were both very charming and friendly.

During tea Gosse told stories about Herbert Spencer. It

appeared that the philosopher used to live as a paying guest with two old ladies who would play the piano for him until he was tired of it. Then, even in the middle of a chord, he would hold up his hand and the music ceased. He had two pieces of cotton wool which he inserted in his ears when conversation bored him, and he was known to make use of the same device at dinner parties, to the general astonishment.

When his works were about to appear in America he wrote to the publisher saying that someone must come to see him to make the final arrangements. The head of the firm accordingly crossed the Atlantic and called on Spencer at Brighton. The great man, however, was not in a very cordial mood, and opened the proceedings by saying: 'I beg of you to state your business as succinctly as possible, as I cannot endure the human voice for more than six minutes'.

On his death bed (this Gosse begged me to note as it was an oral tradition he would not willingly let die) Spencer raised himself up on the pillows, to the surprise of everybody present, who thought he was dead already, and said: 'Conscious as I am that this my body will probably shortly be transported across the water . . .', and fell back dead. Gosse thought he had in mind the recent transporting of the body of Queen Victoria from the Isle of Wight, and imagined that something of the sort was to happen to him.

Gosse had recently been to America and did not like it. There were cultured and delightful people in the United States, but they were 'surrounded and beleaguered by the forces of barbarism'. His American adventures reminded him of a story about Woodrow Wilson. Mrs Woodrow Wilson, talking one day to Clemenceau, remarked: 'Woodrow is a very wonderful man but, do you know, when he proposed to me I almost fell out of bed with laughing'. Apparently he had proposed by letter and she had read it over her morning coffee; but Clemenceau put the natural French construction on the remark and told everybody. Even that failed to win for Woodrow Wilson the affection of Paris.

As I took my leave Gosse, with great affability, offered to support my candidature for the Savile Club and added: 'Come and see me one Sunday, and I'll take you to dine with George Moore.'

What fools young men are! If he really wants me, I thought, he will ask me for a definite date. Yet, after all, it was my business to chase him, not his to chase me. I was too proud, or too shy, to take him at his word. And so I never dined with George Moore, never, indeed, set eyes on him, except at some theatrical first night. It is one of my regrets.

It is not (to be honest) that I have ever fallen flat on my face in admiration of George Moore. In his reminiscences he is delightful. And I can read, and re-read *The Lovers of Orelay*. But are his imitations of the French 'Naturalists' as good as they were once supposed to be? And when he becomes obsessed with 'Style' he can be quite intolerable. To my mind at least *The Brook Kerith* is one of the most boring and pointless books ever written.

Perhaps he will survive as a character. Miss Hogarth told me that when he saw the portrait Sickert had painted of him, he was much annoyed.

'You have made me look like a booby', he said.

'But you *are* a booby', was Sickert's answer.

Sylvia Gosse (whom I now met for the first time at her father's house) was another of Sickert's women pupils. She had learned from him to etch and produced some admirable plates of her own. Years later she presented her splendid collection of the Master's etchings to my Department at South Kensington.

The day after the visit to Gosse I met another lion. Will Rothenstein, whose studio was in the same building as my own office, sent over an invitation to meet Yeats, of whom he was making a drawing. I found the poet standing in front of the fire in the studio, very tall and shaggy, with floppy tie and broad black eye-glass ribbon. We spoke of the Rhymers Club and Ireland. He thought the clergy were losing their influence there. Someone had remarked to him that the Church in Ireland was walking the plank. 'Yes,' said Yeats, 'and the Church in England is *treading the boards*'. He was delighted with this witticism. He complained, not very bitterly, that the Shamrock Tearoom, where he had lodged in Oxford, was now called the Yeats Café.

Rothenstein's relations with some of my Museum colleagues were, I think, a little strained, but he was always very kind to me, bringing me in whenever he had a distinguished visitor. My diary records:

'Rothenstein sent up a note asking me to meet Max Beerbohm and his wife at lunch in the Museum. I sat next to Mrs Beerbohm and Ashton opposite, next to Max. Rothenstein sat at the end of the table. I did not hear the beginning of his conversation because I was busy with Mrs B., but when Hardie came and sat on her right and began to talk about Rapallo I was more free to listen. They had arrived at Conrad and his efforts to write a play.

'*Rothenstein*: "They are all mad to do it and they all make the most ghastly failure of it – James, Meredith, George Moore . . ."

'I chipped in with the remark that *Gabrielle* was to be produced some time in the Autumn.

'*Max*: "That's Moore's play, isn't it? Not much chance for that." '[1]

'The talk drifted to Conrad's entourage and the "boosting" of Press agents. Wells had told Rothenstein that Bennett had made £7,000 on royalties alone by his trip to America – such was the stimulus imparted to sales . . .

'Rothenstein declared that too much money was going to Museums and not enough to the encouragement of contemporary art. "Finally, the Museum gets everything," said Ashton. I proposed the Chinese method: the desecration of the ancestral tombs at every change of dynasty. The absurd prices brought by fifth-rate Knellers – himself a third-rate artist – were discussed and Rothenstein remarked that he would like

[1] It was indeed 'the most ghastly failure'.

to see John "get his boom. He needs money for that expensive family of his."

'*Max*: "How many of them are there now?"

'*Rothenstein*: "Nobody knows – not even John."

'Beerbohm laughed in his peculiar way, shaking his left shoulder. He is bald now and rather plump-faced with a reddish moustache slightly curled upward.

'*Max*: "I suppose when it got into three figures he stopped counting."

'*J.L.* (making his supreme effort): "Augustus the Physically Strong . . ."

'*Rothenstein*: "John is wearing a little, of course. He is no longer so startlingly handsome, although his head is still magnificent. He can look very effective in blacked boots and well-cut clothes, and he still makes people uncomfortable when he comes into a room."

'*Max*: "I know. They sit on the ends of their chairs and gaze at him."

'Orpen was now most respectable and no longer wore that little coat straight across the throat. Most attractive! I remarked that Shaw was a white venerable old man and quite well dressed.

'*Max*: "But still hygienic in Jaeger."

'*Rothenstein*: "Drinkwater has begun to dress well." (I saw him, indeed, at Simmonds' puppet with an actor-manager collar of astrakhan.)

'*Rothenstein*: "It is a great mistake for artists to become well-dressed as they grow prosperous. Gordon Craig is unchanged."

'Mrs Beerbohm remarked that Craig sometimes wrote a note (exquisitely worded and spaced) to borrow some English stamps to receipt his bills. Someone called him uncharitable, but Rothenstein defended him as a man who had, after all, failed and was liable to contrast other men's half-successes with his dream-perfections.

'I asked after the Goldini Theatre which Craig had run for some years in Florence and was told that it had been abandoned years ago. "Do the Craigs go about much?" someone asked, and Max dwelt on their poverty, but said he had seen them studying the map, finding some minute Italian town with a theatre, and going off to it *en pélérinage*. They reminded him of the scene in *David Copperfield* when Micawber had declared that there was nothing for it but suicide: "Self-destruction, my boy," and had been seen by David next day on the top of the coach cracking nuts and at peace with the Universe. So, too, Craig, one night in the depth of depression, is off next morning on one of his expeditions, with the wind in his cloak.

Hardie: "I know that cloak of his. I remember his setting out with his wife and daughter and son, they in thin things and over-burdened with his baggage. Then a shower came on and Craig was the only dry member of the party – and he went to bed with a chill."

'The conversation went down a blind alley after Craig's son. Charming, Max thought him, and I agreed. Hardie mentioned a pathetic letter from him in which he said that his father had "only three people working for him now instead of the dozen he needs". Most of us thought him very fortunate, and Max began a tale about a Russian-American lady who had been drawn in and had worked for six months. Mrs Craig was afraid she would go away and tell America that she had been working for Craig. Max thought it a small price to pay for an unpaid and proficient typist.

'*Rothenstein*: "These helpless men of genius make a system of it. Conder had twenty women round him, each persuaded that she alone had kept him from starvation."

'*Max*: "Yes, his staff of nurses certainly looked after him."

'*Rothenstein* (turning to Mrs Beerbohm): "Your sex, Florence, is so ready to mother a man of genius."

'*Mrs Beerbohm*: "How forgotten Conder is now. Nobody seems to care about his work at all."

'*Rothenstein*: "That is because he was not a Negro." '

Max's conversation was not exactly witty. It was the slow, deliberate manner with which he built up his effects which fas-

The author with Douglas Fairbanks Jr and Dolores del Rio

Veronica Turleigh

cinated me. I once heard him take twenty minutes to describe the purchase of a 'velvet hat' at Lock's. It was hard to say what the charm consisted of, but it was certainly there. Anyway, I was grateful to Will Rothenstein for having given me the chance of listening to him. This was the time of his exhibition at the Leicester Galleries which caused so much excitement because of the bitter caricatures of Edward VII. They were withdrawn after public clamour, and I must confess that they shocked me a little. Max seemed to lose his usual urbanity whenever he depicted King Edward. Was there some personal reason for the virulence of his attacks? I suppose we shall never know.

Rothenstein himself was an excellent raconteur, and, after all, he had much to recount. He had something to say about Verlaine and the Goncourts; he even had some new stories about Wilde. I liked the one of Wilde visiting a thieves' kitchen – a real one – in Paris. One of his friends, who was rather drunk, announced his intention of protecting 'my friend Oscar Wilde' against all the world. 'Be quiet,' whispered Wilde, 'you are defending us at the risk of our lives.'

Rothenstein spoke enthusiastically of Wilde's wit, denying that he owed anything to Whistler, but he admitted that his appearance, when he knew him, was frightening. The bloated, red-brown face, the swollen lips, the vast bulk, all contributed to the startling nature of the vision which appeared suddenly in the doorway of his studio in Paris.

Wilde apparently spoke very bad French, and the French themselves could make nothing of his peculiar brand of humour. He was once present at a French version of some Shakespeare play, preceded in the programme by a ballet. He kept remarking during the ballet that it was 'not a bit like Shakespeare's masterpiece', and his companion, a French lady, kept on explaining patiently that Shakespeare was to come 'afterwards'.

In the same *genre* was his refusal to accept an invitation from (was it?) Degas, on the ground that the hour named – nine in the morning – was much too late. *'Je suis beaucoup plus*

bourgeois que vous, Monsieur. Je me couche toujours à quatre heures.'
The Frenchman went away marvelling at Wilde's thick-headed-
ness.

After his release from prison, Rothenstein visited him, in
France, and was received with gratitude. Wilde told many
amusing stories of his prison life – it is a mistake, of course, to
suppose that the *Ballad* represents his only mood in Reading
Gaol – particularly of the warder who tried to improve his
literary education by talking to him.

'And Mr Charles Dickens, would he be considered a great
writer, Sir?'

'Oh yes! You see – he's dead.'

'And Miss Marie Corelli, Sir. Would she be considered a
good writer?'

'My dear man, I would not for worlds say anything against
Miss Corelli's moral character. But, for her writing – why, she
ought to be *here!'*

I knew that Rothenstein had brought Verlaine to England.
He told me how glad his hosts were to see him go; how he had
parted with the £80 earned by his lectures to a harpy in Dieppe,
so that the harpy in Paris got nothing; how Rothenstein and
Ray Lankaster, the scientist, had celebrated Verlaine's fiftieth
birthday, and how his wit used to flash out in the midst of his
most banal conversations.

Rothenstein seemed to have known everybody, as indeed he
had. He told me that walking once with 'that old satyr Rodin' in
the garden of what is now the *Musée Rodin*, the sculptor said, *à
propos* of nothing: 'They accuse me of thinking too much about
women. What else is there to think about?'

Alphonse Daudet came to England with his son Léon and
dined at Christ Church. Wolsey was mentioned and Daudet
asked his son who Wolsey was. *'Le Chancelier de Georges III,'*
came the incredible answer. Daudet visited Meredith, and when
they parted, Daudet being already in the train, they embraced
in French fashion. Unfortunately both men suffered from loco-
motor ataxia and they could not unclasp their arms. The train

started, and there was nearly an unpleasant accident for poor Meredith.

Rothenstein, in spite of his own very comfortable background, thought that dirt and squalor were useful to the artist in protecting him from aristocratic patronage. He instanced Augustus John, diverted from his natural task of painting gypsies to producing Society portraits. The French artists of the 'seventies and 'eighties never obtained any footing in polite society at all. I suggested that Degas was, surely, an exception, and he agreed.

He surprised me by saying that when Max Beerbohm made his famous descent of Oxford he was universally detested. He had in those days a very bitter tongue, and it was he who made the terrible remark about Beardsley: 'Even his lungs are affected.'

There were many other stories: of the cheap bouquet which Sickert weighted with lead and flung to Ellen Terry, and which fell among the costly flowers with a most alarming thud; of George Moore in the Café Royal denying that John had any talent, and then when the latter lurched in, sat down at a table and began tracing shapes with his finger in spilt wine, Moore bristled with eagerness and saying: 'If you wish to draw me, I am perfectly willing to sit.'

Rothenstein himself was a curious blend of the conventional and the unconventional. I once met him at Hyde Park Corner, in the early afternoon. To my astonishment he was wearing an opera hat. He explained that he had just been presenting his son John[1] at Court. He had bowed to the Establishment in such a major issue as this, but, having no silk hat, thought an opera hat would do just as well.

I met the whole family in due course, at the big house in Sheffield Terrace on Campden Hill. Simmonds' Puppets, already mentioned, were presented there to a very distinguished assembly, including Shaw and Arnold Bennett. It was the first time I had heard the Irish brogue of the one and the high-pitched

[2] Now Sir John Rothenstein, Director of the Tate Gallery.

squeak of the other. Mrs Rothenstein, as she then was, had a Rubenesque beauty. Her sister had married William Orpen and soon I met him too at the Savile Club, where Rothenstein took me to lunch. I met there for the first time J. C. Squire, then the influential editor of *The London Mercury*, the novelist W. L. George, and Gosse, once more.

The Club had not yet moved to its present inaccessible position in Brook Street, but was situated in Piccadilly, next to the St James's Club, in the little pot-bellied house, since demolished, from which, the legend ran, Blücher had watched his troops marching through London. It was a friendly, slightly fusty place. I liked it and was shortly elected a member, proposed by Rothenstein and seconded by Gosse. Unfortunately, having paid the entrance fee and subscription, I was so short of funds that I could hardly ever afford to use it.

However, an unexpected gift (from L.D.H., of course), and finding that I had already earned a little official leave, decided me to go to Florence in the autumn of 1922. Rothenstein at once offered me a letter of introduction to Bernard Berenson; and armed with this I set off.

When I crossed the frontier I was, at first, completely bewildered by what seemed to be going on. At Milan the train suddenly filled up with men in black shirts and tasselled tarbushes. The fat man who sat opposite to me had also a pistol and a long knife stuck crosswise into his belt. Innocent of Italian politics and never having heard of Mussolini, I had arrived on the day of the March on Rome. Still, Florence was quiet enough. Apart from bands of children singing 'Giovinezza' and a couple of *Communisti* being chased through the streets I saw nothing unusual, and settled down to explore the beautiful city at my leisure.

Rather nervously I telephoned to *I Tati* and, after mentioning my letter of introduction, was invited to luncheon. I made my way to Settignano and, at the end of an impressive avenue of cypresses, found the Berenson mansion. There was quite a large company, all gazing on the Master with awe, as indeed I did myself. He was royally gracious to one whom he must have regarded as an infant-in-arms, and we soon adjourned to a kind of summer-house for the meal. What chiefly impressed me was the gold (probably silver-gilt) plates for the fruit, and the white gloves of the serving men.

'B.B.' as everybody called him did most of the talking. He was inveighing against the historical method in art criticism. He confessed that his own early essays had been 'crassly Morellian', but he had now come to see how fruitless it was merely to determine 'who painted, or carved, or built, whatever it be'. What was needed was a 'qualitative', not a 'quantitative' judgement.

I listened to this with some astonishment. It was all very well for Whistler, the practising artist, to declaim against those: 'sombre of mien, and wise with the wisdom of books, who frequent museums and burrow in crypts; collecting – comparing – compiling – classifying – contradicting.

'Experts these – for whom a date is an accomplishment – a hall-mark, success.

'Careful in scrutiny are they, and conscientious of judgement, establishing, with due weight, unimportant reputations, discovering the picture by the stain on the back – testing the torso by the leg that is missing . . . disputatious and dictatorial concerning the birth place of inferior persons – speculating, in much writing, upon the great worth of bad work.'

But Berenson was himself the King of the Connoisseurs. Who more than he had frequented museums and burrowed in crypts, contrasting, comparing, compiling? He was a genius at it. And in nothing had his genius, with its curious blend of scholarship and business acumen, been more clearly shown, than in his decision to group all the works of the disciples of Botticelli under the invented name of Amico di Sandro. That this was perfectly legitimate had been explained at length as long ago as the beginning of the century. After all, each anonymous painter in question must have been, in some sense, a 'friend' of the great Florentine. The fact remained that pictures labelled Amico di

Sandro brought very much higher prices in the saleroom than pictures labelled School of Botticelli. I looked around me at the luxurious villa, at all the evidences of his success, with wonder.

He was courtesy itself. He saw me to the door and into the taxi which he had ordered to take me back to Florence. He complained that his car had been requisitioned for the day by the local Fascist bosses. 'Not that there is anything new in that,' he said. 'The Communists used to do the same. The curious thing is that the order was signed by the *same people*!'

Rothenstein had given me also a letter of introduction to the architect Geoffrey Scott, who was living at the Villa Medici. This I found a somewhat less awe-inspiring establishment than Berenson's. The house was smaller than I had expected and the drawing room, to my surprise, was pure Louis xv chinoiserie. Lady Sybil Scott and Miss Cutting, her daughter by a previous marriage, received me very kindly and everything was very easy and informal. Geoffrey Scott himself was, in a different way, as brilliant as B.B. I had, of course, primed myself by reading his *Architecture of Humanism*, the first book I had ever come across in which 'baroque' was not a dirty word. Reared on Ruskin I – like almost everybody else, including Baedeker – had regarded it as a term of abuse. Geoffrey Scott's book and Sacheverell Sitwell's *Southern Baroque Art* turned the tide, and, a generation later, the taste for baroque is a commonplace. Yet even now when I enter Browning's 'Church of St Praxed's' in Rome I can't help regretting that it was thought necessary to baroquise *everything*. I would give the whole of the rest of the building, and half-a-dozen other Roman churches besides, for the one surviving Chapel of St Zeno with its exquisite sixth-century mosaics.

In those days, not having yet seen Rome, my acquaintance with baroque architecture was slight enough, and I was not likely to see much of it in Florence. I did not care. I could say, with Browning:

> But at any rate I have loved the season
> Of Art's spring-birth so dim and dewy,
> My sculptor is Nicolo the Pisan,
> And painter – who but Cimabue?

I had first become aware of what Florence meant when, as a schoolboy in Liverpool, I had walked down Bold Street and gazed entranced into the window of the Medici Society's shop. Botticelli, Ghirlandajio, Filippo and Filippino Lippi had long been familiar names to me, and here, at last, I found their actual works. Florence in the third quarter of the fifteenth century was where, and when, I would have chosen to live.

Unfortunately the companion of my walks through the city, when we penetrated into

> dim San Spirito
> Or was it rather the Ognissanti,

or into that most magical of churches, Or San Michele, was a New College friend who was not interested in the Renaissance at all, early or late. What enthralled him were the 'towers of the nobles'. Such towers, of course, still exist at San Gimignano and in other Italian towns but in Florence they had long been swept away. 'Just think,' he would say, 'what an interesting building they pulled down to put *that* up'. *That* was Giotto's campanile. I realized what fanatics art-historians can be, and what a streak of sheer lunacy runs through connoisseurship.

Indeed, when I got back to the Victoria and Albert Museum and began to know the connoisseurs and collectors, it soon became plain to me that many of them were more than a little mad. I came to the reluctant conclusion that collecting as such, divorced in many cases from any kind of aesthetic appreciation, is a pathological activity. Fortunately the Victoria and Albert Museum does not concern itself with postage stamps. But I was visited by collectors of match-box labels (phillumenists was the grand name they gave themselves), jam-jar labels and even orange-wrappers. The justification for these pursuits is that they assemble material for a history of design, but I could not help wondering at what point this legitimate interest shaded off into mere magpieism.

One of the benefactors of the Museum was a man with a famous name who left us in his will a collection of drawings. Collecting drawings is a very respectable hobby, but when I went to Harrods' repository to see his drawings there were 20,000 of them. There is no point in possessing 20,000 drawings. If one spent all one's spare time looking at them, it would take years even to glance at the individual items. It was obvious that most of the drawings, once bought, had never been looked at again. Indeed, many of them had never been looked at at all, for they were still in the brown-paper parcels in which they had been purchased. My Director would only allow me to accept fifteen hundred of them, and even these took three months to select and classify.

Can one be said to possess a thing one never sees? It is related of William Randolph Hearst that, coming across a photograph of a fine piece of silver in an old catalogue, he cabled to his representatives in Europe, 'Find it. Buy it. Spare no expense.' They spared no expense and, after a long interval, cabled back that this particular piece had been in Hearst's own collection for the last ten years.

When the Benedictine Fathers of Ampleforth purchased Gilling Castle for their preparatory school it contained a very fine Elizabethan panelled room. They sold this to Hearst for a little less than the price they had paid for the whole house. When Hearst died the room, dismantled, was found in a London store. The Benedictines raised a subscription and bought it back. It is now in its original position. The good monks in fact got the room – and the castle – almost for nothing. God moves in a mysterious way. Private vices (and private lunacies) can sometimes be public benefits. But I suppose Hearst had never read the 'Fable of the Bees'.

Some of the connoisseurs' aberrations took strange forms.

There was the man who had come to believe that all (or almost all) works of art in the world were by Turner. By looking long enough, through a powerful lens, he had discovered, or imagined that he had discovered, an occult and microscopic signature. It could not, of course, be seen by everybody, but he could see it, and he found it everywhere.

'Come into the gallery,' he said.

I followed him and he struck an attitude before our little water-colour of 'The Borgia Children', by Rossetti.

'Who painted that?' he asked.

'Rossetti?' I suggested.

He shook his head.

'No. Turner.'

Then he pulled from his pocket an illuminated initial from a sixteenth-century manuscript on vellum.

'Who painted that?'

'Turner?' I said.

He beamed, and nodded emphatic assent.

'Early manner?' I asked.

'Yes,' he replied. 'Very early manner.'

It was quite plain that argument of any kind was useless, and yet this man was, or had been, quite a distinguished connoisseur. He told me that before he stumbled on his great discovery he had only possessed three Turners. Now, he had three hundred.

An even stranger case was that of the Frenchman who thought that everything in the world was by Leonardo da Vinci, even, incredible as it may seem, a large axe or chopper which he had in his possession. Leonardo had 'signed' this axe, by microscopic notches on the blade, in half-a-dozen places, and not Leonardo only, but all the distinguished men of the period, artists and statesmen, cardinals and poets had scratched their names on Leonardo's axe. It was a kind of universal autograph album and, of course, priceless. But when anyone but the owner examined the blade he couldn't see any signatures at all. Another scholar cherished the somewhat Freudian complex that if you looked long enough at the specifically male organs of Michelangelo's nude figures you would see the monogram of the master!

These strange aberrations were paralleled by those of the Diagonalists, to coin a word for those who believe that great masterpieces of painting have all been constructed on strict mathematical principles. Chief of these was a man who held that if you joined the third finger of the left hand of all the principal figures in Raphael's paintings you would obtain a series of geometrical figures bearing constant relations to one another.

He was certainly a little mad; but my complete scepticism of the ideas of what might be called the 'Golden Section School' has since been modified. Matila Ghyka, in his monumental book *Le Nombre d'Or*, has, I think, shown convincingly that some of the Renaissance painters at least had such a notion very much in mind when they were constructing their pictures. But, for the moment, I had other things to think of.

Very soon after my arrival in the Department a letter arrived from Vancouver, signed A. H. Palmer. The writer, who was very old, said that he had a large number of the works of his father, Samuel Palmer, and he offered to lend them for an exhibition. Nowadays, of course, everybody admires Samuel Palmer, but it was very different in the early 'twenties. He was dismissed as a Victorian painter who had once, in a vague way, been a disciple of Blake. His elaborately worked etchings had been driven out of favour by the fashion for Whistler and Seymour Haden, his pen-and-wash drawings were almost unknown, his oil paintings could be bought for a song. The authorities agreed to hold the exhibition and Hardie left the organizing of it very largely to me.

We carried on an enormous correspondence with A. H. Palmer, an irascible old gentleman who once cabled to Hardie that I was to be 'instantly dismissed', and who later (Hardie himself having fallen from favour) implored Laurence Binyon, then Hardie's opposite number at the British Museum, to take the whole affair out of our hands. I have never seen a more embarrassed man than poor, shy Binyon who came to enquire what on earth he was to do about it.

We really did not deserve this treatment. I ruined my eyesight establishing the 'states' of all the Palmer etchings (they are still known as 'L.58, State 3' or whatever it may be), and I delved deep into the record of the 'Old Etching Club,' the manuscript minutes of which happened to be in our Library. I came to love the etchings, especially *The Bellman*, and when the small sketches arrived we were astonished at their beauty. We were able to buy some of them after the exhibition; the show itself was a great success and started the Palmer vogue. I suppose I could, in those days, have bought one of the oils for about forty pounds – but I hadn't got forty pounds. Now that I am richer, Palmers are still out of my reach. This is the carrot that a wise Providence dangles forever before one's nose.

I enjoyed all this work so much that I sometimes wondered why the Museum authorities paid me to do it. Oughtn't I perhaps to pay *them*? My conscience was a little stricken that I was getting so much pleasure out of life and doing so little to share it; and so, when, one day in 1924, a circular appeared on my desk asking for volunteers to teach at the Working Men's College, I was in a mood to respond.

The College had been founded by Frederick Denison Maurice about a hundred years before. Ruskin and Burne-Jones had taught there, and it was where Rossetti was supposed to be (but wasn't) on the night Elizabeth Siddal took an overdose of laudanum. Its Principal was General Sir Frederick Maurice, grandson of the founder, and the active spirit was Ellis Franklin, nephew of Lord Samuel. I thought I would go along to Camden Town, where it was now located, and have a look. Rather nervously, I made my way to the common room. Of course I met Franklin (he was there, I think, every night) and, of course, having met him, my fate was sealed. Before the week was out I found myself taking a class in English literature for students preparing for the London Matriculation.

One of the things I found rather distracting was the practice (the admirable practice, I think now) of bringing meals into the classroom. For those who came late from work it was a very necessary arrangement, but I was put off my stride when an old man in the first row started eating a kipper during my discourse on Wordsworth. I couldn't help feeling that if Providence had really foreseen this contingency it would have produced a kipper with fewer bones.

For a couple of years I plugged away at English, gradually learning more and more about the College and entering into its life: a little fencing, a few debates and lectures. Then Franklin asked me to reorganize the Art Class. It was a big undertaking. It is no reflection on those teaching at the time to say that their methods were a little out of date. The tuition was mostly in 'shading from the Antique'. There was no life class at all.

I consulted Rothenstein and he was, as always, most helpful. He did a very real service to me and to the College by putting me in touch with Percy Horton. Percy Horton was the real creator of the Art Class. One of his first actions was to break up the clutter of casts, to simplify the whole set-up, to provide adequate 'donkeys' (I remember the ridicule I met with in the Studies Committee when I clamoured for money for 'donkeys', the combined stool and easel used by artists), and most of all to provide a living model. We were later to expand our activities and to have an exceptionally brilliant team of teachers, notably, Geoffrey Rhoades and Barnett Freedman. Geoffrey was as quiet as Barnett was ebullient. Both of them, and all the art teachers, did wonderful work for the College, but it was Percy Horton who was the pioneer. I am glad to know that their labours at Mornington Crescent did not prevent these men from developing their own talents, in fact I like to think that it helped them.

Horton was a born teacher and ultimately became Principal of the Ruskin School at Oxford. Barnett Freedman, a rumbustious and heroic figure, fighting ill-health for the greater part of his short life, was a good painter and an excellent book illustrator and lithographer. I once made a selection of book-jackets for an exhibition and found that about three-quarters of them were by Barnett Freedman. For his work as a war artist he made several dangerous trips in submarines and was as popular ('I'm an East End Jew and proud of it') with the officers as with the men.

There was, however, one perhaps unfortunate result of the very success of the art teaching at the Working Men's College. Some of the pupils became so proficient that they began to win scholarships at the Royal College of Art and elsewhere. Is one really doing a service to a working printer by encouraging him to give up his job and launch himself on the stormy sea of art? One such man took the plunge and was provided with a small income to carry him through his years of training. I would like to record that the names of the providers were Eddie Marsh and Lady Juliet Duff.

Meanwhile my writing activities were somewhat in abeyance. I wrote short stories and verses and sent them to *Punch* and other magazines, but without much success. Soon I had a varied and interesting collection of 'rejection slips'. Then, one day, Martin Hardie showed me a letter he had received from Wilfred Partington, editor of *The Bookman's Journal* (not to be confused with *The Bookman*). Partington wanted someone to write 'etching criticism'. How old-world that sounds! Who cares nowadays whether etchings are criticized or not – or produced or not? But the 'twenties was the heyday of the great etching boom, and the leading etchers: McBey, Griggs, Gerald Brock-hurst, W. P. Robins, etc., were taken very seriously, and their works competed for. A single impression of McBey's *Seven Sisters* was sold for £400; whereas one could have bought the original drawing from which he worked for a tenth of that sum. It was the absurdity of these inflated prices that finally killed the etching boom.

Hardie asked me if I would be interested. 'Of course,' he added, 'I don't know if you can write'.

I wrote a preliminary piece for Partington and then went to

see him. He had an office in Fleet Street, and he received me with a certain amount of one-upmanship (although the word had not yet been invented): keeping me waiting, pretending to be desperately busy, and the whole performance which a surprising number of people seem to think necessary to build up their prestige. But he was genial enough when we got down to business. He offered me a retaining fee of £25 a year; and I was to write a minimum of six articles at £5 each. Fifty pounds a year! Prospects of unlimited wealth opened before my eyes. I walked back along Fleet Street as if I owned the place.

The Bookman's Journal was by no means a negligible publication at that time. Its contributors included Arthur Symons, Vernon Blake, William Poel, Gerald Gould and Michael Sadleir. It is amusing to find, in one of the early numbers to which I contributed, a letter from Thomas J. Wise:

'Sir, – May I be permitted through the columns of *The Bookman's Journal* to enter a warning against two impudent forgeries of rare books . . . the first editions of Shelley's *Adonais*, printed in Pisa in 1821, and *Hellas*, printed in London in 1822'.

In view of what we now know of Thomas J. Wise's own 'impudent forgeries' this is pretty rich.

Partington was a publisher as well as an editor and, after a few articles had appeared, he suggested that I should write a novel. I did so, and I am very glad now that it was never published. Like nearly all first novels it was autobiographical, and writing it got something out of the system, so that when I came to write my second novel, *Nymph Errant*, I was able to be completely objective. But this was long after 'John Castle' (as Partington's firm was called) had gone out of business.

Partington then suggested that I should write a book about modern artists and, rashly, I agreed. In consultation with Mary Hogarth a list was drawn up, a list which makes rather odd reading today. Sickert, as Mary Hogarth's master, was in, of course, and so was Duncan Grant. Vanessa Bell and Roger Fry fell into the same group. Brangwyn and Sargent we felt had to be included, as well as George Clausen and Cayley

Robinson. Augustus John was in as well as William Nicholson and James Pryde, Tonks and Wilson Steer, William Rothenstein and Sir Charles Holmes. Epstein, Frank Dobson and Eric Gill represented sculpture. Paul Nash, who was then teaching at the Royal College of Art, I got to know quite well, once I had overcome his resistance to being in the book at all. I went to see James Pryde in his studio in Westbourne Terrace and found him in bed on a little balcony recovering from a motor accident. He received me kindly and allowed me to use a self-portrait as one of the illustrations of the book. So did Rothenstein, Orpen, Steer, Clausen, Nicholson and Duncan Grant. Eric Gill and Wyndham Lewis drew portraits specially for the book and if it has any interest today it is largely for these illustrations. Henry Lamb, Ambrose McEvoy and Lucien Pissarro completed the list.

Not quite! For Partington had thought of what he considered a wonderful title: *Portraits in Oil and Vinegar*. I disliked this intensely, and vainly protested that there was no vinegar in the book, which was a serious attempt at the appraisal of contemporary artists' work. Finally it was decided to include the President of the Royal Academy, Sir Frank Dicksee, about whose work I could be as vinegary as I chose. 'British art is going back a long way if it is going back to Dicksee' was about the best I could manage; but it did justify the title. On the title-page was an (alleged) quotation from Brillat-Savarin: '*Dans la vie comme dans la salade il faut de l'huile et du vinaigre: beaucoup de l'une, très peu de l'autre*'. I say 'alleged' because no such sentence is to be found in *La Physiologie du Goût*. Like Walter Scott with his 'Old Ballad' chapter headings, I made it up myself.

The book came out early in 1925 and most of the reviewers were kind. The notable exception was Clive Bell in *The Athenaeum*. He tore the whole thing into little pieces ('Mr Laver is a man of some wit and no aesthetic sensibility whatever') and flung them to the winds. I had not yet met him but did so shortly afterwards. We have long been friends, and it is a sign of the magnanimity of his character that he bears me no malice.

CHAPTER 5

Coast of Bohemia

At this time of my life I knew far more artists than men of letters, a situation natural enough perhaps to a man in a museum. The two worlds do not always overlap, and to help them to do so was one of the functions of the Omar Khayyàm Club. The Club had been founded in 1892 and among the early members were Barrie, Anthony Hope, W. W. Jacobs and Max Pemberton. In the second generation had come in Arnold Bennett, Chesterton, de la Mare, W. J. Locke and Sir Henry Newbolt. The best-known members in 1925 were Philip Guedalla, David Low the cartoonist, Harold Nicolson, E. V. Lucas, Ralph Straus, Arthur Wimperis, Humbert Wolfe, and J. C. Squire. Squire was in the chair at the first meeting I attended, and Guedalla made a speech. Martin Hardie was my host.

We met by tradition at Pagani's in Great Portland Street, and I noted in my diary: 'Pagani's is a sort of Aladdin's Cave of all the worst works of art that could possibly be collected. If it could only be preserved untouched for a thousand years!' Alas! Fate willed otherwise, for Pagani's was completely destroyed by a German bomb in 1940, and since then the Omarians have had no settled home.

I looked about me with a certain awe. There was W. W. Jacobs, as *small* as life. His illustrator, Will Owen, was about the same size, but as fat as Jacobs was thin. There was Guedalla looking like a Spanish bull-fighter rather out of condition; Anthony Hope and E. F. Benson – names which had been familiar to me since my school days.

It was customary for one of the artist-members to design the

Pamela Brown and James Mason in *The Heart Was Not Burned*

Authors versus Actresses—Mr Priestley's XI

Front row: A. J. Cronin, Sir Arthur Bliss, J. B. Priestley, Sir John Squire, Ralph Straus.
Back row: Gerald Gould, Miles Malleson, the Author, C. K. Sherriff, Alec Waugh, Ivor Brown.

menu, for one of the literary men to pronounce the Fitzgerald
Oration, and for another to compose a poem in honour of Omar.
Within recent years the poets had included Walter de la Mare,
John Drinkwater and Aldous Huxley. The standard was high.
But it was Arthur Wimperis who provided the most amusing
verses, and some of them remain in my memory:

> There was a Door to which I found no Key,
> There was a Veil past which I could not see;
> Then my inverted Bowler hit the Kerb
> And Someone hiccoughed twice – and it was Me!
>
> Forsworn alike the Ruby and the Rose
> I sought those blessed Doors that never close
> Where Heppell brews the old familiar juice;
> *He* knows about it all – Eno's – ENO's.

This seemed to me excellent fooling. I liked the Club, was put
up for membership, duly elected and in the fullness of time
became President. We still have excellent speeches made by
members such as E. V. Knox, R. H. Mottram, Cyril Ray and
Malcolm Muggeridge, amusing (or serious) verses by Richard
Church and D. B. Wyndham Lewis, and clever pictures by
Fougasse, Ronald Searle and Osbert Lancaster.

Gradually, I began to go to parties and 'discovered' Chelsea.
It still retained something of its character as a *quartier artiste*,
that is to say, artists could still afford to live there, which is
hardly true today. My first Chelsea character was a fellow-
contributor to *The Bookman's Journal*, a North of Ireland
journalist named Louis McQuilland. With his high collar and
old-fashioned double stock, he was a familiar figure, in both
King's Road and Fleet Street. He lived with his unmarried
sister over a shop in the former thoroughfare, and once a week
he held receptions in a little parlour so crowded with furniture
that once you had squeezed yourself into a seat you were there
for the evening. Strong tea was provided, and, for the chosen
survivors, Irish whiskey.

The company was mixed. A few Fleet Street colleagues on the literary side of their papers, a young girl or two who might have been secretaries or 'on the fillums', a Russian actor named Boris Ranevsky, who gave lurid accounts of his escape from the Bolsheviks over the frozen Baltic, and two middle-aged Irish-women whose identity I did not, at first, gather. One of them swore dreadfully, although perhaps one should add that with Irish people it is often hard to say whether they are swearing or uttering pious ejaculations. Every sentence contained an invocation of the 'Mother of God' and once, turning to me, she asked for a light 'fer the luv of Our Lady's Son'.

When the time came for her to sing (for everybody was expected to contribute to the entertainment) she rendered with enormous gusto a song which surely deserves to be preserved:

> I'm Bigamy Liz. I'm Bigamy Liz!
> If I'm not married then nobody is,
> I've husbands in the Argentine
> Husbands in Japan
> Five or six at Armentiers (*sic*)
> And some in the Sudan.
> Perhaps you've heard of the old woman who once
> lived in a shoe?
> She had so many children that she didn't know what
> to do,
> Well! I've as many husbands as there are monkeys
> in the Zoo!
> Gee whiz! I'm Bigamy Liz.

The other Irishwoman then rose and recited, most movingly, a piece called 'The Mother's Heart'. The name of the comic genius was Maire O'Neill; the other, her sister, was Sarah Allgood.

Maire (or Mollie as she was called by her friends) seemed to take to the rather academic young man sitting in the corner, and she invited me to a party at her own house in Walpole Street the following Saturday. She was married, I learned, to the well-known journalist, George Mair.

I had expected from her free and easy manner at the McQuillards' to find a very Bohemian crowd. It was a grave miscalculation. I had put on a soft collar and loose tie; I found most of the company in full evening dress. The drawing-room was beautifully furnished and on the walls were several Bakst watercolours and a large painting of a curiously triangular applewoman, by Mark Gertler.

The company was impressive. The man with the raucous voice and the prize-fighter's face, squatting on the floor, was James Agate; the distinguished-looking gentleman in the check trousers was Ashley Dukes; the vivacious little woman (his wife) who gave an imitation of Sarah Bernhardt in *Phèdre* was Marie Rambert. The man who sang so beautifully was John Goss. The shambling, sheepish-looking man in disreputable clothes was our host.

About midnight Nigel Playfair, with his baby face and high voice and eyes beaming through gold-rimmed spectacles, arrived with his wife from Hammersmith, where Edith Evans was still drawing the town as Millamant in *The Way of the World*. A discussion arose about Robert Loraine's performance as Mirabel. Agate said it was wooden and without any touch of gallantry. Who on the English stage could have done it better, asked Playfair. Herbert Marshall, perhaps, but he was engaged elsewhere. Then a warm argument developed between Playfair and Dukes concerning the merits of Henri Bataille as a dramatist. Dukes thought him not worth translating. The odd thing about the evening was that our hostess absented herself from the party for three hours, only reappearing at almost two o'clock in the morning to bid us good night. I walked back to my lodgings feeling that I had begun to penetrate the arcana of Chelsea.

It was impossible to go to Chelsea parties without, sooner or later, encountering 'Gwen'. Her full name was Gwendoline Otter; she was sometimes referred to as 'the Last of the Chelsea Hostesses', but everybody called her Gwen. I had been watching with some curiosity the strange little figure dressed in the extreme fashion of the 'twenties (a fashion she retained until her death): short, tubular dress, short hair and long strings of amber beads. She was extremely plain; some of her friends said she looked like a rather sad chimpanzee. She herself claimed to be descended from Pocahontas, so perhaps it would be kinder to say that she resembled an Indian squaw.

For some reason, I made a remark about the Marquis de Sade, and she took to me at once. Anything odd, or unconventional, had an immediate appeal to her. Had I known any practising sadists? I said 'No', which seemed to disappoint her a little. However, she invited me to lunch, and, the following Sunday, I presented myself at the house in Ralston Street where she lived alone, with 'a couple' to look after her. It was as well that somebody looked after her, for she was quite the untidiest person I have ever met.

The drawing-room had a blue ceiling studded with golden stars. There was a grand piano, and a large quantity of books. On the walls were reproductions of the more sinister Beardsley drawings, and a framed portrait by Augustus John. She believed it to be a drawing, but it was, in fact, a lithograph. The sitter had been drawn with his head thrown back and his eyes closed. His name, she told me, was Aleister Crowley.

Had she known Crowley? Yes, indeed, and for many years. A friend had said to her one day: 'I know you like extraordinary people. I will take you to see the most extraordinary man I have ever met.'

He took her to a studio in Victoria Street where there were a lot of people dancing round a brazier. Crowley was 'in robes' and when Gwen arrived she thought: 'What has happened here? This is the most sinister atmosphere I have ever known.'

Later Crowley moved to another studio in Fulham Road, and Gwen said to him:

'You haven't got the same atmosphere here. That other place was very peculiar.'

'Ah, you noticed it, did you?' said Crowley. 'You see, we'd forgotten to do a banishing rite.'

116

Crowley had formerly been married to Grace Kelly, sister of Gerald Kelly. She was already engaged to somebody else when he saw her at a party. He walked straight up to her and said:

'I hear you're engaged to be married. Within a month you will be married to *me*!'

And she was! Who shall say where 'personality' ends and 'magic' begins?

When Gwen met him he was with a woman named Lela Waddell; 'a perfect darling, with a strong Australian accent'. Her official title was 'Mother of Heaven', and Crowley used to say to her: 'Oh, Mother, I wish you'd get rid of your Australian accent. It sounds so bad in the ceremonies.' And poor Lela said to Gwen: 'Will you tell me when I sy anything in Austreyelian?' She called Crowley 'I.C.' and said to Gwen: 'I.C. wants me to devote my life to magic, but I don't think I want to.'

Gwen had attended the Mass of the Phoenix and the performance Crowley put on at the Caxton Hall called the Rites of Eleusis. Gwen thought them 'rather beautiful', but she had no illusions about Crowley himself. Victor Neuburg once said to her: 'How lucky you are to have known Crowley for so long, and he has done you no harm.' 'How could he?' said Gwen. 'I was not in love with him, and I have never lent him money.'

Crowley took Lela to Paris and when they were short of cash would send her out to get some. 'Crowley was really rather a pig,' was Gwen's comment, and I marvelled at her moderation. But Lela continued to be devoted to him and was genuinely distressed when she found herself replaced. She used to play the violin 'rather indifferently, and it was a rather indifferent violin'. It was arranged that the new woman should give her a new violin, and have Crowley. Lela took to the stage and went to Russia with the 'Seven Ragged Ragtime Girls'. Ultimately, she found her way back to Australia and died there. I thought it a sad story.

Crowley's disciples used to take analonium, the effect of which was to enlarge the consciousness and give 'a different dimension'. Even those who weren't exactly disciples were sometimes given packets of the drug. Katherine Mansfield was a friend of Gwen's. They even wrote a little play, or sketch, together called *Mimi and the Major*, which they acted, with Gwen as the Major and Katherine Mansfield as Mimi, at the Passmore Settlement, an idealistic institution, the hall of which could be hired for special performances.

Gwen gave a party afterwards at which Crowley, Lela, and others, were present. Both Gwen and Katherine took a dose of analonium and for a while nothing happened. Crowley, Lela and Katherine left together, but Crowley brought Katherine back again.

'The stuff is beginning to work,' he said. 'She's not going to be interesting; she's only going to sleep.'

Katherine lay on the sofa and lit a cigarette. She threw the match on the floor and it lay crookedly on the carpet. This caused her such acute distress that Gwen put it straight. 'That's much better,' said K.M. 'Pity that stuff had no effect.'

Then she began to talk, about a princess who lived at the edge of the sea and when she wanted to bathe she just called to the waves . . . It was as wonderful in its creation of atmosphere, thought Gwen, as one of her short stories.

Gwen got rid of the last guests and returned to find K.M. standing rather unsteadily in the middle of the room. 'Where are the others?' she said. 'Have they gone on deck? It's lucky it is such a smooth night. Pity that stuff had no effect.'

Gwen lent her a nightgown and helped her into it. 'But we can't do up all those buttons,' she said.

'Oh yes, we can,' said Katherine, 'if we talk to them very gently'.

Gwen got ready for bed herself. She washed in a basin that seemed miles away, and brushed her teeth with an arm that went out to infinity. The upper part of the body was very cold.

She could not sleep and when the dawn came at last she was frozen. She got up and went to see Katherine Mansfield, who said she was hungry. While munching biscuits she remarked: 'A pity that stuff had no effect.'

Crowley himself seemed to be immune to drugs but 'he always had a little handy' for his friends. Gwen had taken it once and driven to the theatre 'in an enchanted chariot'. She said she would like to take cocaine and go to hear *Tristan*, but, so far as I know, she never did.

I understand the impulse. After a minor but painful operation, I was once lying in bed in a nursing home, a wretched tangle of jangled nerves. A nurse came to look at me.

'Are you all right?'

'Yes,' I managed to say, with a grimace of pain.

She went away and returned with a syringe of morphia. A little prick and in a moment, instantaneously, the Gates of Heaven opened and I floated through on a pink cloud. But I have never willingly poisoned myself with anything but alcohol and tobacco, and both in moderation. The clinical history of those drug-addicts I have known – and I used to meet Brenda Dean-Paul at Gwen's table – is not encouraging.

Gwen's luncheon parties were never without interest. I met *chez elle* Alec Waugh and Evelyn, not yet famous, and Ernest Thesiger, whose aristocratic nose, stylized gestures and superb enunciation had already impressed themselves on my mind when I saw him play the Dauphin in the original production of *St Joan*. Ernest asked me to lunch and when, at the end of the meal, he suddenly poked a finger inside his collar and brought out the string of pearls which he always wore round his neck, I knew I had been accepted into his circle of friends. He was one of those actors whose stage personality and real personality seem to coincide.

Could one say the same of Robert Farquharson, another fellow-guest at Gwen's? Robert Farquharson was his stage name; his real name was Count Robin de la Condamine. In ordinary life he had an engaging stammer (sometimes used, no doubt, for deliberate effect); on the stage there was no hesitation in his speech at all. He seemed to regard acting as an elegant pastime rather than as a profession.

'M-M-M-Matheson Lang,' he said, 'w-w-wants to put on some *theatricals* in the West End. He has asked me to h-h-help him.'

The 'theatricals' in question consisted of a play called *Such Men are Dangerous* and Robin was to play the Mad Czar. This was just the kind of part he liked: he loved playing sinister roles like Paul III and the Cenci, and played them very effectively too.

In private life he liked to startle and score off people. Although Stephen Potter had not yet invented the term Gamesmanship, Robin knew all about it, and never let an opportunity pass. I once happened to mention that I had been reading Maeterlinck's *L'Intelligence des Fleurs* and, rather naïvely, asked him if he liked Maeterlinck.

'Oh, n-n-no!' he said. 'I d-d-don't like my f-f-facts served up with saliva sauce.' I have never been able to read Maeterlinck since. Trying to get my own back I said, 'I suppose the only flowers *you* like are orchids'. 'Oh, n-n-no,' said Robin. 'I think they're Nature's b-b-bedpans.' That finished orchids.

I have now known him for more than thirty years and in all that time his appearance has hardly changed. Many people thought he wore a wig and, on one occasion, a theatrical manager who was discussing a possible part for Robin concluded the interview by saying, 'I wonder, Mr Farquharson if you would mind removing your wig!'

'N-N-Not at all,' said Robin, 'but it's rather t-t-tight. Would you h-h-help me?'

The manager pulled and pulled with no result, for what looked like a wig was, in fact, Robin's own hair.

A propos of wigs, Esmé Percy used to tell the story against himself that he once ran across Robin at Gustave's the famous theatrical wig-makers, and 'like an idiot' asked Robin, 'Do you come here for your wigs?'

'Oh, n-n-no,' said Robin. 'Do *you*?' (with immense surprise). 'I come here to look at the p-p-portraits of B-B-Bernhardt.'

Another visitor to Ralston Street was the well-known gynaecologist Norman Haire, one of the founders of the League for Sexual Reform. Haire's attitude to sex was a simple one: he thought there ought to be a great deal more of it. His ordinary method of greeting any young man was to clap him on the shoulder and say, 'Well, my boy; sex all right?' And he loved to startle dinner parties by remarking with enormous conviction: 'Incest? Very good thing!'

Haire was a great mountain of a man, and in striking contrast was another of Gwen's guests, the painter Stuart Hill. He was tall, thin and handsome, with a little red beard which appeared to be dyed, and indeed was. He looked as Holman Hunt's Light of the World might have looked after a visit to the barber, and was known as 'the Christ of Chelsea'. He was rumoured to have been engaged at one time to a Royal Personage and, for all his affectations, was a most charming and kindly man.

He was not a very good painter but he excelled in all the minor arts of life. His exquisite linen was laundered with his own hands; his studio in Glebe Place had been largely built by himself, and it was in this studio that he entertained, with lavish hospitality, a wide variety of friends. His parties were famous and not without reason. Where else, I wonder, in Chelsea or elsewhere, then or now, could one applaud a *private* cabaret in which the artists were Delysia, Florence Mills, Layton and Johnston, Paul Robeson and 'Hutch'? Robeson and Hutch would sit down at the piano together and, while Robeson played a serious piece in the bass, Hutch mimicked and mocked him in the treble. A good many of these people were Gwen's friends also and were to be met at her Sunday luncheons.

An occasional visitor was a rather frail old lady (as she had now become): Violet Hunt. 'The Immodest Violet', Gwen called her, because she was so eager to tell the world about her love affairs. The love of her life had been Ford Madox Ford, and, when she was well over seventy, I have seen tears come into her eyes at the mention of his name. She had made something of a sensation in the 'nineties with her novel *The Maiden's Progress*. Her heroine, nicknamed significantly Moderna, tells her fiance that when she is married she intends to read Maupassant and Zola, and he replies that he had rather his wife lay dead at his feet than that she should read Zola. She 'paints a little, scribbles a little, skirt-dances a little, and very nearly visits a music-hall'. The novel was written entirely in dialogue, thereby anticipating the work of Ivy Compton-Burnett. In *The Flurried Years* Violet Hunt put aside the mask of fiction and was frankly autobiographical.

She was not a relation of Holman Hunt, but was the daughter of that lesser-known follower of the Pre-Raphaelites, William Hunt. Her house on Campden Hill had many relics, including a rather horrible crayon drawing by Frederick Sandys of Charles Augustus Howell. This interested me because of the ambiguous part played by the 'Portuguese person,' as Rossetti called him, in the affairs of Ruskin, Rossetti and Whistler. That he forged Whistlers, or got Rosa Corder, his mistress, to forge them is undoubted. According to Violet Hunt, he was found dead in the Euston Road with a knife in his back and half-a-crown clenched between his teeth.

She wanted to sell the drawing and asked me how much it was worth. The Director of the Birmingham Art Gallery was coming to see it. I said 'about £30'. Next day she telephoned me:

'He offered £30, but as you had told me to hold out for a hundred, of course I didn't sell.'

She was full of information about the Pre-Raphaelites. According to her book *The Wife of Rossetti*, the accepted version of Elizabeth Siddall's death—that she accidentally took an overdose of laudanum—was false. She maintained that when Ford Madox Brown, summoned by Gabriel, entered the dead woman's bedroom he found something which no-one else had noticed, a small piece of white paper pinned to the front of her nightdress. And on the paper was written: 'My life is so miserable I wish for no more of it.' Brown suppressed this evidence and the question of suicide was raised at the inquest only to be brushed aside. But the secret was known to the inner circle of the Pre-Raphaelites, and one or other of them had mentioned it in the presence of a sharp-eared little girl . . .

This was fascinating; but was it true? Was Violet Hunt to be relied upon? I am afraid she was not. I was once walking with her along King's Road, Chelsea, when she pointed to the window of a house and said: 'That is where Miss Blank (a famous literary lady) had her affair with Augustus John.' I know that there was no foundation for this story whatever.

She was supposed to be writing a life of Howell, and I have often wondered what happened to the manuscript. Douglas Goldring had her papers when she died, and now he too is dead, and a satisfactory life of Howell has still to be written.

I was myself engaged on a life of Whistler at this time, and I took considerable pains to get hold of authentic material. People were still alive who had known Whistler: Will Rothenstein, for example, and I naturally consulted him. He put me in touch with Jacques-Emile Blanche who, with French old-world courtesy wrote me a whole series of lengthy letters. Miss Alexander, the subject, when she was a child, of one of the Master's most exquisite paintings, *Harmony in Grey and Green*, still lived on Campden Hill and I called upon her, and was most kindly received. It was even more remarkable to be able to have tea with the rather formidable old lady who, as *Annie Haden*, had posed for what is perhaps Whistler's greatest etching. As Annie Haden was then a girl of twelve or thirteen, and as the etching is dated 1859, I felt that I was really getting in touch with the past.

I followed my usual practice, an essential practice, I think, when writing a biography; it is also, as I have already remarked, one of the great pleasures of life. This is to follow in the footsteps of the man one is writing about, in the district where he lived, and with a map of his period. I went to Paris, armed with a guide-book of 1855, when the Quartier Latin was almost as it had been in Murger's youth, when there were tumble-down houses with neglected gardens between the Sorbonne and the Luxembourg; when there was no Boulevard St Germain and no Boul' Mich'.

It was impossible for me to visit St Petersburg, but with a map of the eighteen-forties I was able to follow Jimmy and his brother from their house in the Galernaia to the Académie Nicolas where they went to school. In Chelsea, of course, it was easy enough. One had only to wander down to the river and *un*-think the Embankment. Fortunately Lindsey House, in part of which he lived with Jo Heffernan, was still intact, even to the fire-place against which he painted her as *The Little White Girl*, and in front of it there still is the clutter of barges which was there in his time. But alas! the old wooden Battersea Bridge was gone; and it was no longer possible to see the rockets exploding over vanished Cremorne.

One of the most agreeable results of the publication of the book was that it brought me the friendship of John Drinkwater and Philip Guedalla. I had not met either of them when we were all present at an OUDS dinner in London, and they both sent their menus down the table with a complimentary message scribbled on the back. Drinkwater was then a little past the crest of his fame. I suppose he had run out of Protestant heroes for his plays—when he tried to write about Mary Queen of Scots he was plainly at sea. His distinguished head and astrakhan collar made him look like an actor-manager of the old school. He invited me to his fine old house at Highgate where I found Daisy Kennedy, vivacious and red-headed, and her daughter, a dark, silent schoolgirl, now known to fame as one of the best of our stage designers, Tanya Moiseiwitch.

Guedalla was equally friendly and hospitable. He had a Regency house in Bayswater, the walls lined with Napoleonic relics and Beerbohm caricatures, and also a country house at Dunmow. I say a 'country house' but it was, in fact, the Countess of Warwick's laundry, and it was in two parts separated by a garden. One dined in one part and then followed Philip, armed with a storm-lantern and wearing a Spanish hat, along a dark and rather muddy path to the sitting-room, holding one's hand over one's brandy-glass to prevent the excellent cognac from being diluted by the rain. And all the time Philip talked; in fact he started talking when one arrived on Friday and was still talking when, on Monday, one said goodbye. And the talk seemed just as good on Monday as on Friday. I admired Guedalla. For all that his style is as baroque as the façade of a Portuguese church, his book on Wellington is a very remarkable achievement. Yet he was, I think, a disappointed man. Had there been an effective Liberal Party he would undoubtedly have ranked high in its counsels. As it was, he never even succeeded in getting into Parliament; and the comic querulousness, which was the dominant note of his conversation, grew gradually less comic and more querulous as the wasted years went by. He died comparatively young with many books behind him but, I think, his real ambitions unfulfilled.

I began at this time to be involved, to some extent, in the musical world. I am not naturally musical. I love music, but would not claim much competence, even in appreciation. On hearing me confess this, my friend Frank Herz decided to make himself responsible for my musical education. His method was to choose the performance he thought I ought to attend, buy the tickets and then charge me for mine. It was an excellent system as far as I was concerned, especially as the late 'twenties was a period of considerable musical activity in London.

Together we attended a whole succession of concerts and operas: Weingartner conducting Beethoven's *Ninth*, the *Rosenkavalier* conducted by Bruno Walter; *Elektra*, Emil Sauer, the Lener Quartet I thought was beginning to understand what it was all about. Then Herz introduced me to his cousin Robert Mayer, who had married Dorothy Moulton, the singer, and in whose house were to be met all the musical celebrities of the day. I found myself a fellow-guest at dinner or soirée with Arnold Bax, Harriet Cohen, Fleury, the great French flautist, and even Weingartner himself. Later the Mayers were to institute the famous 'Children's Concerts', conducted by

Malcolm Sargent, and to provide generous funds for musical scholarships.

In 1926 the busy but agreeable life I had been leading was suddenly interrupted by the General Strike. I thought, and still think, that this was a Great Mistake and so, as it now transpires, did most of the leaders of the Labour Party. I was an utterly unpolitical animal and was, indeed, forbidden by my terms of employment as a Civil Servant to take any active part in politics. But I considered such a strike to be a revolutionary attack upon our Parliamentary institutions and I had no hesitation in volunteering, with the approval of the Authorities, as a special constable. If there were going to be barricades, I knew that I was going to be on the side of Law and Order.

We were assembled in a barracks in Westminster, provided with steel helmets and batons and held in readiness in case of 'serious trouble'. The serious trouble never came and after a week or so we were disbanded. With excessive conscientiousness, I handed back my pay as a special constable, on the gound that the Government was already paying me as a Civil Servant. I was quite certain that I was doing the right thing, but I was a little disconcerted by some of the people who were doing the right thing with me: the strange collection of ex-Black-and-Tans and proto-Fascists who had flocked together for the saving of Society. It was with a sigh of relief that I returned to my work at the Museum and to my other activities.

These were more various than ever. I was writing regularly for *The Bookman's Journal*, running the art teaching at the Working Men's College, concocting an elaborate *History of British and American Etching*, sending some poems to *Punch* (and having them returned), and trying to write short stories for the magazines. Most of the magazines rejected my efforts. And then, one day, I sent a story to *The Strand*. By return of post I received a cheque for £50 and an invitation to lunch with the editor.

He turned out to be a large, fat, genial man called Reeves Shaw. We met in the bar of the Savage Club, then in a nice, frowsty old house in Adelphi Terrace. I don't think that the Savages have ever really recovered from transferring themselves to their present grandiose premises in Carlton House Terrace where the disapproving eye of Lord Curzon looks down upon them with a damping effect on their high spirits. Be that as it may, they had few inhibitions in their old house.

Reeves Shaw invited me to have a drink. I accepted, and was astonished to see *eight* sherries appear on the bar-counter. I looked round for his other guests, but there were none.

'I always order things in fours,' said Reeves Shaw. After a well-lubricated lunch I foolishly accepted the suggestion to 'have some port'. Eight glasses of port appeared – or was it sixteen? I am not quite sure. I decided that my constitution would hardly stand the process of writing for *The Strand*, profitable as it might be.

Shortly afterwards, I had my first real piece of luck as a literary man. For my own amusement and without very much hope of publication I had written a Popeian poem called *A Stitch in Time*. It was quite frankly a pastiche of *The Rape of the Lock* but transposed into modern times. I showed it to my Director, Sir Eric Maclagan, who seemed to like it. I then showed it to Herz, who passed it on to Dorothy Moulton Mayer. She happened to be a friend of Stephen Gooden, who was then producing his miraculous line engravings for the publications of the Nonesuch Press, and she invited him to dinner to meet me and hear the poem. He carried it off to show to Francis Meynell and to my astonishment and delight Meynell offered to publish it.

It appeared, with the Nonesuch Press imprint, in the autumn of 1927. Meynell had set it in a late seventeenth-century fount with a title-page which was a masterpiece of its kind. It was a very beautiful book and its success exceeded my most sanguine expectations. Arnold Bennett, whose column in *The Evening Standard* was then very influential, devoted to it the greater part of an article. Other papers noticed it favourably. The small edition was soon exhausted and it became something of a collector's piece, so that even *The Financial Times* was moved to comment upon the bullish qualities of a publication which had risen in price, in a couple of weeks, from 3s. 9d. to 35s. My own satisfaction was somewhat modified by the fact that I had to buy several copies at the enhanced price to give to my friends.

The New Statesman had already reviewed it, and then, a week later, there was a very kind reference to it in the column signed 'Affable Hawk'. 'Affable Hawk' (although the name meant nothing to me) was indeed so very flattering ('A sparkling, vivacious trifle has been added to permanent literature') that I did what I have never done before or since: wrote a letter of thanks. The letter I received in reply was signed Desmond Mac-Carthy. He said he hoped we might meet.

Then began an extraordinary game of hide-and-seek. Those whom Bennett had called 'the alert, lettered élite' began to issue invitations. Eddie Marsh asked me to lunch at Raymond's Buildings, Gray's Inn. The other guests were Lady Birkenhead, Lady Colefax and Evan Charteris. To my astonishment they all seemed to have read *A Stitch in Time*. I said I wanted to meet Desmond MacCarthy, and Charteris kindly said he would arrange it. But when I lunched with him in Mount Street a week later there was an empty chair beside me. 'Desmond must have forgotten,' said my host, with an understanding smile.

At Lady Colefax's, *même jeu*. Eddie Marsh was there, Augustine Birrell and Raymond Mortimer, Hugh Walpole and, if I remember rightly, Bennett himself. But no Desmond Mac-Carthy. I began to think that I was fated never to meet him. Then he wrote inviting me to lunch at his house in Chelsea. And I thought: at last it has come.

But, on the day before, he telephoned to ask me not to come to lunch on the morrow but to dine with him the following week. *That* day came and I was preparing to set out when there was a ring at the door of my flat. When I opened the door I found a rather breathless lady, who explained that she was Mrs Desmond MacCarthy, and would I mind postponing the dinner until the same day the following week.

Once again, when the time came, I was about to set forth when

I had another visitor. This time it was Desmond himself to explain that he couldn't possibly have me to dinner that evening. 'All right,' I said, 'now you are here, why don't you dine with me?'

To my surprise, for I had imagined that he had some important engagement (the joke is that he probably had!) he agreed at once. He stayed until well after midnight, talking – enchantingly.

I have known some good talkers in my day, but no-one else to whom I have ever listened has given me as much pleasure as Desmond MacCarthy. He seemed to wander on like a placid stream, but a stream full of lights and shadows, an occasional bubble of humour, a glint of gold in the hidden depths. Reminiscences were blended with literary judgements. And, in literature he was startlingly up to date. He knew all about the rising young men and he managed, with infinite courtesy, to suggest that you were among them.

He did better than that, he gave one active encouragement. I blush today to think that I once gave a Sunday afternoon lecture at the little Gate Theatre on 'The Meaning of Cocteau'. But MacCarthy came to hear it (on Sunday afternoon!) and even printed it in *Life and Letters*.

Apart from his kindness and his conversation, what chiefly impressed one about him was his untidiness. He had elevated lack of system into a principle. His clothes were a joke. Someone once asked Gwen Otter if Mr MacCarthy was 'very, very poor'. 'No,' she replied, 'just very, very untidy'.

At one time, out of the kindness of his heart, he employed an ex-convict as a man-servant. A well-meaning friend gave the man an old overcoat, but, said MacCarthy, 'he didn't like it – so he gave it to me'. It was not that he was in revolt against the conventions; most of them he simply ignored. But occasionally he felt moved to make a protest. He had come to the conclusion that chambermaids in great country houses (and he was always staying in great country houses) should not be called upon to perform certain services for visitors which were in fact, in the absence of modern plumbing, quite usual at the period. These services he resolved to perform himself.

Unfortunately, he was a late riser, and so the entire house-party (minus one), coming upstairs in a body after breakfast, was astonished to meet him, progressing slowly along the Great Gallery in a dressing-gown, and carrying – what the prudery of the period called an 'article'. It goes without saying that he was completely unperturbed.

When I first knew him he had been living, I think from the beginning of the century, in Wellington Square (the 'Sycamore Square' of Jan Struther, who lived in a corner of it) in Chelsea. When Desmond first went there it was little better than a slum, and I am sure he got his house at a very reasonable figure. He always maintained that there had been a murder in it. A servant had murdered his master, an old clergyman, and buried the body in the garden.

In 1934 I moved to Wellington Square myself, immediately opposite to MacCarthy's house. My own had been inhabited for the previous forty years by a French journalist, Paul Villars, the London correspondent of *Le Journal des Débats*. He had a large wine cellar, but no bathroom, which showed, perhaps, a sensible attitude to life. MacCarthy told me that Villars had frequently entertained George Moore to dinner in the little back room on the ground floor which now became my study.

MacCarthy's study was at the top of his house and, as the square was a narrow one and my house was immediately opposite, it was possible to watch him at work. He seemed to do most of it walking about, and his progress became noticeably more agitated late on Saturday night. He was, in fact, composing his weekly article for *The Sunday Times*!

I think he wrote with difficulty for, like so many Irish people, his natural medium of expression was not the written, but the spoken, word. Posterity is the poorer for that.

CHAPTER 6

In the Wings

I suppose it was partly my Puritan upbringing which gave me
my passion for the theatre. As a child I was allowed to read
plays and even, surprisingly enough, to take part, at school in
our annual theatricals. My 'first appearance on any stage' was as
Miss Hardcastle in *She Stoops to Conquer*. This must have been
around Christmas 1914; and my chief memory of the occasion
was that I was so tightly laced that I could hardly breathe or
speak. 'Laver,' said the critic of the performance, 'acted with his
eyes.' I was never inside a theatre until I was grown up, except
the Winter Garden at New Brighton, into which we ventured by
mistake, and therefore the theatre was to me an undiscovered
country, a new and magical world.

I arrived at the Victoria and Albert Museum at a fortunate
moment. The great International Theatre Exhibition had been
transferred there from Amsterdam and was shown in my
Department. It contained examples of the work of all the leading
Continental and English designers and one was presented, as it
were, with an encyclopaedia of décor and costume. There were
designs by Claud Lovat Fraser, Charles Ricketts, Paul Nash,
Alexandre Benois and other famous artists, as well as some by
Louis Jouvet, and models by George Sheringham, Robert
Edmond Jones and Gordon Craig. Craig's model for *Hamlet*
was made of concrete and immensely heavy. He himself was
still about and he would come and sit in my office poring over
seventeenth-century drawings: an impressive figure with his
long, white hair. His son, Teddy Craig (aged sixteen) had contributed a marionette to the exhibition, and, looking through

the catalogue recently, I was interested to find a 'Fantastic Design for a Small Theatre' by John Gielgud.

When the exhibition was over the authorities purchased a large number of designs and models (including Craig's), and it was decided to make these the nucleus of a comprehensive collection of the Art of the Theatre. I was put in charge of it, and welcomed the chance to make stage design one of my special interests.

I devoured all the available literature of the subject, although there was very much less then than there is now, and most of it had to be sought for in the pages of learned periodicals. I went to Paris and had a look at the Musée de l'Opéra where so many of Bérain's designs have been preserved. Bérain was so influential in Paris towards the end of the seventeenth century that it might almost be said that he *was le style Louis XIV*. We had some Bérains too as well as work by the Bibiena family, that astonishing dynasty of stage designers which dominated Europe from the middle of the seventeenth century to the middle of the eighteenth. By a lucky chance – which I shall describe in another connection – we purchased for £20 four large theatrical drawings which turned out to be the work of Bernardo Buontalenti for the Florentine *Intermezzi* of 1589 – probably the earliest designs for perspective scenery in the world.

By another lucky chance I discovered, in a mass of uncatalogued drawings by James Thornhill, his designs for the first Italian opera produced in London: *Arsinoë, Queen of Cyprus*. Also, uncatalogued, was a number of cut-outs made by Philippe de Loutherbourg for Garrick. And we possessed as well the splendid series of watercolours commissioned by Charles Kean when he was elaborately producing Shakespeare at the Princess's Theatre in the eighteen-fifties. I made it my business to try to fill in the gaps so as to make available to the public examples of stage design and stage costume from the sixteenth century onwards.

While this was going on we received a visit from Mrs Gabrielle Enthoven. This remarkable woman, with her short grey hair and her clear-cut classical features, had for years been collecting playbills. Gradually they had accumulated and overflowed until she could no longer house them. She offered the entire collection to the Museum, and proposed that she should be given an office where she could go on with the cataloguing, assisted by a group of helpers to be paid by herself. In spite of the generosity of this offer, the authorities hesitated (all museums suffer from a perpetual lack of space), but in the end it was accepted. Mrs Enthoven and her staff were duly installed in my Department and for a quarter of a century worked away at their task. On her death the authorities appointed a paid staff of its own, so that, today, the public has access to a collection which includes not only every playbill (with a few exceptions) issued in London since about 1730 but a mass of press-cuttings, photographs and letters of all kinds.

While she was working in the Department, Gabrielle, as I was soon instructed to call her, would refer to me as her 'boss', but no one was less likely to allow herself to be bossed by anyone. She was the Queen of her section and ruled her little kingdom with a sceptre of iron. But she was one of the kindest of women, indeed embarrassingly so. If one happened to say that one had a cold or felt under the weather, as likely as not one would find a dozen bottles of invalid port waiting on one's doorstep when one returned from work. She was very hospitable and gave excellent dinner parties, always with a theatrical flavour, at which one might meet John Gielgud or Barry Jackson. We became great friends.

She had one curious characteristic: an inability, especially as she grew older, to distinguish between what had really happened to her and what she would have liked to happen. Her father *had* been a distinguished official in Egypt; but had she really shared a tent with General Gordon in the desert? She herself had certainly belonged to what is now called the Establishment; but had she been quite as intimate with Queen Victoria as she liked to make out? I began to wonder; and when she gave a graphic account of how, disguised as a boy-jockey, she had won a race at

Ascot, I realized that she had just been reading *National Velvet*.

When she was ill in the last days and friends came to see her in the nursing home, she lamented to them that she was 'ruined'. This meant, in Edwardian language, that she would shortly have to draw on her capital. John Gielgud, with characteristic generosity, got up a subscription to defray her hospital expenses. When she died she left £20,000 to the Ministry of Education for the purpose of expanding her collection. Even this was not without its irony, for she decreed that, if the Ministry should refuse it, the money was to come to me, personally. And I was the official who had to sign the form recommending the Ministry to accept it! This is the nearest I have ever come to receiving a legacy. I am not complaining. I have always been treated by 'Whitehall' with consideration and even generosity; and, in the Autumn of 1927, I was sent, with expenses paid, to Magdeburg, to report on the great Theatre Exhibition which had just opened there. Having duly inspected it, I paid my first visit to Berlin.

Berlin in 1927 was an exciting city. The 'twenties indeed have been called Berlin's Golden Age – 'almost as creatively anarchic as Italy in the Quattrocento.'[1] In painting, Expressionism (much as I disliked some of its products); in the cinema, *The Cabinet of Dr Caligari* and *The Student of Prague*; in the theatre, Ernst Toller and Bertholt Brecht. Max Reinhardt's interests had already shifted to Vienna and Salzburg, but he still controlled four theatres in Berlin: the Deutsches, the Kleines, the Kammerspiel and the Grosseschauspielhaus. I was eager to visit them all, as well as the Piscatorbühne, where the most revolutionary methods of stage production were being tried out. I had been a reader of *Der Querschnitt* for years, and had even contributed articles to it. I knew, or thought I knew, what to expect.

Deciding that the Adlon was too grand for me, I put up at the Hotel Fürstenhof. 'Earl's Court,' I said to myself, but, if the names meant the same, the two districts were very different.

[1] John Maunder, *Berlin: The Eagle and the Bear*, Barrie and Rockliff, 1959.

The Kurfürstendamm was as gay as a Paris boulevard, with the curious difference that a considerable number of the prostitutes were men. But there was more music in the cafés, and better music too.

I explored the city on foot, as I always do, but the back streets of Berlin, unlike those of any other capital city, were extremely dull: architecturally dull, I mean. They were busy enough; thronged with men who might have come out of the caricatures of Georg Grosz; thick-necked and paunchy-men with absurd little hats perched on their shaven heads, and each with a despatch case under his arm. (At that period, what the Germans call a *Mappe* and the French, rather oddly, a *serviette* was unknown in England; Englishmen carried an attaché case.) They were all smoking cigars, usually, as I noted with naïve disapproval, with the band on.

I escaped from the whirlpool of the streets into the calm of the Kaiserfriedrich and also into the Künstgewerbemuseum. Here was (for alas! it was destroyed in the War) the largest collection of Engraved Ornament in the world. The second largest was in my own Department at South Kensington. The great Dr Jessen was dead but I made contact with his successor, and was able to put in some useful work in the *Kupferstichkabinett*.

The night-life of Berlin at this period was notorious, chiefly for its homosexual flavour. The dance halls where all the dancers were men have often been described. I found the ordinary joints in the Jägerstrasse more interesting. One of them, with typical German scientific thoroughness, had installed a table-telephone system. Beside each table-telephone was a large number on a stand. I looked across the room and noted which of the girls sitting alone seemed attractive, and I dialled her number:

'Number achtzehn? Wollen Sie tanzen mit mir?'

'Jawohl, Herr Einundzwanzig.'

We danced and shared a bottle of hock. She then suggested that I should pay for her supper – which she had already had. When I demurred she said I was 'Kein Kavalier'. Anxious to wipe out this slur on my equestrian prowess, I paid. I was glad to have had this opportunity of seeing Berlin before the Nazis took over and, by driving out the Jews, destroyed most of Berlin's cultural life.

Meanwhile, my contacts with the theatre were becoming more direct, and once more Frank Herz played an important part, just as he had done in introducing me to music. It so happened that his uncle, Ernest Mayer, ran the International Copyright Bureau, which was largely concerned with importing German musical successes into England. Frank took me to see Mayer in his Mayfair flat. The décor, I recorded in my Diary, was startling. The main room had black walls and a black floor, a huge divan covered with multi-coloured cushions, a grand piano, several black armchairs, and numerous standard lamps with shades of deep crimson. The air was heavy with incense. Through a high Greek doorway could be seen another room, apple-green with a silver ceiling and on a pedestal a reproduction of the Victory of Samothrace – bright blue. In short, an interior *à la Bakst*. There were even Bakst drawings on the walls but, having examined them, I whispered to Frank that they were fakes. Ernest Mayer suggested that I should translate some German plays for him, 'without obligation', as he was careful to insist, and I carried off a copy of Klabund's *Der Kreidekreis* to see what I could make of it.

Frank's next intervention in my life was to have more far-reaching consequences. He had procured tickets for the Queen's Hall for August 18, 1925 (why should I not remember the date?) and when we met there, on the promenade, he introduced me to Veronica Turleigh. She had been, I gathered, leading lady at the Oxford Playhouse, the theatre established in what had been in my time a big game exhibition. Under the management of J. B. Fagan it had become a veritable forcing-house of theatrical talent, having among its players John Gielgud, Robert Harris, Elissa Landi and others afterwards famous. Veronica was now playing at the Kingsway Theatre in Barry Jackson's modern dress *Hamlet*. I asked if I might 'come round' after the play, and take her out to supper.

This was my first acquaintance with stage doors and dressing rooms and with such theatrical *rendezvous* as Rules'. At that time the little restaurant in Maiden Lane, opposite the stage doors of both the Vaudeville and the Adelphi, was always full, at supper time, of actors and actresses. It had (and has) preserved its Victorian décor, its plush seats and heavy curtains, its marble statue behind glass, its framed playbills and caricatures. We drove home in a hansom (the driver told me that fifty still remained in London) through the curious patch of fog at Knightsbridge: the ghost of the Westbourne, now buried underground in sewer pipes.

Veronica introduced me to various clubs such as The Bullfrogs and The Cave of Harmony. The latter was somewhere behind Goodge Street in a room which had once, perhaps, been a stable. It was run by Elsa Lanchester. I remember her as a girl with a slender figure, 'the wittiest legs in London', eyes that seemed perpetually open in surprise at the strangeness of the world, and an irrepressible fund of Cockney humour.

I don't think she ever made a penny out of the club; it seemed to me to be a kind of benevolent institution for the entertainment of the down-and-outs. It was very amusing, none the less, and she put on little plays, such as *The Man with the Flower in his Mouth*, acted by herself and her friends. Of course, she danced and gave her imitations. Behind what was called the bar, which consisted of a square hole cut in a partition, stood a tousled-haired figure, in indescribable clothes, selling coffee. This was John Armstrong. Some of his paintings have since sold for high figures, and he has done a certain amount of decorative work, not only for the stage (notably at the Old Vic) but for the films also.

Shortly afterwards, Elsa started another club in Seven Dials and I went there one evening. A small revue was being performed with Harold Scott singing songs at the piano: *My Libido Baby*, *My Very Complex Kid*, and similar classics. Elsa herself sang the well-known ballad *Frankie and Jonnie*, which I have always found rather affecting. She had as her partner in this performance a young man I did not then know. He was curiously stout of figure, with a large moonlike face and extremely intelligent eyes. He sang his part in the song with a strangely sinister humour, and I could already see that he regarded Elsa as something more than his mere chance companion of the improvised revue stage. Shortly afterwards, they were married. The young man, of course, was Charles Laughton.

Charles and Elsa lived for a time in a flat in Percy Street, off Tottenham Court Road, but Charles's growing success soon made it possible for them to take a country house. Characteristically, they chose, not the ordinary country house, replete with all modern conveniences, but a fantastic structure built aloft in four fir trees in the thick woods behind Newlands Corner, approached only by a track over fields. The whole place looked like a house out of Hans Andersen. It had been built for his children by Clough Williams-Ellis, the 'founding father' of Port Meirion village in Wales. Williams-Ellis had never intended the house to be anything more than a summer house, but the Laughtons made it their home and entertained their friends there. In the end, even they had to fall victims to the weakness for modern comfort, and build another little house nearby of solid brick, where they could retire when the weather was too inclement.

Laughton asked me to translate a play of Jules Romains for him, which I did. I was sorry when nothing came of it, for the part of the principal character, Monsieur Trouhadec, with its superficial simplicity and fundamental cunning, would have suited his style of attack extremely well.

When the modern dress *Hamlet* came to an end, Veronica joined the Irish Players, taking the part of Kate in *The White-headed Boy* and Mary in *Juno and the Paycock*. I was able to renew my acquaintance with Sarah Allgood and Maire O'Neill. Another Irish friend was Kate O'Brien whose first play, *Distinguished Villa*, scored a remarkable success. It was at her flat in Bloomsbury that I met Sean O'Casey. He seemed to regard me in my dinner-jacket with considerable dislike. I suppose he thought me a typical member of the Establishment he despised so much. He himself was wearing a black sweater up to the throat, thereby anticipating the fashion of thirty years later.

Veronica's next job was at the Gate Theatre. Peter Godfrey had started this in a most dangerous room in Floral Street, Covent Garden. It was a wonder that the London County Council had ever granted him a licence, for it was on the first floor of a kind of warehouse, up a rickety staircase, and I couldn't help thinking as I sat in a penitential seat under an excruciating yellow light, that if a fire were to break out not one of us had a dog's chance of escape. Cedric Hardwicke was one of the main attractions.

The members of the Gate Theatre Club soon became so numerous that it was decided to move to larger premises in a disused billiard saloon next door to Gatti's old music hall in Villiers Street, and here the enterprise continued to flourish. Godfrey performed a very real service to the theatre-going public, for he provided plays which could not have been seen any- where else in England. His function was very similar to that of the Royal Court Theatre a generation later, with names like Ernst Toller and Georg Kaiser instead of Brecht and Gênet. Most of the plays produced were those of the German Expressionist School and one of the most successful was Kaiser's *From Morn till Midnight*, in which Peter Godfrey himself played the part of the absconding bank-clerk. He also put on some plays by French dramatists, among them Lenormand's *Mangeur de Rêves*. One of the most successful of the plays at the Gate was Alfred Savoir's *English as She is Eaten*, in which Ernest Thesiger took the part of the imperturbable Englishman. Beatrix Lehmann and Gwen Ffrancon-Davies were others who appeared at the Gate. Veronica took the part of Celeste in Simon Gantillon's *Maya* and of Death in Cocteau's *Orphée* – Death in immaculate hospital white with rubber gloves. I admired this play so much that, as I have already mentioned, I undertook to give a Sunday lecture to explain it to the general public. I wrote the programme notes for nearly all the plays.

By this time Veronica and I had decided to get married, and the ceremony was duly performed (with what Shakespeare calls 'maiméd rites – for I was a heretic) at St James's Spanish Place on January 28, 1928. After much searching we had succeeded in finding a flat – in Piccadilly Circus, on the top floor of the building which, at street level, was the first of Lyons' teashops. The flat had been constructed by Dorothy Warren, founder of the Warren Gallery. D. H. Lawrence's paintings were exhibited there, and the police raided the place and seized them as they were alleged to be obscene. Unfortunately they also seized a number of works by William Blake.

The flat consisted of a very small bedroom, a still smaller kitchen, a tiny bathroom and one magnificent room with a fireplace at each end and two windows looking out on Piccadilly. We lived there for two years, as it was very convenient for the theatre. Our friends quickly got to know it, and regarded it as a kind of oasis in the busy whirl of Piccadilly. They got into the habit of dropping in for drinks after the theatre. It was pleasant enough for a time, but however hospitable one may feel, that kind of thing rapidly becomes a menace to individual peace. Hardly an evening passed without some visitor and as I was by no means rich, I found the expense of alcohol considerable. Peter Godfrey surely holds the endurance record, for he stayed until breakfast next morning. When he had gone, there was nothing for it but for my wife and me to go to bed and try to recover as best we could. My cellarette stood empty until the next windfall.

I was looking about for means of increasing our income, and chose the unlikely medium of verse. I composed the rhymed clues for a 'motor treasure-hunt' round Gleneagles Hotel. This brought in five pounds. I sent a weekly poem to *The Spectator*. Sometimes it was accepted and when the regulation two guineas arrived we were so pleased that we spent it on supper at the Ivy. For a very short time I wrote dramatic criticism for *The New Statesman*. For a month or two I ran the book page of *The Sphere*. As I was busy at the Museum all day, literary work of any kind had to be done in the evening, but there was no difficulty about this as Veronica was pretty continuously in the theatre. When I got tired of writing I would wander out into the West End or perhaps go round to the Gate to see Margaret Rawlings do the dance of the seven veils in Wilde's *Salomé*. Certainly, as one contemporary critic put it, she attacked the part 'in no prudish spirit'.

Sometimes friends would borrow our flat for an after-theatre party, and one such occasion is still vivid in my memory. The party was Sarah Allgood's but her sister Molly was 'not to be told'.

Sarah's friends duly arrived, hardly any of them on the stage and all extremely quiet and well-behaved. Suddenly there was a ring at the bell. I opened the door and there was Molly. Somehow she had got wind of the affair and was determined not to be kept out. I offered her a cocktail; she sipped it and made a grimace. 'Do y' call that a cocktail? For Christ's sake, give me the gin!'

It was like the irruption of the bull into the bull-ring. She dominated the scene; she danced; she sang *I'm the Queen of the Fairies*. She certainly livened up the proceedings, but Sarah's friends left, quietly, one by one.

I felt that I was getting more and more involved in the theatre but had not yet seen anything of my own on the stage. The translation of *Der Kreidekreis* which I had made for Ernest Mayer had been accepted and I had even received £20(!) on account. But several years had gone by and I had heard no more. And then, at last, early in 1929, I learned that Basil Dean was proposing to present it at the New Theatre as *The Circle of Chalk*.

Dean asked me to go to see him and we discussed plans. At his request I had conferences with Ernest Irving, who was to write the music, with Aubrey Hammond, who was to design the scenery, and with Quentin Tod, who was to devise the dances. Irving, basing himself rigorously on the Chinese mode, produced some exquisite settings of the lyrics. Hammond used to drag his huge bulk up the innumerable stairs to my Piccadilly flat and, having been refreshed with brandy, would spread out his drawings on the floor and stay discussing them until the small hours. I liked his costumes very much. I was not so sure about the designs for scenery. Hammond's idea (or Dean's) was to have in the centre of the stage a little house on a revolving stand and to make the scenic changes in full view of the audience, the scene-shifters simply pushing the house round when the moment arrived. I would have preferred a simpler solution – screens, perhaps, painted with grey Chinese landscapes, something more remote and dream-like, against which the reds and golds of the costumes would have stood out with even greater brilliance. As the programme note had it:

'Fast falls the snow amid a world of white. Night in the sky and in the bosom, night! Footsteps and voices! Travellers through the snow appear like shadows, and like shadows go.'

There was nothing shadowy about Hammond's scenery. I went with him to see it being made. It was my first experience of a theatre atelier and I was overwhelmed by the elaboration and complication of everything. It did not seem possible that the work would ever be done.

I did not attend many rehearsals, partly because I had my own work to do at the Museum, and partly because I did not think authors were wanted. Dean himself was kind to me but I still found him rather alarming. He used to wear a Russian blouse and sit in the Upper Circle, from where his deep voice would suddenly come down to us: 'If you don't mind, this is *my* rehearsal.'

For the principal part he had engaged Anna May Wong, who was then making her first stage appearance, although she was already a star in films. She was a beautiful girl, tall and willowy, a charming and cultivated woman. The cast also included a young man then at the very beginning of his professional career, who played the Young Prince. His name was Laurence Olivier.

This was my first experience of being involved in a real play in the West End, and although I was not really the author but only the translator, I experienced all the pangs of authorship. On the first night I had to be given brandy in the wings, and let

142

no one who has not lived through a similar experience despise me for that confession of weakness. Some writers of plays refuse to go to their first-nights at all, and I am not sure that they are not wise, but others, like myself, couldn't possibly stay away. To have put your entire fortune on an outsider in the Grand National may provide a comparable thrill, but I doubt it. It is the only chance the author gets of that immediate contact with his public which is the actor's daily lot. You can *hear* the applause, or you can do as I did, on that occasion, stand behind two people at the bar in the interval and hear them say: 'My God, what a play!' and not in admiration either.

The reception indeed was 'mixed'. Some of the critics objected to Anna May Wong's American accent, some to the method of presentation. The 'procession' called for in the script became a rickshaw ride round the central house and on the first night Bruce Winston (who weighed about twenty stone) was shot out of his vehicle into the orchestra. And it was pointed out (quite rightly) that the play had passed through too many hands. A twelfth-century Chinese original, translated by a nineteenth-century French missionary, adapted by a modern German poet and finally Englished by me. The fact that I had translated it from the German did not prevent my being referred to in the Press as 'the eminent Chinese scholar'.

Much as I liked and admired Anna May Wong, I could not help regretting that it had not been possible to secure the services of Elizabeth Bergner, who had made a great success of the leading part in Germany; but the Hitlerite pressure had not yet brought her to this country. The play did not last very long in London but was revived many times during the next few years: at the Arts Theatre Club, at the Birmingham Repertory, at Piscator's Studio Theatre in New York, in Australia, and indeed all over the world. I even received a few rupees as royalty on a performance in Allahabad. Heinemann's published it as a book. Brecht's *Caucasian Chalk Circle*, recently played in London, is founded on the same Chinese legend but has nothing to do with Klabund's version, or mine.

Meanwhile, in collaboration with Frank Herz, I had adapted another German play, Carl Sternheim's *Die Marquise von Arcis*. It was produced on a Sunday evening by *The Venturers*, with Marie Ney in the principal part. Sternheim was at this time one of Germany's most popular and successful playwrights, but, as a Jew, he found Hitler's Germany impossible and he came to England. He asked me to meet him and I am ashamed to confess that I took an unreasonable dislike to him. It was natural enough that he, a darling of the public, suddenly finding himself in exile, should be pernickety and querulous. But when he asked me to revise my work I declined. He got Ashley Dukes to make a new version. It was produced under the title of *The Mask of Virtue* – and it launched Vivien Leigh.

Somewhat discouraged by these varying theatrical fortunes, I decided to write a novel. It was to be the story of a girl returning from her finishing school in Switzerland who takes a year to get home, because of all the adventures that happen to her *en route*. I intended to call it *Finishing School*, but I was at the same time preparing for the Nonesuch Press a collection of my verse satires, the provisional title of which was *Nymphs Errant*. Suddenly, I realized that *Nymph Errant* was the perfect title for the novel, and it was under this name that I submitted it to Heinemann's.

I was astonished by the warmth of their reaction. They gave me a handsome sum on account of royalties, and I received an even larger cheque from Alfred Knopf, who had agreed to publish it in America. The book duly came out on both sides of the Atlantic, and the reception was more favourable than I had dared to hope; even if *Time and Tide* did describe it as 'the most unpleasant book of the year', and the Irish censorship put it on its black list as a work 'prejudicial to public morals'. I was amused to note that among other books included in the same condemnation was H. G. Wells' *History of the World*. Years afterward, at a dinner party in Dublin, sitting next to a member of De Valera's Cabinet, I ventured to joke with him on the subject of the Irish censorship. 'What can I do?' he said; 'I'm between the Divil and the Holy See.'

Hardly had I recovered from surprise at the reception of my novel than I received another agreeable shock. A letter arrived, forwarded to the Museum by my publisher. It was dated from the Adlon Hotel, Berlin, and at first I could not make out the signature. Finally, I did so. It was that of Charles B. Cochran, and he suggested that I should go to see him at 49 Old Bond Street when he got back from Germany. Few young men today realize what a dominating position Cochran occupied in the theatre in the late 'twenties and early 'thirties. A little earlier, some of the critics had regarded him rather sourly. Even James Agate, who later became a great admirer, was writing of 'bold, bad Cochran', who was supposed to be sapping the seriousness of the English stage, bringing in unheard of novelties and generally sacrificing everything to spectacle.

It is still possible to see what they meant. Cochran was a showman, and proud of it. In his early days he would transform Olympia into a cathedral for *The Miracle* or take the Albert Hall for a prize-fight, both with equal zest. When he visited Spain in order to bring over the Flamenco dancers, the Spanish press refused to believe it, and continued to refer to him as 'Don Carlos Cochran, promotor of box-fights'.

Yet no one could say that he neglected the serious drama. He was producing Ibsen in New York in the 'nineties; he pioneered the plays of Brieux; he produced *Cyrano de Bergerac* (so lavishly that it couldn't have made a profit even if every seat in the house had been occupied every night); he brought over Duse for her last appearance in England. He introduced the famous Russian revue known as the *Chauve Souris* to London; he sponsored the Guitrys.

But it was by his revues and musical plays that he was best known, and he mounted a series of spectacles such as no other manager, until then, had attempted. Once he was absorbed in a production, nothing was too much trouble, nothing too expensive. Was there a period of three minutes in the show when nothing much seemed to be happening, there was no question of 'filling in' with the orchestra. 'Who are the best adagio dancers in Europe? Wire for them to Budapest!' The backers didn't always like it, and, from their point of view, the backers were sometimes right.

All this I knew, or had divined; and so it was with suppressed excitement that I presented myself at his Bond Street office, lined with photographs and theatrical posters, some by Toulouse-Lautrec. (All these have now been safely steered into the collections of the Victoria and Albert Museum.)

His appearance was no surprise to me, for his face was familiar from a dozen caricatures; but mine seemed to be a surprise to him. He had, apparently, expected somebody quite different. However, he was genial enough. He said his wife had given him the book to occupy him during his long journey to Berlin and take his mind off the theatre. As if anything could! He thought he could make a play out of it, and he offered me a contract there and then. Would £100 be acceptable, on account? It would.

As he was leaving he said: 'I'd like to see some more of your work. Have you written anything since *Nymph Errant*?'

'Yes,' I said, 'I've written a life of John Wesley'.

Cochran's original idea was to turn the novel into a straight play, but early in the New Year he changed his mind and decided to produce it as a musical. Romney Brent was to make the adaption and Cole Porter to write the words and music of the lyrics. The leading lady was to be Gertrude Lawrence.

Romney Brent I had met at a party of Mary Ellis's and had been filled with a kind of dumb wonder. He seemed to be perpetually the centre of a laughing group, and, indeed, I have never met anyone whose conversation is more consistently amusing. He is not witty exactly, but high-spirited, and with odd angles of vision on people and places. Strangely enough, in spite of his wise-cracking, he was not born an American. He is a Mexican; his real name is Romolo Larraldi.

Cole Porter I knew only as the author of *Let's do it*, – a song which had swept the sophisticated cabarets a short time before. The world fame of *Night and Day* and *Begin the Beguine* was yet in the future. He lived in Paris and Cochran suggested that Brent and I should meet him there to 'collaborate'.

When Cochran asked him for his address in Paris he replied, 'Ritz Bar'. 'Yes,' said Cochran, 'but if I want to send you a letter or a telegram—?' 'Ritz Bar,' said Porter. I found out afterwards that he had no banking account. He deposited his money with Harry, the barman, and when he wanted cash he simply drew it from Harry over the counter.

A strange taste! The Ritz Bar has never been my idea of a cosy hide-out. On the rare occasions when I visited it, I was alarmed by the very efficiency of the service. No sooner had one deposited a fragment of cigarette ash in an ash tray than a waiter swooped down, removing it and replacing it with another. I began to put my ash surreptitiously under the seat, hoping that no-one would notice. And I regarded the *jeunesse dorée* playing back-gammon all around me with more astonishment than delight.

Mrs Porter had a beautiful seventeenth-century house in the Rue Monsieur on the South Bank, and here Cole occupied a studio when he was not in the Ritz Bar or at some smart cabaret where, silent and motionless, he cultivated that exquisite sensation of being broken-hearted at the Ritz, which was the ground-swell of his most successful work. He had none of Romney's vivacity, but was friendly and genial enough. His appearance was that of an American college boy, a rather solemn college boy, as if he had something on his mind.

We duly collaborated – in the studio, for there was a piano there, and on it Cole Porter picked out the tunes which I thus heard for the first time, and which were afterwards to become famous. I was delighted with them – and with the words. Surely no-one since Gilbert has written such ingeniously witty lyrics. One of them concerned a cocotte at Neauville (Deauville), lamenting the pressure of amateur competition:

> A busted, disgusted cocotte am I,
> Undesired on my tired little bottom, I

Watch these fat *femmes-du-monde*,
With the men that once I owned,
Splash around like hell-bound hippopotomi,
Since only dames with their names on their cheques
 appeal
To modern men, instead of sex, I now have
 ex-appeal.
What will Ma say to me when she learns I've
 turned out to be
An annoyed, unemployed cocotte?

The 'tired little bottom' was afterwards replaced by a less vivid phrase, but this was the refrain as I first heard it. There were other lyrics destined to be even more popular: the *Doctor's Song* with which Gertrude Lawrence brought down the house, and *So-o-o-o-olomon* sung with such effect by Elizabeth Welch.

Halfway through the morning we were invited to have a drink, and this, in Cole Porter language, always meant a bottle of champagne. Then, at lunch time, we ascended to the first floor where, in a room decorated with very good Chinese paintings, Cole Porter's wife was entertaining a chic party including an Italian duke or two. It was an amusing contrast to the modern studio below.

At the end of our stay in Paris, the Porters decided to make their annual trip to Carlsbad, 'to get the champagne out of their system'. Brent went with them, but I was unable to do so. I saw the whole caravan off from the Gare de l'Est, and remained for several days in Paris.

Before they went, we interviewed in Cole's studio a few of the prospective cast. One of the characters in the play, Madeleine, was a French girl, and for this part we interviewed, I never knew why, a beautiful young Spanish actress who, in order to prove to us that she could speak English sufficiently well, brought for our delectation a song called *Aufwiedersehen*.

I, left alone, thought I would entertain the Spanish girl to lunch. We met at Prunier's. I found her extremely interested in the trio of young men who had interviewed her in Porter's studio. I explained to her that Cole Porter was a musician and song-writer, and that Romney Brent was an actor who occasionally wrote plays.

'*Et vous, M'sieur?*' She wanted to know why I had not accompanied the others to Carlsbad, and I replied that I must return to London to my *métier*.

'*Et quel est votre métier, Monsieur?*'

'*Je suis conservateur de musée.*'

She wouldn't believe me.

Back in London, we were soon in the thick of rehearsals, and I came to know, and to admire more than ever, that incomparable artist whose name was Gertrude Lawrence. She could light up the stage with a smile, and put more into a chuckle than anybody else in the business. She danced deliciously and if she didn't always sing *quite* in tune, somehow it didn't matter. She gave herself with both hands, and never seemed to tire. When chorus girls wilted with fatigue she, who had borne the whole weight of the show on her elegant shoulders, was as fresh as ever. I was moved to write her a sonnet:

> How can you know so much, and yet keep clear
> The bubbling well of laughter in your heart,
> Which rises with a sudden gush and start
> Into sweet air? . . .

She had it framed and kept it in her dressing-room as long as she lived. A light certainly went out when her untimely death deprived the theatre of her gracious presence.

Agnes de Mille was to devise the dances, and Oliver Messel was to be responsible for the décor and costumes. Cochran had employed him when he was still very young to make some masks for a revue, and later he was to clothe and decorate *Helen*! perhaps the most beautiful of all Cochran productions. For this I was pleased to be able to draw his attention to the splendid engravings for the *Caroussel de Louis XIV* with their delightful blend of the Roman and the Baroque. His stylised *maquette* for the scene outside the walls of Troy is now in the Victoria and Albert Museum.

I went on several occasions to his studio in Yeoman's Row. It was littered with models of stage sets, half-finished pictures, designs of all kinds, but it wasn't the usual huddle. It had an unmistakable air of elegance: odd pieces of furniture, carefully chosen; flowers, exquisitely arranged. This was partly due, no doubt, to the devotion of his sister, now Countess of Rosse, whom I once found down on her hands and knees scrubbing her brother's studio floor, because she could not find anyone else to do it to her satisfaction.

Once, when Oliver and I were alone in the studio, and he was ill in bed (with a disease contracted in North Africa, where he had gone to get 'atmosphere' for the 'harem scene' in the play), there came a ring at the front door. I looked out of the window and called to the invalid: 'There's a young man just getting out of a taxi. He has scarlet moccasins, no socks, a white tie and a lily in his hand.' Without a moment's hesitation Oliver called back: 'It must be Cecil.' And Cecil Beaton it was.

Unfortunately, Oliver's illness prevented him in the end from finishing his work for *Nymph Errant*. The time came when Cochran could wait no longer. He had to take the job away from Messel and give it to Doris Zinkeisen.

I was already aware of her work for Nigel Playfair, notably in *The Insect Play* and *The Way of the World*, the production in which Edith Evans triumphed as Millamant, and I had imagined Doris Zinkeisen as a typical *femme artiste*. To my surprise, she was a woman of extreme elegance, and a furious rider to hounds. Shortly afterwards she had a nasty fall in the hunting field; her mount fell upon her and broke her pelvis in four places. She went on painting in the nursing home, and, when she came out, rode the same horse to take a first prize in the Richmond Horse Show, painted the creature's portrait and had it hung in the Royal Academy. She showed the same determination in the rushed job which faced her for *Nymph Errant*. In a month everything was ready.

I collaborated with Brent in the writing of the play, and I found him a most agreeable and understanding man to work with. He never fought for his own ideas, but was willing to consider every suggestion on its merits. One of the problems was how the nudist scene was to be put on the stage, and there was much discussion about this with Cochran and Frank Collins, his unflappable production manager. Whatever was proposed (diagonal hedges above which the heads of the nudists could appear, and similar devices), Collins would suck at his pipe and say 'It'll be seen from the side boxes, Mr Cochran.' But when we agreed to abandon the nudist scene altogether Cochran said, 'Leave it in, leave it in'. It was only later that we understood. When the play was presented to the Lord Chamberlain's office there was (not unexpectedly) a tremendous to-do about it. It was declared to be 'impossible'. There were objections to other scenes too. After much argument, Cochran made his grand gesture.

'Very well,' he said. 'If we agree to withdraw the nudist scene, will you pass the rest of the play?' And this compromise was happily accepted.

The real fun came when the whole outfit, including two tons of scenery and the cast of eighty, transferred itself to Manchester for the preliminary trial run. Let no-one speak unkindly of Manchester. To me it is a most exciting city, although I admit that my acquaintance with it is limited to the Opera House on one hand, and the Midland Hotel on the other. There was an amusing incident during our stay at the latter place of entertainment. It happened that the huge City Library of Manchester was still in course of construction and opposite to the entrance to the hotel was an enormous hoarding. Cochran's advertising agents decided to take the centre position of this hoarding for a large advertisement of the play. Unfortunately, they had reckoned without the Nonconformist Conscience. That particular hoarding belonged to a man who 'didn't hold with t'theatre'. Unwilling to lose the excellent site, the Cochran management, in collaboration with Messrs Heinemann, decided to advertise the book, merely. As the author of the book, I saw no objection to this arrangement, but Brent, Cochran, Cole Porter and Gertrude Lawrence herself were confronted, every time they left the hotel to go to the theatre, with an enormous advertisement of *Nymph Errant* in which there was no reference to them at all.

I have already written of the agonies of first nights even for an author. But the author can, if he wishes, drink himself into stupor in the bar or even stay away from the theatre altogether. What of the actors, especially those on whom the whole weight of responsibility for the success of the show rests? On the first night of *Nymph Errant* I took Gertrude Lawrence in a taxi to the Opera House. She sobbed in my arms, crying 'I can't go on! I can't go on'. Of course, she did go on and in two minutes had the audience at her feet. The combination of Cochran and Gertrude Lawrence was, indeed, irresistible.

I suppose I shall never be involved, in any capacity, in a more 'glamorous' affair. Manchester had suffered an invasion of fur-coats and orchids and white ties. The Fairbanks had taken a whole row of stalls for themselves and their friends. The London critics attended in force, and when we got back to the Midland Hotel the stairs leading up to the dinning-room were lined, five deep, with people clapping and cheering Gertrude Lawrence. One of the press men asked me what *I* had to do with the show, and I replied: 'Not much. I merely wrote the book.'

The first night in London was even more dazzling, and the inadequate foyer of the Adelphi was full of well-known faces, from Somerset Maugham to Elsa Maxwell, from Lady Lavery to Cecil Beaton. And at the Savoy afterwards the scenes at Manchester were repeated. I suppose it was natural that I should have been made a little dizzy by all this, especially as my share of the royalties was rather more than ten times the amount of my official emoluments. The film rights were purchased by Twentieth Century-Fox. I began to toy with the idea of giving up the Museum and living by my pen. It was as well that wiser thoughts prevailed, for, in the following year, I paid out in income tax more than my entire earnings from all sources.

CHAPTER 7

Occupations: Various

During the whole run of *Nymph Errant* I seemed to be living
a curious kind of double life. It was not only that I spent my
days on official duties and my evenings in the world of the
theatre but that I found myself, against my will, divided into
two distinct personalities, at least in the minds of other people.
To my colleagues at South Kensington I had become a cigar-
smoking, Savoy-supping, enviable but slightly disreputable
character, hobnobbing with chorus girls and hanging round
stage doors. To Gertrude Lawrence and her friends I was something 'in a Museum', engaged in mysterious and apparently
useless activities quite outside their comprehension; a character
out of *The Old Curiosity Shop*, hardly fit to be let out alone.
Perhaps, unconsciously, I played up to both these delusions.
One evening I was in 'Gee's' dressing room with Douglas
Fairbanks Jnr and half a dozen others. A dispute was in progress as to whether the British Government was justified in
spending £100,000 on the Sinai Codex, and I was appealed to
as the obvious authority on such matters. 'I don't know anything
about it,' I replied, in all innocence. 'I am an iconographer not
a palaeographer.' This was considered extremely quaint.

I became very friendly with Doug, as he insisted on being
called, who was at that time in his early twenties and at the
very beginning of his career. He had just founded Criterion
Films and was proposing to make a picture based on Jeffery
Farnol's *The Amateur Gentleman*. He asked me if I would be
prepared to act as technical adviser on questions of costume and
social history.

I had already had some experience of working with film people. With Anthony Kimmins I had been employed by an American firm making 'quota' pictures in Great Britain to write a shooting-script. The story we were given to work on was some kind of Ruritanian romance, but we had no sooner set to work on this, than the producer came into the office which had been provided for us and said: 'Boys, I've just seen a picture full of old English songs. What this film needs is a lot of old English songs.' Soon after he appeared again and said, 'Boys, I've got Wally Patch on contract. (Wally Patch was well known for his rumbustious Cockney characterizations.) You've got to work him in.' When he had gone Kimmins and I looked at one another, tore up what we had written, and started again. Seeing that we were in difficulties, the producer thought he would give us some further help. 'Boys,' he said, 'I've got an idea. There's a boy, and he meets a girl, and they fall for one another in a big way. Do you follow me? Then something comes between them. Do you get the idea? But it's all right in the end. Work on that now.' The one solid point in this fluid situation seemed to be Wally Patch, who had to be worked in. We started to work out an entirely new story, and it went into production. Some two years later I was watching a film in my local cinema and halfway through suddenly realised that this was *our* picture. A single phrase was all that remained.

Doug's proposition seemed to me entirely different. To be an author for films is to be less than the dust beneath their chariot wheels; to be a 'technical expert' is to be a man of power. One has only to say 'out of period' and the whole show stops. The Production Manager comes to you with tears in his eyes and says: 'Please, *please*, say it's in period. We've got a hundred extras on the set at £2 a day, eating their heads off.' It is necessary to be firm. I tried to persuade Doug to shave off his moustache, assuring him that no one but a hussar really wore one in 1812, which was supposed to be the period of the picture. He declined to do so but in every other respect was most helpful and co-operative.

Sacrificing my entire annual leave, I spent long days at the studio. As there was a prize fight in the picture I had to instruct Doug and his sparring partner in Broughton's Rules, the Queensberry Rules not yet having been invented. For the gambling scene, I was able to provide two unbroken packs of contemporary playing cards. I forbad the smoking of clay pipes in polite society. I went out 'on location'.

One of the scenes involved a chase across country in coaches. Authentic coaches had been hired – the only disadvantage was that they had no brakes – and the coachmen in costume were ready to take their place on the box. The problem was to find a bit of country road and a village in which there was nothing to be seen which could not have been there in 1812. This is not easy within a fifty mile radius of London. I set out in a car with a well-known American cameraman to explore the countryside. He would stop the car and say, 'This is a swell village.' And I would answer, 'Yes, but that wire fence is modern,' or 'That porch was put up in 1840'. After this had happened several times, he looked at me with respectful exasperation and said, 'Gee, you must have been very well educated'.

Finally we found, more or less, what we were looking for at Latymer, a village artificially preserved; and we spent a harassed day – one of the horses shed a shoe and we had the greatest difficulty in finding a blacksmith – staging the chase, with stand-ins in place of Douglas Fairbanks and Elissa Landi. I do not know if the picture made money, but at least I had the satisfaction of knowing that there was nothing in it too glaringly 'out of period'.

The standard of historical accuracy in costume pictures is now of course very much higher than it was thirty years ago, and I like to think that the Victoria and Albert Museum has had a hand in this, so far as British Pictures are concerned. Certainly if any film people came to consult us at South Kensington, we gave them all the help we could. In *The Amateur Gentleman* I was fortunate in having as Art Director Edward Carrick, the son of Gordon Craig. Some of his admirable designs I was able to incorporate in the collections of the Victoria and Albert Museum.

Fairbanks was a charming if sometimes disconcerting companion. One Saturday morning he rang me at the Museum and suggested that we should go to 'The Ball Game'. I am not a football enthusiast but I agreed to meet him at his office at one o'clock. At 1.30 we were watching a film 'In Bond', with a view to importing it and making a new version. At 2.30 we were having lunch at Claridges. At 3.30 we were drinking whisky with an American journalist in his flat in Piccadilly. At 4.30 we were all (American journalist included) in the Hammam Turkish baths. And we never got to 'The Ball Game' at all. I began to think that I lived an excessively tidy life.

Shortly afterwards he asked me to 'do a Cyrano'. He wished to present Marlene Dietrich with a complimentary poem and thought I might write it for him. I was amused and sent him the following:

> When you shall tire, as even you must tire,
> Of lights, and noise and glory and success,
> And having one need only, quietness,
> Find your own room, and silence, and a fire,
> Can you forget long labour, golden hire,
> The acted joy, the all too real distress,
> Can you, as simply as you loose your dress,
> Put off the burden of the world's desire?
>
> I think you can, for there is in your eye,
> A calm, a stillness by the world unguessed;
> By fame unspoiled, by flattery undefiled.
> And I could swear you put your glamour by,
> And with a silent mind lie down to rest,
> And go to sleep, abruptly, like a child.

Of course Douglas admitted it was I who had written the sonnet, and I still have Marlene's charming letter of thanks.

I wrote two more novels in rapid succession, but neither had the success of *Nymph Errant*. I may have hindered the publicity of one of them, *Background for Venus*, by my own action. Meeting William Foyle at one of the Literary Luncheons organised by his daughter Christina, he told me that he would have given a display of the book in one of the windows of his shop, 'But I couldn't with that book jacket'. So immoral a dust cover, it appeared, had not been seen for many years.

I was pained by this, for I had taken the trouble to design it myself. With infinite care, I had cut out columns from *The Times* describing art sales, current events, fires in Bond Street and various other incidents vaguely reflected in the book, and had slapped across them the cut-out figures of Botticelli's Venus. As this was the only book jacket I had ever designed, or am ever likely to design, I was excessively proud of it, although I had to confess that a whole row of the books seen across the road did have a somewhat startling appearance, as of a row of dancing girls at the Folies Bergère. Still it *was* Botticelli, and I was sorry to think that the figure which had passed without comment in Renaissance Florence should have proved altogether too stimulating for the citizens of modern London.

I was also at work at this time on an annotated edition of the Poems of Charles Churchill, the third of the great English satirists, but a long way behind Dryden and Pope. My interest in Churchill lay largely in his first poem *The Rosciad*, which deals with the state of the London Theatre in 1760, with satirical pen-pictures of the leading actors. As the Enthoven Collection was in my own department at the Museum I was able to study a playbill for every performance which Churchill had attended before he sat down to write. Annotating the other poems involved going through the files of *The Gentleman's Magazine* in the Museum Library. All the material I needed for the task was there. But one of the poems, *The Times*, deals with homosexuality which Churchill, as is the manner of satirists, considered to be particularly widespread in his own day, the truth being, of course, that it was as familiar to the Greeks and Romans as to the North-American Indians, and as frequently to be met with in the Baghdad of Haroun-al-Raschid as in the great cities of modern times. The Victorian editor, remarking that, 'A depraved few have occasionally imported from abroad crimes at the mention of which every good man must shudder,' refused to annotate the poem at all. I thought that it was the duty of an editor to elucidate his text, even at the cost of pursuing through the quagmires of contemporary scurrility the mention of 'those crimes at the mention of which every good man must shudder'. I found a good deal of what I wanted in the Dyce Collection in the Museum, and with the aid of such books as *Sodom and Onan*, which is a satire on Samuel Foote, was able to fill in most of the blanks.

The work was very handsomely brought out by Messrs Eyre & Spottiswoode, and Lord Iddesleigh, who was then connected with the firm, and who lived in what is probably the house once occupied by Churchill in Westminster, gave a party in honour of the occasion. On the invitation card was printed the phrase: 'To meet Mr James Laver'. I duly arrived. I had never met Lord Iddesleigh before, but had a long conversation with him. He seemed rather *distrait*, and kept looking round the room. Finally he said, 'Would you know Laver if you saw him?'

The day began to seem all too short for the tasks I had undertaken and it was some time before I tumbled to the obvious conclusion, which was to lengthen it by getting up earlier. One day, in the spring of 1935, I received an envelope with the Cracow postmark, opened it, since I knew no one in Cracow, with considerable interest, and found a letter from an old Polish professor enclosing a review of one of my books, together with some of his own of which he had taken the trouble to make an English summary. I couldn't help feeling that there was some misapprehension. He had detected in *Nymph Errant* a depth of meaning and a seriousness of purpose which, I fear, were not really there. The theme of his own works might be summed up as 'Jesus Christ and the Polish Problem'. I do not intend this as a sneer; in the tragic history of Poland religion and politics are inextricably – and inevitably – intertwined. A friendly correspondence followed, and in one of my letters I told him that all my writing had to be done in the evenings, when my day's work was over, and in reply he said, 'Why not try getting up at five in the morning? Try it, and it will soon become a happy habbit.'

I suppose it was the phrase 'happy habit' that did it. That, and what seemed to me the desperate nature of the advice. If he had told me to get up at six or seven I should probably never have listened to him, but there is virtue in extreme measures.

I bought a cheap alarm clock – the quietest I could find – so as not to wake the rest of the household. I had a divan-bed installed in my small study. Coffee was left ready for me in a thermos flask, and I was all ready for my experiment. To anyone who feels inclined to follow this austere example I would offer two pieces of advice: when the dentist's drill of the alarm bores into the sleeping mind, don't stop to think. Get up! And when you are up *wreck your bed*. Make it impossible to get back into it with any comfort, or without a great deal of trouble. Moral athletes might not need to do this, but for ordinary mortals it is a great help.

The practice has two disadvantages, medical and moral. If you are a smoker it is almost impossible not to light a cigarette, and then another, and another. It cannot be good for anyone to smoke a packet of cigarettes before breakfast. The other danger is more subtle. Early rising induces a feeling of quite intolerable moral superiority. I found myself looking with self-righteous contempt on people who merely got up for breakfast in the ordinary way.

Some of the friends to whom I confided my discovery of this fine new weapon in the eternal battle with Time, seemed doubtful of its value. 'Surely,' they said, 'your work must suffer. You can't for the first hour, at least, be properly awake.' The answer, I think, is that one isn't and that *that* is a positive advantage. For the first hour I wrote little or nothing, but merely sat with my manuscript book before me, brooding over the problem in hand. Literary invention seems to be independent of the conscious will; some of one's best thoughts come between sleeping and waking. In that penumbra before the cold, critical light of day has dispersed the shadows, shapes move, ideas take form and substance, the buried images of the mind have leave to rise and speak.

I kept it up for a year or two and then found, when I wanted to give it up, that breaking habits is almost as difficult as forming them. I no longer set my alarm clock at five o'clock, but I woke up at that hour just the same – with a horrid little pain in the midriff. Then in an endeavour to make up for the time thus lost I procured a dictating machine. This was an old-fashioned Dictaphone with cylindrical records like those of the phonograph. I used to carry a cruet of these to the typist when I had filled them, and on one occasion I dropped the cruet and broke all the records. Six thousand words gone in an instant! Still the machine did enable me to record my book on *French Painting and the Nineteenth Century* in two desperate days.

The use of the machine had one amusing result. It happened that we had a new nurse for the children and on her way down to the kitchen she paused in astonishment outside my little room. Within I was dictating a chapter of *Taste and Fashion*. Awed, she went down into the kitchen and said to the cook: 'Mr Laver's in the study talking to himself about women!'

I became very much interested about this time in the French painter, James Tissot. There had been an excellent exhibition of his work at the Leicester Galleries and Michael Sadleir asked me to write a book about him. I accordingly saw as many of his pictures as I could, and collected reproductions of them. Gradually I pieced together the details of his life. It was a romantic story. He had worked in Paris in the 'sixties and had been a friend of Degas. Coming to London after the Commune, he set up house in St John's Wood and began to exhibit at the Royal Academy. His pictures were either of nautical scenes or scenes of smart society; sometimes a combination of the two, as in his delightful painting 'A Ball on Shipboard'. His pictures were characterised by great attention to the detail of dress, and it is this which gives them much of their charm today.

Early days in television. The author with J. G. Leinks, the furrier.
Alexandra Palace, 1939

Veronica Turleigh as the Goddess Hera in *The Rape of the Belt*

Soon he was prosperous enough to set up an elaborate establishment at 17 Grove End Road, and here, in the house afterwards to be occupied by Alma-Tadema, he lived for the next nine years. In the garden, which was big enough to contain a lake, he constructed a charming little colonnade which he had copied from the one in the Parc Monceau. It appears in several of his pictures, including the one in the Tate.

In 1876 Tissot was at the height of his career as a fashionable painter, and as a diner-out. And then, suddenly, something happened. The tradition was that he was dropped by Society on account of his open *liaison* with a beautiful model. She appears in a whole succession of his pictures for about five years. Then she died. Tissot fled from the house, not even troubling to take his colours and brushes with him, and in 1882 he left London altogether. He devoted himself to religious painting and finally entered a monastery. There seemed to be enough material here to make an interesting life. Who could tell me anything about Tissot? I got in touch with Miss Laura Alma-Tadema. She told me a good deal about the house but she did not know the name of the mysterious model and she could not tell me why she died. She thought perhaps she had committed suicide. I damaged my eyesight by going through the lists of suicides in *The Times*, but could find nothing. I was therefore compelled to leave the mystery unsolved.

Shortly after the publication of the book I received a letter; it was headed A1 Albany (surely one of the proudest addresses in the world) and signed William Stone. I had already had the 'Squire of Piccadilly' pointed out to me: a sprightly old gentleman in a choker collar and brown bowler hat. He lived to be more than a hundred and is reported to have bequeathed to the world this recipe for longevity: 'Never marry, never do any work, and never stand for Parliament.' He was nearly eighty when he wrote to me in a firm old-fashioned hand and said: 'I have just read with great interest your excellent biography of my old friend James Tissot, who I knew very well in the late 'seventies and early 'eighties of the last century on coming down

L

from Cambridge . . . I was a good deal up at 17 Grove End Road and often had tea in the garden with Tissot and the lady.' He ended by inviting me to visit him in Albany and of course I eagerly accepted. He had three Tissots hanging in his hall; he called them drawings, but they were in fact etchings. An elaborate Victorian tea had been set out for my benefit, with lace tablecloth and cream in a silver jug. A liveried manservant was in attendance. He told me how he used to 'ride up to Sinjun's Wood' and he added, cackling and tapping the side of his nose: 'It's my belief he wanted to get rid of that girl on me.' Unfortunately he could not remember the lady's name or anything about her except what I knew already. He had all his faculties except that, like so many old men, he had lost the sense of time.

'There was a johnny called Millais,' he said to me, 'did ye know him? Did ye know him?'

Did I know Rembrandt?

It was not until some years later that the mystery was solved, and it was solved by an enterprising young woman journalist called Marita Ross. By some means she managed to track down an old lady living in Clapham whose name was Lilian Hervey. As a little girl she had appeared in several of Tissot's pictures and was the niece of the mysterious model. The name of the latter was Kathleen Irene Newton.

'She married a wealthy Doctor Newton many years her senior, in India, when she was sixteen. The marriage was unhappy and my aunt returned to England after a few years, with her infant daughter, and lived with her sister (my mother) at Hill Road, St John's Wood. Mr Tissot had a luxurious studio near us. Struck by my aunt's beauty, he followed her one day and asked permission to paint her. Later, much to her father's grief, Mrs Newton went to live with Mr Tissot. Although her husband had divorced her, they were never married because both were strict Roman Catholics. After several ideally happy years, during which many of Tissot's former friends dropped him, Mrs Newton died of consumption. She was twenty-eight.' The whole story was revealed at last.

Marita Ross came to see me at the Museum, and I congratulated her on her flair and pertinacity. Her own story was interesting enough, and she told it in a most lively and amusing manner. She had formerly been a model and in her younger days had posed for many artists, including John B. Souter. His picture *The Breakdown* had been the sensation of the Royal Academy of 1926, and I had actually reproduced it in an article for *Country Life*. The picture showed a Negro in evening clothes and opera hat, sitting on a prone and broken classical statue and playing a saxophone. Beside him was a nude girl dancing – she appeared to be dancing the Charleston. The notion of a white girl dancing naked in the presence of a Negro was too much for some of the critics. I believe there were actually 'representations' from the Colonial Office, and the picture was withdrawn.

'Such a fuss,' said Marita. 'As if any artist would hire two models to pose at the same time! And, as a matter of fact, I posed for the Negro too.'

Although withdrawn from the Academy, the picture attracted the attention of an Indian rajah, who, in his palace, had a large private collection of European nudes. When Souter realised this, he destroyed the picture and, according to Marita Ross, never painted again.

She gave an amusing account of her own work as a model. 'Most of the professionals are all right,' she said. 'It's the amateurs you have to look out for. And if they bring out a tape measure and calipers, make for the door!'

I would like to have possessed a Tissot or two, but it was the usual story. I missed my opportunities of purchasing them while they were cheap, and the combined effect of the book and the exhibition at the Leicester Galleries was to stimulate public interest and to push up their prices far beyond my reach.

CHAPTER 8

Nunc te, Bacche, canam

I suppose that like most men of my generation I owe my first impulse towards an intelligent appreciation of wine to George Saintsbury's immortal *Notes on a Cellar Book*. The young man of today has a whole library of vinology at his command, but, forty years ago, unless I was particularly stupid or blind, it was by no means easy to obtain a working knowledge even of the most famous growths and vintages. I already knew that 1906 and 1911 were good years for champagne, but L.D.H., who was responsible for my education in these matters, hardly ever ordered a bottle of red wine. Saintsbury's masterpiece (for it will survive, I think, most of his other writings) came out while I was an undergraduate and of course I immediately bought a 'cellar book' of my own, although the entries in it were to be lamentably few for some years to come.

It was not until the 'twenties had almost run their course that I took the first important step to wider knowledge. 'When the student is ready the Master appears,' says the Hindu proverb; and my *guru* in these matters was none other, as they say, than Vyvyan Holland. In his shy way he introduced himself to me at a party, with generous praise of my satirical poem, *A Stitch in Time*, which had just been published by the Nonesuch Press. It is perhaps not surprising that I took to him at once, and I was soon dining at the house in Carlyle Square which was for so long the scene of his discriminating hospitality.

I soon found that Vyvyan was not alone. The Wine and Food Society and the Saintsbury Club were not yet in existence, but the little group of civilized men from which both were to spring

164

were already dining in one another's houses and were held together by ties which, if not yet formally acknowledged, were already effective. To meet Vyvyan was also to meet André Simon, Curtis Moffat, and, of course, A. J. A. Symons.

Symons was one of the most extraordinary men I have ever met. With his great height, his striking features, his mop of carefully disarranged hair, his deliberately precise speech, he would have been a striking figure in any company. I met him in a crush on the stairs at a party at Vyvyan's, and he immediately plunged into a discussion of first editions, humanistic scripts, musical boxes and, of course, wine. He took to me in spite of my somewhat prosaic, Civil Service appearance. 'You are the only one of my friends who doesn't look like an intellectual,' he said to me later. He was quite cross about it but it did not prevent him from taking a real interest in my education.

Not that his own was of any long date. He was a wonderful assimilator and *improvisatore*. Vyvyan Holland told me (and I can easily believe him) that when Symons started the First Edition Club he knew almost nothing of first editions, and when he helped to found the Wine and Food Society he knew precious little about wine. But he learned, and he learned quickly. The one thing he never really learned anything about was music. At a time when he was famous for having the world's largest collection of musical boxes he could hardly distinguish one tune from another. He had a genius for 'living on the country'. Once he had started organizing gastronomic functions he probably never sat down to a meal without an excellent bottle of claret. I think it hastened his end. One cannot with impunity be the secretary of *every* dining club in London.

He was always founding new societies, literary or convivial or both and, in the summer of 1929, he came up with a new one. I received an invitation to a dinner, beautifully engraved (who, nowadays, gets an *engraved* invitation even to a wedding?) from his own exquisitely mannered script. The wording was typical of Symons' love of mystification:

'You, James Laver,/are bidden to a banquet to be/held by the

165

Corvine Society on/Thursday June 27th 1929./Compliance with this mandate should/be confirmed to the secretary of the society/at 27 Conduit Street, whereupon you will/be informed of the time & place of meeting/& the costume to be worn./During the evening the Grand Master,/or one deputed to speak for him will/proclaim a eulogy of Baron Corvo/and subsequently the secretary, or one/speaking in his place, will report on the/ State of Corvine Studies.'

I asked Vyvyan Holland what it was all about and he confessed that he was almost as much in the dark as I was. Needless to say, we accepted and were informed that the banquet would take place at the Ambassador Club in Conduit Street, then a restaurant but now the headquarters of the Royal Society of Painters in Water-colour.

We walked through the pillared hall and went upstairs where we found A.J.A. in his element receiving the guests. I cannot make out all the signatures on the signed menu which I have preserved, but they include those of Shane Leslie, Grant Richards, Sholto Douglas, Ralph Straus, and Professor Dawkins.

Around the room were displayed the original manuscripts of Corvo's books, in his extraordinary Elizabethan script. Some of the guests were well known to me, but others were not, and there were no introductions. We sat down, about twenty of us, to one of the most remarkable meals I have ever eaten. No doubt in Edwardian times it would have been reckoned a 'small dinner', but to our modern starveling eyes it has an air of almost unbelievable lavishness. I am tempted to set it down *in extenso* as an historical curiosity.

MENU

Caviar d'Astrakhan
Cantaloupe

Consommé Madrilène en Gelée

Homard Américaine Riz Pilau

Epigram d'Agneau Pio Nono en aspic

Aylesbury Duck Farcie Palermo
Sauce Pommes

Terrine de Petit Pois de Jersey
Pommes Noisette

Volaille Rose de Mai
Salade d'Asperges

Poire Mary Garden
Délice Friandise
Canapé Ambassador

The list of drinks was even more remarkable:

Vodka

Gonzalez Sherry Tio Pepe

Montrachet, 1916

Chambertin, 1915

Krug Private Cuvée, 1919

Château D'Yquem, 1906

Crofts, 1904

Toast Wine (Corvo Gran Spumante)

Courvoisier, 1811, *Grande Liqueur*

'The selection of food and drink' (says the elaborately printed 'True Recital of the Procedure') had been 'made by an unnamed but important neophyte, possessing extensive gastronomic knowledge and an impeccable palate for wine; and the table was garlanded with white and yellow flowers in conformance with the Papal predilections of the author of Hadrian the Seventh.'

When the meal was finished Shane Leslie pronounced a Eulogy

of Baron Corvo in which he claimed that Frederick Rolfe (for that was Corvo's real name) was not so much a spoiled priest as a spoiled Pope. He was followed by A.J.A., still keeping up the fiction that the real secretary of the Society was not present; and then those who had known Rolfe: Pirie-Gordon, Dawkins, Grant Richards and Sholto Douglas.

The meeting, to quote A.J.A., 'did not so much end as deliquesce' and I made my way home wondering who had paid for the feast. It must have cost *somebody* about £500. I was, therefore, all the more astonished when, a few months later, I was bidden to the Second Corvine Banquet. The fare was as lavish as before, but there were some new faces: Francis Meynell, Ambrose Heal, Sturge Moore, Tancred Borenius, Maurice Healy, Earle Welby and Wyndham Lewis. Shane Leslie delivered another Eulogy and A.J.A., who spoke once more for the Secretary, informed us that 'the identity of the Grand Master himself is never disclosed, even to the members.' I didn't care who the Grand Master was, but I was still curious to know who paid for the dinners. I felt that I ought to be asked for a subscription or something, and I pestered A.J.A. until he said: 'If you must know, it was – Maundy Gregory.'

A.J.A. had made his name with a brilliant book *The Quest for Corvo* which is not so much a biography of the strange disreputable eccentric who called himself Baron Corvo as a kind of detective story of how he discovered the facts about his life. In it he recounted some of his dealings with Maundy Gregory, a figure, in his way, as extraordinary as Corvo himself. Had he not run at one time an office for the sale of 'honours'! Gregory was certainly present at both dinners (which is not unreasonable, seeing that he was paying for them) and I must have spoken to him. For I think it was surely he who inscribed my menu '*Magister Magnus Soc. Corvo.*'

A.J.A., if he had lived, would have been the ideal man to write the Life of Oscar Wilde. But there was a difficulty. Lord Alfred Douglas survived him; and so long as he was alive, if you wanted the Queensberry papers, you had to back Bosie's case. I do not see how any conscientious biographer of Wilde could have done this. Bosie *had* no case.

I met him at Cathleen Queensberry's. Cathleen Mann, the painter, was at that time married to the Marquess of Queensberry. She was a clever stage designer and had worked for Cochran for the show following *Nymph Errant*. We became friendly and she invited Veronica and me to spend a weekend in a house which she and her husband had taken for the summer.

The house party consisted of young people, theatrical mostly. I remember that Anton Dolin was among them. But there was also a quiet old gentleman who seemed rather out of things and who spent most of his time in his own room. It was Lord Alfred Douglas. I sat next to him at luncheon and told him, quite sincerely, how much I admired his sonnets. He was pathetically grateful to me for knowing that he was a poet at all. The young people seemed never to have heard of him: never even to have heard of 'the scandal'. He had outlived both his fame and his *infâme*. When the weekend was over we exchanged books and letters; and one of his letters contained the surprising phrase: 'When I was thick with Oscar Wilde . . .'

When Alfred Douglas was dead, Francis Queensberry collaborated with Percy Colson in the book entitled *Oscar Wilde and the Black Douglas*, which, I am afraid, exposed 'Uncle Bosie' as the villain of the whole tragedy. The Wilde story is now familiar to everyone (a play, two films and Micheál Mac Liammóir's astonishing performance) that people have forgotten that, even in the 'thirties, much of it was obscure. I had known Vyvyan Holland for years before he even mentioned his father. Who would have thought that, in the nineteen-sixties a film credit-title would link the name of Oscar's son with that of the great-grandson of the Queensberry who hounded him to prison and death?

Percy Colson was a strange little man. I imagine that he wrote almost the whole of the book, Francis Queensberry merely supplying the information. Colson wrote several books, including a history of White's. He came, unannounced, into my office one day and said he was writing a book about English eccentrics. He was one short and demanded suggestions. I suggested the eighteenth-century scholar Dr Parr, and a short life of him was duly included in the finished work. Colson was a Brother of Holy Cross a charitable foundation in Winchester, a gentleman-pensioner (or whatever the correct term may be) and seemed to be very comfortable in his lodgings. He made frequent visits to London and would invite one to lunch at Leoni's restaurant in Soho. I noticed with some embarrassment that he never paid the bill. It was, indeed, never presented. I imagine that he had done Leoni some service, in his early days as a music critic. He was witty and very malicious.

'It is quite untrue,' he said, 'that Melba told Clara Butt to sing muck to the Australians. Such advice to Clara Butt would have been totally unnecessary.'

I gathered that the ecclesiastical authorities at Winchester regarded him with a somewhat unfavourable eye, chiefly because he never attended any of the services in the Cathedral. 'Are you a religious man, Mr Colson?' asked the Dean, looking down upon him from a great height. 'No! No!' said Percy brightly, 'Church of England.' When he died he 'provided' generously in his will for a young man who had been his protégé; but, alas! the kind intention was all. There was no money to meet the bequest.

A. J. A. Symons was tireless in literary and gastronomic activities. Having already, with André Simon, founded the Wine and Food Society, he then started the Saintsbury Club. The former now has branches all over the world; the latter was confined from the beginning to fifty members. The idea was that they should be either wine merchants, connoisseurs of wine or literary men, or any combination of these. The chairman at the first dinner was J. C. Squire, at the second, Hilaire Belloc. George Saintsbury himself, although still alive, was now too old and feeble to make the journey from Bath, but for some years the dinners were attended by friends and pupils of the Master, and a 'Saintsbury Oration' is still part of the proceedings. On

election a member was supposed to contribute wine to the
cellars – the splendid medieval cellars under the even more
splendid Vintners' Hall with its Grinling Gibbons carvings. The
first hall was destroyed in the Great Fire of 1666; the Charles
II hall survived, I am glad to say, the Great Fire of 1940. By
permission of the Master of the Vintners' Company we still
meet there, twice a year.

Involved, in his casual way, in all these affairs was Curtis
Moffat, the well-known interior decorator. He was as passive as
Symons was active. He lived in Fitzroy Square in a flat with
what seemed in those days a startlingly modern décor. But his
real interest was food and drink. He was gentle, soft-voiced and
modest; and I suppose the most complete Sybarite I have ever
known. His taste in claret and the fineness of his taste-buds
were remarkable.

It was he who telephoned to me early in the 'thirties to suggest that I should join a party going down by car to Bray to dine
with Mine Host Barry Neame at the Hind's Head. The party
consisted of Curtis Moffat, Ivor Stewart-Liberty, A. Van der Poel,
A. J. A. Symons and myself. Symons was, of course, the real
organiser, but we met at Curtis Moffat's place and, wisely
refusing his sherry, which no doubt was excellent, proceeded, as
the police witnesses say, to Bray where we arrived in time for a
walk round the garden before the light faded.

I was meeting Barry Neame for the first time. He was a large,
genial man who looked like a quartermaster sergeant – which,
I believe, he had actually been. He had no pretensions to culture,
but he was an excellent host and he certainly knew about food
and drink. It was his policy to serve the simplest English fare.
Sorrel soup, boiled salmon, roast chicken, asparagus, cheese
soufflé, strawberries and cream – no 'made dishes', nothing
fancy, but everything exquisite. The service was deliberately
slow, to enable us to appreciate the wines; and what wines they
were! After Tio Pepe drunk with 'appetizers' – small slips
of toast bearing buttered shrimps or hung beef, home-made
cheese biscuits and home-made sausages, and a bottle of 1921

Oberemmeler Agritisberg with the salmon, we passed to a noble succession of clarets: Cantenac-Brown, Cheval-Blanc, Château Latour, all of 1920, and a Léoville-Poyferré of 1870. It was the first time I had heard claret discussed as if it were a problem of metaphysics and by people who really knew what they were talking about. The Cantenac-Brown, (or rather that particular bottle of it) was rejected as being unworthy of its companions, but the 'old gentleman' of 1870 had survived all the vicissitudes of history and had come to table in perfect condition. I began to understand the prestige of 'pre-phylloxera'. With the strawberries came a Rauenthaler Berg Feinste Auslese of 1921, followed by two brandies, Hine's 1906 and Martelli's 1904. But I must not be tempted to linger over one particular dinner. This one lasted four hours, and we rose from the table at midnight, 'refreshed'.

Another *simple* dinner which I recall with pleasure was given by the painter Richard Wyndham, not at Clouds, his ancestral home, but at his charming country 'cottage', Tickerage Mill, near Blackboys, in Sussex. Richard Wyndham was just as extraordinary a character as A. J. A. Symons, with the difference that A.J.A.'s eccentricity was deliberately composed and Wyndham's was quite natural, in the grand tradition. When he entered a hotel on the Continent the first thought of the management was to throw this somewhat tramp-like figure into the street. Two minutes later the reception clerk was eating out of his hand. The man had realised that he had to do with a genuine specimen of the eccentric English milord. I once met Wyndham in Bond Street. He had no hat, no collar and tie, and on his feet was a pair of ancient carpet slippers. He carried a large parcel done up in newspaper. 'Where are you going?' I asked. 'The Sudan,' he replied, and it was true. I am sure he arrived at his journey's end in precisely the same condition. He was shot by a sniper in Palestine and with him perished an astonishing knowledge of fine wines.

But on this occasion, when he was host, it was not he but Curtis Moffat who gave the most convincing proof of the fineness of his palate. For, to accompany the *selle d'agneau à la mie de pain* and the *truffes au Xérès*, Wyndham had provided five splendid clarets, of which the two most outstanding were both of pre-phylloxera vintages. And as we were sipping the first Curtis Moffat said: 'Oh, but Dick, you've got them out of order. This is not the Lafite 1874; it is the Margaux 1870.' It was even so; and I had to ask myself how many times would one have to taste these wines – and how seldom ordinary mortals would have had the chance to do so – in order to identify them with such certainty and precision.

I know that a great deal of nonsense is talked by people who profess to know about wine and I have often watched with amusement how they will take a sip from some indifferent bottle and roll it round their tongue with all the grimaces of the connoisseur. I have even been wicked enough to lead them up the garden path by changing labels. But there are people who really do know, who seem to have some special fineness of perception and who, perhaps one should add, have enjoyed quite exceptional opportunities of developing their taste. I have been privileged to know half-a-dozen of these wine-savants: Curtis Moffat and Dick Wyndham, Vyvyan Holland, Maurice Healy, the well-known advocate, Ian Campbell of Airds, and, of course, André Simon. I love wine myself but, in such matters, I simply don't compete. Dare I confess it, I have always felt that the real purpose of good wine is to stimulate people to talk about – something else?

This happy purpose was perhaps most completely realised at the table of Vyvyan Holland. In my notes of meals which I have enjoyed as his guest I find that some dinners were 'claret dinners' in the strict sense. Their purpose was to compare old wines, and the company was assembled for that very purpose. But much as I enjoyed these, I think I enjoyed even more the dinner parties at Vyvyan's which were not quite so specialised. All the guests, of course, loved wine; otherwise they would not have been asked at all, but they were chiefly known for other things. I remember one such party at Carlyle Square very vividly. There were six of us. Vyvyan nearly always limited his parties to six, contending quite rightly that 'the bottle wouldn't go round' any more, and on this occasion the six included H. G. Wells, Julien Green and Alec Waugh.

Wells was certainly no great connoisseur of wine. On the last occasion that I saw him he was sitting at the next table at the Café Royal, and he insisted that I should share the wine he had already ordered. It was Australian and he tried to persuade me that it was 'just as good'. At Vyvyan's he didn't talk about wine at all, although he talked a great deal, chiefly about Frank Harris. Rather to my surprise, he wouldn't admit that Harris had any talent at all. He was, no doubt, in the largest sense of the word, a fraud; but he cut quite a wide furrow through the fields of literature in his time.

Julien Green, whose remarkable novel *Leviathan* Vyvyan had translated from the original French, said very little; and as for Alec Waugh, his voice is like his handwriting, minuscule, and he could hardly have made himself heard against Wells. Not that he wanted to, for he is the most modest of men.

André Simon, when he founded the Wine and Food Society, and began issuing its admirable journal *Wine and Food*, invented a new literary *genre*; the 'Memorable Meal'. It was a composition as stylised in its way as a *chant royal*, and sooner or later we all tried our hands at it. It was not too difficult to learn the language, and my own efforts in this direction had a flavour of affectionate parody which did not in the least diminish my respect for the model and its creator. An example may not be without interest (what would one not give for a similar piece composed in 1760 or 1820?):

MEMORABLE MEALS

The place: 41 Carlyle Square, S.W.
The date: 6 May 1936, 8 p.m.

The host:	Vyvyan Holland
The guests:	André Simon, Maurice Healy, J. Murray Easton, James Laver
The fare:	*Œufs de Pluvier*
	Consommé aux Tomates
	Truite Saumonée; *Sauce Hollandaise*
	Selle de Pré-salé; *Purée d'Epinards*;
	Purée d'Oseille; *Pommes Nouvelles*
	Soufflé au Fromage
	Dessert
The wines:	*Montilla Sencillo Fino*
	Château Latour 1920
	Château Haut-Brion 1906
	Château Durfort-Vivens 1899
	Château Lafite (avant 1874)
	Château Lafite 1870 (*mise de Cockburn et Campbell*)
	Mortier, fine champagne 1865
	Mortier, fine champagne 1875

When I arrived, punctually on the stroke of eight, I found my host and Maurice Healy in the dining-room shaking their heads over the Château Durfort-Vivens 1899. Holland thought he had detected a trace of corking on decanting; Healy denied this and was upheld by André Simon arriving *à propos* to dissuade our host from opening something else instead. We adjourned to the drawing-room, where Murray Easton joined us (Charles B. Cochran, the other guest, was prevented from coming) and we tried the sherry, a dry wine with a curiously sweet after-taste.

The plover's eggs were excellent, André Simon assuring us that while it was illegal to sell them in England it was certainly not illegal to eat them. The *consommé aux tomates* is a *specialité de la maison*. Its crystal clarity, like Tavel Rosé, is apparently a secret of Holland's cook, but an open secret, for it is performed by making a purée and clearing it with the white of an egg and the shell.

The Latour is a great gentleman, there is no other 1920 to compare with it, but we were lucky to drink it when we did for it will probably never be better. Its sugar is all gone, and, like all the 'twenties, it has no future. André Simon declared that we should be quite unable to come back to it after the other clarets, but I was sorry that I finished mine, as it later, in the opinion of the other guests, developed unsuspected qualities.

The Haut-Brion 1906 was a most remarkable wine. Maurice Healy claims that he discovered it in 1925 and produced it at the Savoy, with unfortunate results. One of the guests once called it 'a first class claret with a dollop of port.' Simon wished to substitute for the word port the word burgundy, and certainly this particular claret has the unmistakable flavour of the cooked grape, the slight *amertume* of over-ripeness.

Nothing much can be said about the *truite saumonée*, which does not mean there was nothing to be said for it. The saddle of mutton was perfectly cooked and was accompanied, beside the new potatoes, by two purées: spinach and sorrel. Maurice Healy, with the amiable frankness which is characteristic of him, was inclined to blame the inclusion of two so similar green vegetables, but our host defended himself on the ground that the flavours of the sorrel and spinach were different and complementary. Certainly *oseille* by itself is a somewhat acid vegetable, with a taste, curiously enough, rather like that of the gooseberry, whose name in French is so similar to its own.

The third claret, concerning which controversy had raged before dinner, proved a very attractive wine. The Durfort-Vivens turned out to be a nice old gentleman, still far from senility. A certain virility was gone but the wits remained. The nose (the bottle had had time to breathe meanwhile) was very gracious and charming, and the colour was lovely. No body at all. In short, a fine wine not quite at full cock. We congratulated ourselves that our host had been dissuaded from turning it away.

The most interesting wine of the evening was the unknown

Veronica Turleigh as the Mother Superior in *Teresa of Avila*

The author with Madame Schiaparelli

(No. 4). The wine merchant had said, 'We don't know if it is *the* Lafite, but it is very old.' As there was no date branded on the cork it was necessarily earlier than 1875, and André Simon, by a process of ratiocination which left at least one member of the party speechless with wonder, decided that it must be 1869. It was a vigorous wine, curiously sweet and seemed much younger than the 1899 which had preceded it, younger even than the 1906.

By comparison the Lafite 1870, which was served immediately afterwards, showed its age. A magnificent wine (our host produced a magnum) but with an undoubted odour of antiquity. It was indeed not in anything like the same condition as the other wines so perhaps it was unfair to judge.

An excellent cheese soufflé was followed by English peaches of a flavour which would never have suggested the hot-house.

Our host professed to know nothing of brandies and produced, almost apologetically, a Mortier '65. This Maurice Healy pronounced, in round terms, a fake. André Simon demurred; said it was a made-up brandy, but well made-up – *de la cuisine mais de la bonne cuisine*, which does not mean brandy whose only sphere is in the kitchen. Holland then produced a Mortier 1875 which was better liked. Maurice Healy enlarged, among various ecclesiastical anecdotes, upon the excellence of very old Irish whiskey and swore that he had frequently deceived connoisseurs into thinking it was brandy.

We rose from the table at eleven o'clock, agreeing that we had been provided with a most interesting *gamme* of wines and that the unknown Lafite was the hero of the evening – perhaps the most interesting wine even the most experienced members of the party had ever drunk.'

Have I left anybody out of my list of wine-mentors, men to whom I should be grateful for whatever finer perception I may have acquired? Yes, indeed: the late Eustace Hoare, whom I met much later than the others I have mentioned, but whose exquisite hospitality is certainly among the most pleasant memories of my life. There were times when I couldn't help wondering why I came into the picture at all; and I was even moved to protest when André Simon included me in the Délégation Britannique which was going to Alsace for the *Fête des Vins*. 'Why do you include me?' I asked. 'Because you are articulate, my boy,' was the kindly answer.

I don't think I was very articulate at the end of the final banquet. It took place in the Town Hall of Colmar, and lasted three hours, during which were served fourteen wines and six liqueurs. At the top of the table was the President of the French Republic, and, immediately opposite to me was the Archbishop of Strasbourg. When the wine waiter leaned over his shoulder with the first wine he covered his glass with his hand and said: '*Non, non!*' and then, removing his hand, '*Un tout petit peu.*' I was amused to note that the same little pantomime was repeated every time the *sommelier* came round!

When the luncheon at last finished we emerged into the sunlight and I found myself standing on the rather steep steps of the Town Hall with Vyvyan Holland. Our only thought was to go quietly home but, to our horror, we saw, stretching in front of us, an avenue lined with French troops. There was no escape. We formed into a somewhat ragged procession and braced ourselves for the ordeal.

'*Vive la délégation britannique!*' cried the crowd. We felt like death.

All the meals, I am glad to say, were not quite on this scale, indeed, some of the most agreeable were small, almost intimate occasions; at the enchanting little town of Riquewihr, where almost every house seems to be provided with a magnificent Renaissance staircase; at Ribeauvillé, among the vineyards, and up in the mountains at Trois-Épis. We were taken on a tour of the Vosges and, standing on a hill commanding a view of the Rhine, we saw around us the trenches and the rusty barbed wire of the Kaiser's War. It was now 1936 and the unspoken thought in all our minds was: would they come again? '*Nous avons besoin de vous, Monsieur!*' said my host, and without another word we turned away.

CHAPTER 9

Towards the Brink

In the second half of the 'thirties I was conscious of a growing and almost intolerable malaise. All these activities in which my years had been consumed, all these pictures seen and plays attended, all this paper blackened, this whirl of casual acquaintance, this 'cultivated life' – what did it all amount to?

Dean Inge once remarked that one is for ever 'a man of' the decade in which one is oneself between twenty and thirty. He proudly proclaimed that he would always be 'a man of the 'eighties'. I was a man of the 'twenties and I suppose I still am. At all events, I soon became aware, as the 'thirties progressed, of an alien climate of opinion. It was plain to me that in the eyes of men who were, at most, ten years younger than myself, I was already a back-number. I belonged, if only just, to the generation which had 'fought in the war'. Worse, I had accepted and even enjoyed the frivolous 'twenties, when writers had not yet realised that their first duty was to ally themselves with proletarian culture, whatever that might be. I had even rallied to the wrong side of the General Strike. At literary parties, and similar gatherings, I often found myself in a minority of one.

I was strangely immune to the contagions of the time. When the Oxford Union proclaimed its unwillingness to fight for its King and Country I was distressed. When Beverley Nichols (keeping up with the age better than I did) demanded 'Peace at any price' I thought he was foolish. The propaganda of the Peace Pledge Union seemed to me misguided and dangerous. All these activities, I am convinced, magnified in the sound-box of Ribbentrop's stupidity, played no inconsiderable part in bringing about the Second World War.

I did not share the 'wonderful Russia' complex of so many of the people I met. I regarded the clamour for a Popular Front as a swindle, as later revelations by ex-Communists have shown quite plainly that it was. I couldn't understand how intelligent men could be taken in, or why they should want to be taken in, as they so obviously did. The most unlikely people fell victims to this Russian 'flu. I used sometimes to go to the parties given by a dear old Edwardian gentleman. He was almost a caricature of the type who, while offering his excellent brandy and cigars, would ask you if you had been to 'Monte' lately. It was at his house that I met Harry Pollitt, the little bald-headed ex-boilermaker who was from 1929 to 1956 the Secretary of the Communist Party in Great Britain and then its President.

Intellectual ladies, over cups of tea, would discuss with relish the coming 'liquidation' of their political opponents. Stephen Spender would be quoted:

'Death to the killers, bringing light to life.'

But who were the 'killers'? While having nothing but hatred for Hitler and all his works I couldn't help noticing that when a Nazi killed a Communist it was murder, but when a Communist killed a Nazi – or a Kulak, or a Liberal, or another Communist – it was merely 'liquidation'. Wonderful is the soothing power of words! So a Chicago gangster who would have started with horror at the idea of murdering a woman, saw no objection to 'rubbing out a dame'.

The Dictatorship of the Proletariat seemed to me neither possible nor desirable, and I was shocked by the self-abasement of the English intelligentsia before this illusion-image. I belonged to a small society called the '63 Club'. It consisted of ex-Oxford and Cambridge men who met (and still meet) once a month in the winter to read and listen to papers on all sorts of subjects. Once a year a Distinguished Visitor is invited, and on one occasion this was Middleton Murry. The subject he chose was 'The Necessity of Communism', and in his paper, which was afterwards published, he said:

'It is quite conceivable . . . that the type which we ourselves may be said to represent – the 'intellectuals' who have perhaps learnt their disinterestedness through their fragmentary opportunities of economic freedom – will not survive. It cannot be helped. But it is not wholly accidental to the purpose of this book that it may teach some of those how to endow themselves with survival value. For there is only one way – to be ready to sacrifice their all. By that readiness they will have earned the right to survive; in virtue of that readiness, if they see no prospect of surviving, they will not care.'

This hysterical appeal for an intellectual suicide-pact seemed to me contemptible, and I ventured to tell him so, with a vigour perhaps incompatible with the courtesy due to a Distinguished Visitor. Poor Murry! In retrospect there is something very pathetic about his career. He could be a good critic, but he was always being carried away by the fatal lure of words with capital letters. And could any man with a grain of humour or self-criticism in his composition have entitled one of his books: *God: An Introduction to the Science of Metabiology*, and remarked plaintively afterwards: 'The title of this book, has, I fear, been an impediment to many.'

The Right seemed to me as unattractive as the Left. Like many other literary men I had received an invitation to join the 'New Party', and the letter was signed by some very surprising names. I suppose it is unfair to judge them, for it was as yet by no means clear where Fascism was leading. I had known Francis Yeats-Brown since the 'twenties, when he used to give me demonstrations of the Yoga-positions. He had had an enormous success with his *Bengal Lancer*, and when he took over *Everyman* he asked me for contributions. I sent him several articles, but the political part of the paper seemed to be going more and more Fascist, and I severed my connection with it. Even Sir Arnold Wilson, the new Principal of the

Working Men's College, was inclined to regard the Axis with a favourable eye. But when the war came, although over age, he joined the RAF as a rear-gunner, and was shot down in one of our raids on Berlin.

With the Left, my only contact was, oddly enough, through the theatre. My wife was invited to take part in a production of W. H. Auden's *The Dog Beneath the Skin*, to be produced at the Westminster Theatre early in 1936. Two years before she had had her first part as a leading lady in the West End in Gordon Daviot's *The Laughing Woman*, the play about Gaudier-Brzska, in which the part of the artist was taken by Stephen Haggard. His early death cut short a promising stage career. In 1935 she had played Miss Jewel in Richard Oke's *Frolic Wind*. In the new play she was to be one of the 'Witnesses', Gyles Isham being the other.

The Dog Beneath the Skin is perhaps the only play I have ever seen, or am likely to see, about a baronet disguised as a dog. Its intention was satirical, its method kaleidoscopic; some of its shafts went wide, and some of its diatribes I thought merely silly. But it had the first essential of a play: it was alive, even violently alive, and when I went over the speeches given to Veronica I had to admit that they were the work of an authentic poet. Auden was at that time a tall, blinking, gawky youth, with tow-like hair, but he was already the leader of 'the Movement', and *The Dog Beneath the Skin* was only the first of his many successes.

Later in the same year Veronica created the part of Harriet Vane in *Busman's Honeymoon*, and we met for the first time its author, Dorothy Sayers, who seemed to be able to turn, without effort, from detective fiction to the higher reaches of Christian apologetics.

Some twenty years later Veronica was to play the Empress Helena in *Constantine*. If anyone had told me that it was possible to put the Arian Controversy on the stage and to make the verbal duel between Arius and Athanasius as exciting as the court scene in a murder trial I would have laughed at the idea.

This astonishing feat Dorothy Sayers accomplished. She affected a rather masculine get-up, with the short hair and the long cigarette holder of the 'twenties, but on first nights would appear in all the splendour of a mandarin's robe. I was never as enamoured of Lord Peter Wimsey as she was herself, but his adventures made an excellent play.

Meanwhile I was nibbling at the theatre again myself, turning out lyrics for revues. One of these, *Haven't Got a Heart* had some success, being sung by Hermione Baddeley in the revue *To and Fro*. It was the lament of a Bright Young Thing for the dear dead days of the 'twenties, and who could have been better qualified to sing it than that incomparable artist? The first performance was a 'midnight matinée', and it so happened that Heinemann's were giving their annual party that evening in the beautiful rooms of their Bloomsbury premises. At Heinemann parties the champagne flowed and I think I must have drunk just a little too much of it for I found myself addressing Somerset Maugham as *'cher maître'* which I don't think I would have done if I had been completely sober.

However, I felt no ill effects and, hurrying off to the theatre, took my place in the stalls. And then an alarming thing happened. When Hermione came on to sing my song, there were *two of her*! I had thought that seeing double was a joke, but here I was doing it myself. I hurriedly left the theatre and took a taxi home.

Hermione seemed to like my work and asked me for some more lyrics. She suggested that I should come to her flat to talk things over, but when I arrived I found her entwined with snakes. This sounds like a dipsomaniac's vision, but it was not. She was standing in the middle of her apartment with a large and vicious-looking reptile round her neck. It seemed that the occupant of the neighbouring flat collected snakes and had allowed Hermione to fondle them. She invited me to do the same. Somehow we never got down to any useful discussion.

Then Herbert Farjeon asked me for a contribution to the revue *Nine Sharp* which he was thinking of putting on at the

Little Theatre in the Adelphi. Although he had been active in the theatre for years he was a most untheatrical-looking person; indeed, with his pince-nez and old-fashioned butterfly collar with rounded corners he looked like a country solicitor. He asked where we should meet for lunch, and I suggested the Ivy, at that time *the* theatrical rendezvous. He told me to my astonishment that he had never been there before. I offered him some lyrics, but he said he preferred his own. I could only agree, for no one ever wrote better lyrics for intimate revue than Farjeon. He asked me for a sketch, and I said I would write one. I remembered the story I had heard of the Second Empire cocotte who is won in a raffle by one of the cadets of St Cyr. They spend together a glamorous night of love. As they are parting in the morning she asks him how he could possibly afford the most expensive cocotte in Paris and he confesses that the cost to him was precisely five francs. She laughs and makes her grand gesture. 'This night,' she says, 'will cost you nothing. Here! take it.' And she gives him five francs.

The sketch, which was called *The Queen of Paris* was accepted by Farjeon and put into production. And then I had a fright. Katherine Hammill, who was to play the lady, said to me casually during rehearsal: 'I suppose you know this story appears in Alexander Woolcott's *While Rome Burns?*' I was horrified and started cabling wildly to America in an endeavour to track Woolcott down. He replied very generously that the story was an old yarn, 'told to me by Gilbert Miller *en route* to a performance of *Journey's End* at West Point. I therefore consider that I have no rights in the matter whatever.' Ironically enough, the *Queen of Paris* was – for its size – one of the most successful things I have ever written. After a long run in London it was transferred to New York, and brought in a steady five pounds a week for years. I was very grateful to Woolcott, for he could certainly have made things difficult for me if he had wished to do so. I only met him once, at the house of a well-meaning hostess who gave a luncheon party for Woolcott, Rebecca West and myself in order, as she said, to hear some good conversation.

I was looking forward to this but as she herself talked without stopping neither of these two formidable conversationalists got a word in edgeways.

Through Gabrielle Enthoven I got to know Barry Jackson, and he asked me to give a series of lectures on stage décor at the Malvern Festival. The God of the Festival was, of course, Shaw, who lent himself to the various social activities in the most genial manner. One of the things to do was to have tea with 'The Lady of the Caravans'. She was a rich woman who took a house near Malvern every year at the time of the Festival, and parked in the drive a series of caravans. They were no ordinary caravans; they were more like the Blue Train. I don't think they had ever been actually used, but it was the custom, after tea, for the guests to go and sit in them and, having admired the fittings, to continue their conversation. I was in one of the caravans with Mrs Shaw and through the window I could see, in the next caravan, my wife closeted with G.B.S. He was talking in the most animated way, but of course I couldn't hear a word. When we emerged I said to my wife, 'What did he say? He had, it seemed, only one topic. He had talked for three-quarters of an hour on 'the danger and folly of using aluminium saucepans'. Alarmed at the thought that she might be poisoning her children, my wife drew Mrs Shaw aside and asked her what *her* pans were made of. 'Aluminium, I think,' she answered.

Then Barry Jackson asked me if I would collaborate with him in a stage version of *The Swiss Family Robinson* to be put on at Christmas at the Birmingham Rep. Alfred Reynolds was to compose the music and Barry arranged a meeting. I was delighted with him. I knew, of course, that he had been largely responsible for the success of *The Beggars' Opera* but, so far as I was aware, I was now setting eyes on him for the first time.

In this I was wrong. As a boy I had visited 'Reynolds' Wax Works', the Liverpool equivalent of Madame Tussaud's. It was situated opposite Lime Street Station and offered an impressive array of tableaux, including the Death of Nelson, the

Murder of Rizzio and other historical scenes likely to appeal to schoolboys' imagination. There were also entertainments of various kinds, ranging from performing fleas to 'Aboma, the African Giantess'. This lady, who was certainly large enough, was made to look even larger by the size of the little man who introduced her. Her arm, extended sideways, came well above the top of his head.

The little man was Alfred Reynolds. The Wax Works had been founded by his grandfather, and was run, at this time, by his father. Alfred, not yet launched on his musical career, was helping out. He had hoped, he told me long afterwards, to present Aboma as straight from the jungle. He wanted her to wear a grass skirt and lion's teeth and to beat upon a tom-tom. She declined to do anything of the sort. 'I's a good Methodist,' she said.

Not only was Reynolds an amusing conversationalist and a good musician but the easiest collaborator I have ever worked with. When *The Swiss Family Robinson* was finally produced it was stated in the programme that Barry Jackson had written the play and that I had written the lyrics. Actually, it was almost the other way round. I wrote most of the play and Barry wrote some of the lyrics. Barry, chuckling with glee, would produce a first stanza. We wanted a duet for Mr and Mrs Robinson. Mrs Robinson was supposed to be extremely excited by the tropical air of whatever island it was she was marooned on. Barry made her sing:

> Oh, get me a scarlet hibiscus,
> To put in my bonny brown hair;
> Or a dago with dank, curly whiskers,
> So dashing and devil-may-care . . .

I suggested that the second stanza might run:

> Oh, get me a scarlet hibiscus,
> To put in my permanent wave,

> For I'm feeling extremely promisc'ous,
> And finding it hard to behave.
> I tell you I'm mad for a swarthy-limbed lad,
> You must do something quick or I'll go to the
> >> bad
> So get me a scarlet hibiscus,
> To put in my permanent wave.

Mr Robinson, in his pedantic way (and since she has asked *twice*) replied:

> If I get you two scarlet hibisci,
> You must faithfully promise and vow
> That you won't get outrageously frisky,
> In a way that no spouse could allow.
> *I* will give you a kiss and you'll promise me this:
> Recollect you're a mother,
> Remember you're Swiss . . .

I found all this great fun, and the play was quite a success as a Christmas musical show at Birmingham and in other cities.

My next theatrical adventure was of a rather different kind. I had known Jonathan Cape for many years, and he had published two of my children's books in the middle 'thirties. One day in November 1938 he telephoned to propose a curious assignment. He asked me if I would be willing to go to Paris the following day, contact Mrs Patrick Campbell who was supposed to be staying at the Hotel Brighton, and buy the Shaw Letters. I could go to £1,000. I agreed, took the Dunkirk Ferry and at nine o'clock next morning emerged from the Gare du Nord, washed, shaved and breakfasted and, having deposited my bag at a hotel, telephoned Mrs Pat. Yes, she would receive me at eleven-thirty.

Arrived in the Rue de Rivoli, I found her awaiting me in a comfortable sitting-room with a bright fire and the sun pouring in at the windows overlooking the Tuileries Gardens. She presented an astonishing spectacle, clad in a rather soiled black satin skirt, a beige lace jumper and a black velvet toque adorned with two or three ostrich plumes dyed Prussian blue.

She began by saying that she had never heard of me and did not know if I was at all capable of undertaking the task of editing the letters which had passed between Shaw and herself. As a matter of fact nothing had been said about my editing the letters, but Mrs Pat seemed to take it for granted.

'I suppose,' she said, 'that you think we ought to have tucked up together. You won't understand what I mean by *amitié amoureuse!*' I assured her that I had a little historical imagination, even if young men of my generation were not much given to cerebral flirtation (of course I didn't call it that).

Then she began to read the letters. She was seated against the sunlight and her superb enunciation sent up a little shower of microscopic saliva bubbles which winked and glittered as she spoke.

'Of course,' she said, 'they are not as good as I make them sound.' And when I finally read them in the printed version I thought she was right. 'Stella! Stella! Stella! Stella!' one of them began, and went on like that for several pages. But they *were* wonderful letters, full of Shaw's curious mixture of blarney and delicate feeling, and the strange vapourized passion which goes, I imagine, with *amitié amoureuse*. Certainly if he and Mrs Pat ever had 'tucked up together' such letters would hardly have been written. She wrote him some letters too and they seemed to me equally good.

My praise appeared to mollify her a little, until, as the morning progressed she was able to envisage me as the man to write what she called the 'connecting tissue'. I was, she said, to 'give up everything' and devote my life to this task, so having at least a humble share in the immortality of the letters. On and on she read, until, about two o'clock, I was fainting by the way.

'Now, Mrs Patrick Campbell,' I said, 'I will take you out and give you lunch, anywhere you say.' I suggested Prunier's, but nothing would suit her but that we should lunch at Rumpelmayer's. I had always thought of it as a place where one had tea, but we went to Rumpelmayer's and Moonbeam, of course, came with us.

Moonbeam was her Pekingese dog and when I ordered lamb cutlets for two, Mrs Pat corrected me at once. 'Lamb cutlets for three,' she said. Moonbeam did not actually sit at the table; he ate his cutlets from a plate on the floor, but the waitresses were kept busy looking after him and one of them was even conscripted to take him outside on a lead and walk him up and down the Rue de Rivoli. And all the time Mrs Pat talked.

She asked me what books I had written to justify Cape's choice of me as an envoy, but, like jesting Pilate, she never stayed for an answer. She said what a sly man Cape was and how little he was offering for the letters after all his gallantry. They had met, it seemed, on the Lake of Garda, and Cape had been most attentive. She spoke of how badly her daughter had treated her (quite untrue) and how she had thrown up a part in London worth a hundred pounds a week because she could not bear to think of Moonbeam in quarantine; she talked about her success as Electra in America, and so back to reminiscences of George Alexander and to stories I had heard before.

When we returned to the hotel she read more letters and I tried to make an estimate of what the book would contain; and it came to about two hundred thousands words without any 'connecting tissue' at all. Finally she agreed to Cape's terms which I had stretched a little beyond his limit. We parted and I returned to England.

We exchanged letters. I sent her my book on Whistler and she was gracious enough – with certain reservations – to approve of it and to add: 'You will do our job excellently well.' And then, suddenly, Cape received a telegram repudiating the contract. Mrs Patrick Campbell remained in Paris for a time but, early in the war, she removed to Pau in the Pyrenees and died there. Meeting her daughter Stella Patrick Campbell shortly afterwards, I lamented that the letters were presumably lost, but she reassured me. 'My mother left copies of them in every capital in Europe.' They were finally, I believe, discovered in a hat box. Now at last they have been printed and the world can read the correspondence of these two remarkable characters and follow the progress of their strange flirtation. But I think Shaw's letters to Ellen Terry have more genuine warmth.

Mrs Patrick Campbell, when I met her, was at the very end of her career. Another theatrical character of some importance was at the very beginning of his – hardly even that, for he was then thirteen or fourteen years old. During my endeavours to get together a comprehensive collection of theatrical designs for the Victoria and Albert Museum, I had made friends with Nadia Benois, the niece of the great Alexandre Benois, and herself no mean artist in this field. Veronica and I dined fairly frequently with her and her husband, whose name was Ustinow and who was perhaps the best raconteur I have ever met. So good were his stories that I was sorry when he suddenly paused and said, 'And now I think it is time for Peter to entertain us.' A guest's heart always sinks a little when the children of his host are brought forward to perform; but Peter duly appeared, went behind the screen and proceeded to give a most extraordinary imitation of European radio, in half a dozen languages, noises off and everything. Now, of course, Peter Ustinov (he changed the 'w' of his father's name to 'v') is world famous, and he still gives performances which are not so very unlike the one I heard him give when he was a schoolboy. One of his astonishing talents was, and is, to give the impression of speaking a foreign language of which he knows little or nothing.

In August 1938 I had the luck to be invited to go on a cruise to Greece and the Greek Islands. All I had to do in return was to give two lectures, one on the Greek Theatre in the Theatre of Dionysus in Athens. The other lecture was to be on Greek costume; and this, with the aid of a sheet off my own bed, two safety pins, and the prettiest girl on the boat in a bathing dress, presented little difficulty. We started from Venice, moved slowly down the Dalmatian Coast and visited all the obvious places, including the enchanted Island of Samothrace. I was much moved and stimulated by the whole expedition. I think Delphi is the *holiest* place I ever set foot in. Thermopylae at first seemed disappointing. The whole estuary has now silted up, and the narrow gorge which the Spartans defended so bravely is a wide plain. It is recorded that, on the night before the battle, they washed their long hair in the hot stream which flowed beside their encampment. As we were walking along I noticed a small stream, rather yellow in colour, and thinking to cool my hands, plunged them into it. It was boiling. It has been boiling ever since! When we came to Mount Athos only the men, of course, were allowed ashore. The ladies were, naturally, furious, and as we sailed away, one of the young girl students was heard to say, 'I think it's very unfair; and when we come to Lesbos, none of the men ought to be allowed ashore.' Everybody looked at her wondering how much – or how little – she knew.

When I returned to England early in September I found the Museum in a turmoil. It seemed that war might come at any moment and preparations were already advanced for getting our treasures out of London. The contents of my own department, being what the Americans call 'flat art', presented a comparatively easy problem, except, of course, that there were about half a million items. I decided that, apart from a few precious things, priority should be given to the catalogues. This may sound crazy, but I reflected that a good many of our prints could be replaced whereas to replace a hundred years of cataloguing would take – a hundred years. The only objects in my department which presented insuperable difficulties were the Raphael Cartoons. These original designs by Raphael for the tapestries in the Vatican were in water-colour and body-colour on friable paper. All seven of them were mounted in huge frames behind enormous sheets of plate glass and hermetically sealed. We found that, as the room in which they were exhibited had been built round them, the doors were too small to allow their egress. There was nothing for it but to pull down part of the wall and enlarge the doors. We had in the basement a so-called bomb-proof store, but it was realised that what had been bomb-proof in the First World War was unlikely to be so in the Second. It was resolved, therefore, with the exception of a few large architectural objects, to evacuate the entire contents of the Museum.

Then came the *détente* of Munich and we breathed again. Or did we? I was extremely unhappy about the whole affair, and when one morning, at breakfast, I read in *The Times* the famous 'stab-in-the-back' leader – 'There is nothing sacrosanct about the frontiers of Czechoslovakia' – I was so angry that I thought I was going to have an attack of apoplexy. I rose from the table, went straight to my news-agent and cancelled my subscription to *The Times*. Then I walked along King's Road gesticulating and talking to myself. People must have thought I was mad. Still, for the moment, there was, if not peace with honour, at least peace. There was nothing to be done except get on with one's own affairs.

It so happened that Norman Marshall, who had taken over the direction of the Gate Theatre, had commissioned a play from me. This was *The Heart Was Not Burned*, and it was finished in time for production before Christmas. The theme had been simmering in my head for a long time, in fact, ever since I came across a passage in one of Edmund Gosse's books in which he speculates on what might have happened if Byron, Shelley and Keats had not died when they did. Well, what would have happened? I pictured Keats (not having died at Rome), safely married to Fanny Brawne and travelling in Italy with his bride. In duty bound he calls upon Shelley who (not having been drowned in the Gulf of Spezia) is now living on the Adriatic Coast in close touch with the Carbonari and frightening that secret society by his intransigent idealism and lack of worldly wisdom. Shelley insists on taking Keats and Fanny out in his boat, Mary Shelley refusing to come. A storm springs up, the small craft is driven across the Adriatic and wrecked on the Albanian coast. The castaways are rescued, or captured, by brigands and taken to the stronghold of their chief. The chief turns out to be (the reader has already guessed it!) Byron, who (not having died at Missolonghi and having failed to liberate Greece) has carved out a little principality for himself on the model of his old friend Ali Pasha.

My interest, of course, lay not in this somewhat arbitrary story but in the chance it gave me of expounding three points of view: that of the artist, man of action and 'Fascist', (Byron), that of the artist who had drifted into an extravagant idealism (Shelley) and that of the artist *pur sang* (Keats) who only wants to be left alone to adore Fanny, to listen to the nightingales and to go on writing poetry. It seemed to me that this might be made a real 'Tract for the Times'.

But I was mistaken. I expounded the theme to Elsa Lanchester, who was driving me back from a television broadcast at Alexandra Palace in which we had both been taking part.

'What a fool you are,' she said, with her usual brutal commonsense. 'What does the Public care about the real lives of Byron, Shelley and Keats, let alone their imaginary lives?'

I suppose she was right. The audience was frankly puzzled. They didn't know much about the biography of the three poets but they knew enough to feel there was something wrong, somewhere. Even one eminent and cultivated theatre manager said to me on the first night: 'You took a lot of liberties with history, didn't you?'

Douglas Fairbanks Jnr, who spent one of his three evenings in London seeing the play, sat up half the night afterwards pulling it to pieces and trying to find the flaw – a gesture which I very much appreciated.

People couldn't understand the title, perhaps not knowing that when Shelley's drowned body was consumed on the seashore of Spezia the heart was not burned. It was perhaps a somewhat too elaborate way of saying that he did not die. One wag suggested that a better title would have been *The Cough Did Not Kill*. If a somewhat older and more celebrated playwright had not already appropriated the title I might have called it *Fanny's First Play*.

Marshall himself liked the piece and took immense pains to have it properly mounted. The scenery and costumes were beautifully designed by Edward Wolfe and Marshall assembled a good cast. I like to remember that the principal parts, that of Fanny Brawne and Byron, were played by two young people then at the very beginning of their careers. Their names were Pamela Brown and James Mason.

The next production at the Gate Theatre was a translation of François Mauriac's *Asmodée*, and Norman Marshall offered Veronica the important part of 'Mademoiselle'. I was a great admirer of Mauriac's novels in spite of their Jansenist tone and the way in which, like Hardy, he seems to load the dice against his characters. *Asmodée* was, I believe, his first play and he came over, with his wife and son, for the English production. He was tall and thin with a stoop and a little moustache; in fact he looked rather like an English schoolmaster. He had no English but seemed pleased with the general effect of the play, and at the French Embassy afterwards where Raymond de Margerie was giving a party in his honour, covered Veronica with compliments saying that she had incarnated his ideal.

A few days later Mary Hinton, who was playing the lead in *Asmodée*, gave a lunch party for the Mauriacs at the Savoy. The other guests were Charles Morgan and his wife, Edward Knoblock, Christopher Sandiman, Veronica and myself. Charles Morgan was looking his most noble, and Mauriac said to me in a hoarse whisper: *'Il porte son génie très haut.'* Morgan at that time, of course, was regarded by most cultivated French people as the leading English novelist. He was even a member of the *Institut*, and theses had been written on his work with such titles as *Le platonisme dans l'oeuvre de Charles Morgan*. I had known Morgan for many years – we were indeed contemporaries at Oxford – and had admired his early books. But I couldn't get on with the later ones at all. So great was his obsession with Style that he was supposed to rewrite each paragraph four or five times. It would have been very much better if he hadn't.

When the lunch was over it was suggested that I should take

the Mauriacs to see Hampton Court, so we hired a car and set off. It was nearly four o'clock before we got there, and I had a horrible feeling that the place shut at four. However, after a little persuasion, we were let in and one of the guardians led us through the rooms with a lantern. The effect was most dramatic, strange gleams of light on the gilding and monstrous shadows hovering over the four-poster beds. Mauriac was much impressed, and I was half-hoping that he would use the scene in one of his novels. But Mauriac was never given to the exotic; he never strays far from Paris and Bordeaux.

In this period between Munich and the outbreak of war the Franco-British alliance was very much stressed, at least in the cultural field. The Comédie Française was in London, and the Margeries gave a series of parties in their honour. I was engaged with Lord Ivor Churchill in arranging an exhibition of French and British caricatures in Burlington Gardens. He was already a sick man and I wrestled with the proofs at his bedside.

On March 15 Hitler marched into Czechoslovakia, and Chamberlain's 'Peace in our time' was exposed as a hollow sham. Britain began, at the eleventh hour, to re-arm. We prepared for the evacuation of our treasures; but we continued to acquire new ones. We already had a large collection of the work of William Morris and, after the death of May Morris, we had been offered the contents of Kelmscott Manor. Late in June I went down in a car to Oxfordshire to see what there was, and Giles the caretaker showed me over the house. I selected what we wanted fairly quickly and was able to appreciate the beauty of the place with its rambling rooms and thick rafters and mellowed stone. I note with some amusement that I entered in my diary that 'it is to be a home of rest for tired intellectuals, so this may not be my last visit'.[1] There was very little trace of Morris except for a few wallpapers and hangings. The small rich garden was very beautiful and the surrounding country exquisite. I wondered what Morris would have thought of the aeroplanes zooming overhead.

[1] I was over-optimistic. The Oxford authorities have now abandoned the idea.

The caretaker turned out to be a character and he had inherited at least a touch of the Master's socialism, for he pointed out a little painting of the late sixteenth century, probably representing one of the Months. In the foreground there was gardening going on and in the background a kermesse. Giles's interpretation was: 'These 'ere are the workers and over there the rich people are enjoying themselves.' He told us lurid stories of Miss Lobb, May Morris's friend, who inherited everything and died a few months later 'of drink'. She weighed twenty stone, Miss Lobb did, 'and they do say as she done away with the old lady.' The Director informed me when I got back, and I had indeed guessed it already, that Miss Lobb's fault, if she had one, was love. She seems to have been a woman of pronounced masculine type who was devoted to the frailer May Morris, and died of a broken heart almost immediately after the death of her friend. So much for village gossip!

Meanwhile the political sky was getting darker and darker. I paid a flying visit to Paris, with the premonition that it might be the last for a very long time. The play by Jules Romains, *M. Trouhadec saisi par la débauche*, which I had long ago translated for Charles Laughton, was put into rehearsal at the Little Barn Theatre, Shere, but I was too busy helping to pack up the Museum to give it much attention. By the end of August most of our treasure had been evacuated to the country. We had stacked the huge Raphael Cartoons like a pack of cards in the middle of one of the galleries and had built a brick house round them. An American visitor appeared at this moment and asked to see them. He assured me that he had it on the highest authority that there would be no war; he was particularly anxious to see the Raphael Cartoons and he offered to pay for the expense of getting them out again. I asked him if he was willing to run to a million pounds if they were destroyed, and declined to oblige him.

On August 22 came the Nazi-Soviet Pact and it was plain that war was now inevitable.

The contents of the Museum had been put in a place of safety, but the staff remained. As we were Civil Servants, it was plain that most of us would be transferred to other Departments. Having declined to remain on the 'skeleton staff', I was sounded by the Director as to my willingness to go to the Treasury. I agreed to do so.

My son was at that time seven years old and my daughter nearly five. All children were being evacuated from London, and we wanted to get ours away too. But where? My friend Ronald Balfour came to the rescue and offered them accommodation in his house in Sussex. I shall always remember the gloom of Victoria Station and the walk back to Chelsea in the wet and the darkness feeling that the end of the world was rapidly approaching.

Next day the sky was full of balloons. I went to the Museum to finish clearing up and in the evening listened to Chamberlain's speech. It was so vague and non-committal that I was filled with apprehension. The next day, Sunday, September 3, I was still more disturbed by the morning's papers. Were we going to rat after all? I don't think I have ever experienced more agony of mind than I felt as I walked through the Park towards Downing Street. There, standing with an immense crowd, I heard Chamberlain's voice on the radio declaring war. Almost immediately the sirens sounded. As we now know it was a false alarm, but if it had been a real one it would still have come as a liberation. I walked back to Chelsea almost happy, and certainly with no regrets.

CHAPTER 10

Wandering Voice

Three days after the outbreak of war I was installed in the Treasury, in the Department of Defence *Matériel*. Why half the title should be in French I never learnt. We were chiefly concerned with the Ministry of Supply which had to seek our permission for its expenditure, and on the first Saturday afternoon, when I was the only officer left on duty in my department, a man came dashing over from the Ministry of Supply with a document which he laid before me. 'Sign that,' he said.

'How much is it for?' I asked.

'Only two million.'

I regarded the paper with a certain apprehension. I had the uncomfortable feeling that they might stop it out of my pay if I were wrong. Of course when I presented it to my chief on Monday he brushed it aside as a matter of no consequence. Chicken-feed!

I was astonished at the inadequacy of the accommodation provided for Treasury officials; I shared a room with a colleague, and all I had for a desk was what looked like the bottom half of a sewing machine. It was impossible to get one's legs under it; I had to sit sideways.

For me it was a strange life. I spent my days on Interdepartmental Committees, and my evenings in my deserted house. On Saturday afternoons I went to the British Museum, for I had agreed to edit an edition of Baudelaire for the First Editions Club of New York. It was proposed to bring this out in two volumes, one containing the French text and the other the best English translations I could find. It so happened that

George Macy, who ran the Limited Editions Club of New York, had found in Paris an edition of Baudelaire with drawings in the margin by Rodin. He had commissioned Epstein to illustrate the English volume. I set about looking for English versions.

I knew that Arthur Symons had produced a considerable number and I turned to these first. I was disappointed to find that they were for the most parts not only extremely bad but bore hardly any relation to the original text. In his splendid, sombre poem 'Don Juan in Hell' Baudelaire describes Don Juan crossing the Styx in Charon's boat and leaning on his sword – a most dignified attitude. Symons makes him lean on his *stiletto* and, in order to get a rhyme, brings in a 'man from the Ghetto' who does not appear in the original poem at all! Most of Symons' versions I had to set aside. Edna St Vincent Millay had produced a complete version but she had translated the French alexandrines into English hexameters, which seemed to me a mistake.

However, I found some good versions by Lord Alfred Douglas, Sir John Squire, James Huneker and others. Sturge Moore kindly allowed me to use some of his, and Humbert Wolfe, with great generosity, made one specially for the book. Finding that there were half a dozen rather unimportant poems which no one had troubled about, I was compelled to translate them myself. The English version came out as a separate volume during the war. The sheets of the French text, which had just been printed when France fell, remained hidden in a cellar for nearly five years, when the two volumes were at last united.

I liked and respected my colleagues at the Treasury, but neither my temperament nor such talents as I thought I possessed fitted me for the work I was called upon to do. Some of the quasi-legal documents on which I was supposed to base my actions were to me almost incomprehensible, and I found it very difficult to take 'the Treasury Point of View'. Perhaps this was due to the quarter century I had already passed in a 'spending Department'. 'Are you on our side or not?' my chief used to ask me sometimes when I returned from a meeting and said I had yielded some point or other.

On one occasion I was being briefed before attending a meeting with the Ministry of Supply. 'I know we shall have to give in in the end,' said my chief. 'But we must put up a fight.'

'Why should we put up a fight?' I asked, 'if we intend to yield in the end?'

He looked at me severely. 'You must realise that you are not called on to be a judge in these matters. You are an advocate. Go along and make the best case you can.'

Looking back I think he was right. At the time I just thought it an appalling waste of time.

I tried to get back into the Army. Couldn't I take up my military career where I had left it, with the dazzling rank of Second Lieutenant, in 1919? I had dreams of becoming a Town Major in France, or being posted to a training depôt. Nobody seemed to be interested in these endeavours.

I lunched with two men from the British Council to discuss the possibility of lecturing for them in the Balkans. Italy, France, Holland and Scandinavia were also mentioned. The irony of this lies in the date: December 11, 1939.

Anyway, nothing came of it for the moment; but shortly afterwards I was invited to go to Copenhagen on behalf of the Council. The only question was: would the Treasury agree to my absence. At first all seemed to be going well and a man arrived from the Colonial Office to take my place. Then the complications started. The British Council was not 'strictly speaking' a Government Department and a civil servant could not be lent to it. The Council had to take over his full salary and pension contribution, and out of its limited budget could not afford to do this. If it had been part of a Ministry of Propaganda there would have been no difficulty and I was so much annoyed by what seemed to me a mere accountant's quarrel that I offered to go to Copenhagen in my own time, that is to say using up my annual leave. But my friend Bosworth Smith, Establishments Officer of the Ministry, intervened.

'You are being very foolish,' he said. 'Suppose *anything happens* while you are in Copenhagen; and you can't get back. You will be considered as over-staying your leave, and your wife and dependants will get nothing while you are away.' Reluctantly I abandoned the project, and it was lucky I did. The man who went in my place was in Copenhagen when Denmark was overrun by the Germans, and he stayed there for four years!

Meanwhile the Treasury had filled my post in 'Defence *Matériel*,' and I found myself transferred to another department with the strange name of 'Law and Order'.

I knew nothing of 'Law and Order' and had no idea even of the kind of thing which fell within its scope. I was soon to learn, although when I tell people nowadays what I was concerned with they refuse to believe me. I am not quite sure that I believe it myself.

The Department of Law and Order was concerned with all the bits and pieces that couldn't be fitted in anywhere else. I found that I was in charge of 'All Islands' and was expected to collect the rates, for example, of the Island of Herm. These were assessed in Norman-French as *treizièmes*, but actually they were fourteenths and not thirteenths, just to make it harder. The owner of Herm declined to pay the rates on his property on the ground that Government regulations prevented him from going there. When the Germans invaded the Channel Islands I am afraid I threw the file into the air with the shout of joy: 'That settles those blasted rates!' I found that I was acquiring a reputation for frivolity.

Another of my duties was concerned with the Heralds' Offices. A man who said he was a Unicorn wrote to me from Scotland: 'Unicorn must have a typist.' I replied that my research into mediaeval lore had led me to believe that it was then the custom to dedicate unicorns to the service of virgins. I understood that my correspondent wished me to reverse this procedure, and I regretted that I couldn't see my way to sanction such a break with precedent.

Even more extraordinary was that part of my duties which

was concerned with the Escheated Estates of Intestate Bastards. I am not making this up. There were enough of these cases to make a permanent file on my desk. The legal position is simple enough. If a man who is illegitimate has no wife and his mother is dead, he has no legal relations at all, and if he dies intestate his estate 'escheats' to the Crown. The Crown, however, does not grab it forthwith; it looks about for 'claimants'. These fall into two categories: the 'putative' brothers and sisters, and the 'uterine' brothers and sisters, and the latter have the stronger moral (or should it be immoral?) claim. Little men in bowler hats would sometimes come into my office and say: 'I am the uterine brother of the deceased.' I found this quite a change from 'Is this a Rembrandt?'

The files of former cases fascinated me. A Scottish servant girl had had two illegitimate sons – at thirty years' interval. The younger claimed the estate of the elder, and got it. But what an extraordinary human story! What was she doing in between?

Even more fantastic was the case of the Vicar of B—. The Vicar of B— was a bastard. Some time in the 'nineties he had become possessed of the advowson and had presented himself to the living. Perhaps this had exhausted his resources, for he went about in rags and never lived in the vicarage; he lived in a room over the Post Office. However, he finally broke into the vicarage and hanged himself there. It was then found that, far from being penniless, he had several thousand pounds tucked away. And he was not intestate, he had in fact left a will. And what a will!

He desired that his money should be formed into a trust for the purpose of providing 'knickers for boys' in B— and its surrounding villages. The boys had to be thirteen years of age and 'not black'. The knickers were to come at least two inches below the knee, to be made of stout serge and lined with un-bleached calico stamped with the words, 'So-and-So's Gift'. If, after a year's wear these words were still legible the wearer could apply to an office in B— to be established for the purpose, and he would then be given another pair of knickers.

The highest legal authority in the land sat upon this astounding document and pronounced it to be the work of a lunatic. The estate then escheated to the Crown, and the Crown, with admirable generosity, allowed the money to be used for the repair of the church which the unhappy vicar had allowed to fall into decay.

No doubt, even after Dunkirk, it was necessary for 'Law and Order' to be maintained, but I could not honestly feel that I was contributing much to the War effort, and I looked about for some means of escape. I went to see Jack Beddington, then in charge of the Films Division at the Ministry of Information, in the hope that he might be able to fit me into his department; I thought there might be some liaison job with the Free French. Then, suddenly, I was invited by Sir Robert Kindersley (as he then was) to join the staff of the National Savings Committee.

The suggested task was a curious one. Meetings were being held all over the country in factories, workshops and coalmines. Every little town and village was proposing to have a War Weapons Week and every little town and village was asking for the King to come and open it. Failing the King, they wanted Winston Churchill, or even (they said 'even') the First Lord of the Admiralty, and so on, down the list. My job was to be a professional substitute for these important people, to be greeted with disappointment wherever I went and, as Kindersley put it, 'to be insulted on every platform in England'. I jumped at it.

My departure from the Treasury coincided with the Fall of France. My days at a desk were over; a new life had begun. It was an extraordinary sensation to walk about London in the summer of 1940. The weather was brilliant and there was in the air a sense of expectancy which, strangely enough, was by no means wholly disagreeable. At any moment attack from the air, even invasion, might come and yet the expression on people's faces was neither miserable nor fearful. On the contrary it reflected a kind of almost mystical happiness. Everyone who lived through that period of heightened sensibility will know what I mean. In my own case it was undoubtedly enhanced by my change of job. For nearly twenty years I had been tied to an office routine. My new work involved constant travelling, much concentrated effort, and considerable physical fatigue. But it gave me leisure and an occasional day which was really free. I was able to wander about Chelsea in the sunshine, to sit in the garden of the Six Bells over a pint, to bathe in the Serpentine in the middle of the morning. I am ashamed to confess that before the War I had always been too much of a snob to bathe in the Serpentine. Now I delighted in it. It was as clean as any river is likely to be, the arrangements were excellent, and there was a large grassy space for sunbathing. The clients were numerous and exciting. There were refugees from Holland and Norway, Free Frenchmen and Poles. Lansbury's Lido had become as cosmopolitan as Mussolini's used to be. The languages were more varied than those once heard on Eden Roc.

I think I enjoyed too the new freedom from social obligations. That sounds ungracious – and ungrateful, but just before the War I had arrived at the ridiculous situation of knowing three weeks beforehand exactly how each evening was going to be spent. There was no room for the chance meeting, the sudden impulse. Now (apart from the obligation to be at Clacton or Cardiff at a given hour tomorrow) I was as free as air. There was no need even to return home at definite meal-times.

A few brave souls continued to give dinner parties, and among these was Vyvyan Holland in his house at Carlyle Square. I remember one such dinner party with six or eight guests and the usual splendid sequences of wines, when everybody pretended not to notice that the ominous thuds were coming nearer and nearer and that the glasses were jumping about on the table. When I left at midnight to walk back to my own house, there was a large hole in the road and a broken gas main was flaring to heaven.

I spent the next four years in continuous travel over the face of England and Wales (Scotland was outside my diocese). I became quite an expert on second-class provincial hotels, which got worse and worse as the war dragged on. I soon learnt that the best thing to do was to make straight for the 'Commercial' and order High Tea. But for days I hardly ate anything at all. I would leave one hotel too late to be served with breakfast and arrive at another too late for the evening meal. Sometimes I would emerge from the railway station in a blackout so complete that I might as well have been blind. I spent long days and nights in trains, mostly in the corridor. I visited workshops with a dozen men grouped around the anvil on which I stood, and an arms factory so vast that it needed a car to get from one side to the other. I talked to Irish labourers in the mud of an airfield in the course of construction, and to miners in the pit-head baths. (Incidentally, that is the only place you *can* talk to miners. They won't wait when they are going on shift and they bloody well won't wait when they are coming off). I watched men puddling steel and girls filling detonators. I saw the gleaming, golden beauty of brass foundries; my eardrums were shattered by the noise of weaving sheds. I knew the dignity of Council Chambers, and the cosiness of Mayors Parlours. (Mayors, by the way, can be divided into two categories: those who have 'a little something' in the cupboard and those who haven't.) I stood in market places and boat builders' yards. I marched in processions: I even took the salute at military parades while everybody wondered what a civilian (in a very shabby suit) was doing there at all. I made nearly eight hundred speeches, travelled thirty thousand miles, lost two stone in weight – and loved it.

No audience is exactly like any other audience, although I had to admit that there was a certain monotony in the Chairmen's remarks. One of them, after expressing the usual regrets that I was there at all, went on: 'But I 'ope you will accord to Mr (hastily consulting his notes) Lahver the same degree of attention as you would have given to the First Lord of the Hadmirality 'ad 'e been 'ere, as we all 'oped 'e would 'ave been.' Then being a decent chap and feeling the need to say something nice about me, he went on: 'Mr Lahver 'ad a very distinguished career in the First World War, rising to the rank of Second Lieutenant. Since then 'e 'as been in a Museum.'

I had always been interested in public speaking, as such, but the only speeches I had made before the war were of the after dinner variety. Here was an unrivalled opportunity to try out some of the theories I had long had in mind. It was an advantage that the conditions were almost as unpropitious as they could be. A pit-head bath at two o'clock in the morning, a factory canteen with a noise of rattling plates, a windy market square: these are not ideal situations in which to woo the reluctant ear. The audience was inevitably prejudiced against me personally; they had hoped for someone more glamorous or better known. The subject did not interest them, and no one particularly likes being asked for money. They were tired – sometimes sleepy. How was I to penetrate the defences of such people? How carry out the task I had undertaken?

My first efforts were not very well received, but after a couple of weeks, I began to get the feel of the audiences, to establish a kind of rapport. Under the circumstances in which I was working it was important to do this very quickly. In a big factory canteen there is only about six minutes between the time when the last arrivals have finished drawing their food from the serving hatch and the time when the first arrivals have finished their meal and are moving towards the door. I soon discovered that you can't address five hundred people – or even fifty people: you can only address *one* audience. Somehow the separate individual must be unified, and to unify them they must be made to do something together. The easiest thing they can be made to do together is to laugh. If I could get a laugh in the first half-minute I knew I was all right. People stopped moving towards the door. They stayed to listen.

A cynical Frenchman has remarked that an audience is always *feminine*, even when it is composed of men, and a successful speech is always a seduction – if not a rape.

I tried to vary my wooing in accordance with the circumstances. In Wales when sharp faces looked at me suspiciously, I would say: 'Now, before we have any speeches, I would like to hear you sing.' They sang, divinely, and when my speech was over, Mr Jones (it was always Mr Jones) would jump to his feet and pour out a torrent of eloquence which left mine in the shade. Sometimes he even got the *hwyl*. With mature men in an engine shed in England I was matter-of-fact and down-to-earth. The fact that they said nothing did not mean that they were hostile; we got very good results. I discovered a rule: the lighter the industry, the lighter the approach must be, and the more inflammatory.

I once found myself facing an audience of two thousand girls making balloon fabrics. They had already been whipped up into a state of almost sexual excitement by an RAF band in one corner of the canteen. 'Give us the tools – *we'll* use them', they shouted as other RAF boys moved among them, distributing Savings forms.

As a child I had frequently been taken to Revivalist Meetings, and I remembered that in one of them the preacher had told the story of the beleaguered city, which had at last been forced to surrender. The terms of capitulation were these: that all the men were to be killed but that the women were to go free; and each woman was to be allowed to carry from the city her most treasured possession. And, as dawn came, the besieging troops watched a long procession of women emerging from the city, staggering under heavy burdens. Each woman was carrying a *man*. I told this story and then, raising my voice and pointing my finger at a girl in the front row, I said, 'And now, when *we* are besieged, and the enemy is at *our* gates, will you carry a box of trinkets – or will you – carry – a Man?' And the girl I was pointing my finger at fainted.

With one part of my mind I was delighted (especially when I learnt that the meeting had raised the membership of the Savings Group from twenty-six per cent to eighty-six per cent), With another (and perhaps better) part, I was more than a little alarmed. The trouble about all public speaking is that one begins to evoke emotions one no longer feels – and that might almost be the definition of a prostitute. I began to understand what Kipling meant by:

'If you can talk with crowds and keep your virtue.' This is a moral problem which I cannot pretend to have resolved even yet.

I was usually met by the Savings Committee's local representative and taken in a little car to the factory where I was to make my speech. The representatives, and the factory managers too, came from surprisingly different walks of life. One of them – a typical retired major I had thought – said to me suddenly:

'You're in the art world, I don't know anything about art, but I'm in the Tate.'

'You're in the Tate?'

'Yes. Do you know the picture by a man called Tuke? Two boys bathing, one with red hair and one with black. Well! I'm both of them!'

One of the factory managers showed me round his works but his mind seemed to be on other things. He told me that he had often been on safari with the great Selous, and in imagination he was on safari still.

'I'll give you a word of advice,' he said. 'If a rhinoceros charges you, think nothing of it. Just step aside, and fire. But a water buffalo will hunt you like a dog. Remember that!' I promised to remember.

Sitting in the lounge of a hotel in Southampton I heard someone enquiring for me. A tall young man, handsome in a rugged way, introduced himself. He said he was a detective in the Southampton Police Force and suggested a drink.

'Ah,' I said, 'but the bar has run dry'.

He smiled and led me to the back of the hotel where, in the chauffeurs' canteen, there was drink in plenty. He took me back to his house where I was astonished to find shelf upon shelf of poetry. He certainly knew far more about English poetry than I did. When I next met him, after the war, he had become the well-known radio personality John Arlott.

At first Lord Kindersley's evangelists were only two in number, Sir Noel Curtis-Bennett and myself. But as the work grew – I once made forty-five speeches in four days – it was found necessary to recruit a larger panel of speakers, and I found myself teamed up with the most unexpected people, ranging from retired admirals to Norwegian pastors, band-leaders, singers, actresses – and Jean Batten. Her splendid solo flights must have required nerves of steel, but crossing a street in Manchester in the black-out she was as nervous as a kitten. Such unexpected *rencontres* certainly helped to cheer me on my way.

I was naturally much concerned with the safety of my young family. When the raids began in earnest Ronald Balfour's house in Sussex ceased to be an ideal place of evacuation. My wife had the offer of a cottage in North Wales and decided to take the children there. The cottage was situated in a beautiful valley in the foothills of Snowdon and about five miles from Penryndeadreth. Slightly higher up the valley was the house of Clough Williams-Ellis and also a romantic structure on a neigh-bouring bluff. When Williams-Ellis' tenants asked him what he would like for a wedding present, he said, 'Build me a ruin'. A ruin was accordingly built and being constructed of granite, still stands, although the house has vanished. Higher still up the valley was 'Parc', a house where Richard Hughes, author of *High Wind in Jamaica*, lived for a time.

There could have been few safer places in the British Isles, but it was inaccessible to an extreme degree. Poor Veronica had to bicycle five miles to Portmadoc to do her shopping. My daughter was still too young to go to school but my son was already installed at Hemingford Grey, in Huntingdonshire where the Benedictines had evacuated their Margate preparatory school. It once took me two days, in the depth of winter, to get him home for the holidays. We began to search for something less inconvenient and remote.

I was friendly with Milton Waldman, the reader for Collins (it was he who got them to commission my book on Nostra-damus) who was then living with his family in the Old Rectory at Fen Ditton, two miles out of Cambridge. It was a fine, early eighteenth-century house with some twenty-six rooms, and some of these he allowed us to convert into a refuge for my family. Veronica and the children stayed there for the greater part of the war. Indeed we outlasted Waldman and various other occupants of the main house.

The most interesting among these were old Sir William Nicholson and Marguerite Steen. I had, of course, known Nicholson's work for many years and had included an article on it in my first rash venture into art criticism, *Portraits in Oil and Vinegar*. I had met him once before when I went, in the 'thirties, to his studio in Appletree Yard, St James's, to negotiate the purchase of his huge design in cut-out brown paper for the great Don Quixote poster. Now, whenever there was a pause in my journeying I was able to get to know him really well. He still had traces of the rather sporting elegance – the white socks, the spotted stiff butterfly collar – which had once made him the dandy of the Café Royal. He was still painting vigorously and producing some of his finest late work at Fen Ditton. It was a pleasure to walk with him through the flat landscape of Cambridgeshire as he studied cloud effects and made notes of colours and 'values'. He was a mine of reminiscence about people he had known in his youth: Phil May and Augustus John and, of course, James Pryde, the other Beggarstaffe Brother. Between them, as I had every reason to know (for what is probably the largest collection of posters in the world was in my Department at the Victoria and Albert Museum) they had founded poster-art in this country. But as his stories have already been reproduced in Marguerite Steen's *William Nicholson* there is no need to repeat them.

Marguerite Steen was then engaged on her immensely successful novel *The Sun is my Undoing*, and her typewriter clicked steadily in the long room overlooking the garden. William, when he was not painting, would busy himself with little delicate tasks which gave him immense satisfaction. He would spend a morning painting a paper butterfly with the same exquisite taste he showed in everything.

As I was still travelling about the country opening Savings

Weeks I was only an occasional visitor to Fen Ditton and except during the school holidays, Veronica led rather a solitary life. She was saved by her friendship with Mrs Mary Hutchinson who, with her daughter Lady Rothschild, lived at Merton Hall, a beautiful half-medieval, half-eighteenth-century house almost in the centre of Cambridge. Here, from time to time, nearly 'everybody' seemed to turn up, from 'Bob' Boothby to Lord Russell and from Cyril Connolly to Noël Coward.

Veronica's theatrical career was sadly interrupted, but the Cambridge Arts Theatre gave her some opportunities, especially in Ibsen's *The Lady from the Sea*. This was the only time I ever met Lord Keynes who, with his wife Madame Lopokova, came round to the dressing room after the first night, and, for half an hour, turned the searchlight of his mind on to the play. I listened entranced to his brilliant analysis of every detail, and began to understand *why* he was a great man.

The theatre during the war offered me no opportunities but I did get involved in a film. John Gielgud asked me to act as technical adviser to *The Prime Minister*, a film just going into production at Teddington with himself as Disraeli. Somehow I managed to fit this in with my travelling, although it once involved walking nine miles through the black-out from Hammersmith, the electric line having been broken by a bomb at Gunnersbury. Bombs fell on the studio one night and killed the manager; but, *tant bien que mal*, the film was made. I do not think Gielgud was ever given sufficient credit for his portrayal of the young, and the old Disraeli.

There were many problems in the course of production. I was asked to suggest the menu of the dinner to be given by Bismarck to Disraeli to induce him not to leave the Congress of Berlin. I decided on caviar and roast goose. A goose was procured but it went bad under the heat of the studio lights and another one had to be found in a hurry. And where, in wartime, could one find caviar? I had often been struck by the resemblance between a tin of caviar and a box of small-shot, and thought it an excellent notion to substitute one for the other.

'Listen,' said the production manager. 'This is a *sound* picture.' And, indeed, one would not expect a spoonful of caviar to *rattle* on the plate. In the end we used pearl barley glued together with blackcurrant jelly!

I was still keeping on my London house, and would return to it after my journeys, twice to find the windows blown in and the floors littered with broken glass. The third time this happened I was at home. But I was lucky, for when a thousand-pounder fell in Wellington Square (I heard it coming and thought 'that's a big one!') there was only a slight thud. The bomb, instead of exploding, had simply buried itself in the ground. Otherwise the charming little square would have vanished, and I would not be writing these memoirs.

Life in London at this period was very strange. There were no children in the streets and most of one's friends seemed to have gone away. But certain aspects of London life had hardly changed at all. The Savoy Grill was crowded at supper time; all the management did, when the siren sounded, was to hang a storm lantern, inconspicuously, on one of the pillars. Nobody noticed it, or if they did they pretended not to. The private clubs continued to flourish and one could still dance at the Café de Paris. Most of the people there thought they were safely underground – until one night a bomb fell right down the well in the centre of the building and killed two hundred of them.

Still it was difficult to make contact with one's friends, and this is perhaps the only time in my life when I have ever felt lonely. I was therefore all the more grateful to my chief, Sir Eric Maclagan, for putting me up for the Literary Society. It was a small dining club meeting once a month, but during the war it met at lunch time, first at the Garrick Club and later at Antoine's in Charlotte Street. An entry in my diary reads: 'To the Garrick Club for the Literary Society Luncheon. Very agreeable function – if not very literary: Bernard Darwin, Alan Lascelles, Stephen Gazelee, E. V. Knox, of *Punch*, Kenneth Clark, Sir Dugald Malcolm, Sir Edward Grigg, General Ian Hamilton. Glad to hear from Lascelles that Walter Monckton is safe. His plane (containing also Litvinov and Quentin Reynolds) was two days overdue at Teheran. Proposed to Clark that someone should go and paint subjects at Waltham Abbey Ordnance Factory, especially the men in ochre-stained white clothes pulling their barges along the little canals. He promised to employ one of his war-artists on the job.'

Ian Hamilton was a wonderful old man, straight as a ramrod and with all his faculties intact. But he was then over ninety, and like William Stone, he had lost the sense of time. 'Do you remember Majuba, my boy?' he said to me, and I had to tell him that I had not, in fact, taken part in the first Boer War. He had been wounded in the battle and I had a vision of the old boy, in 1882, climbing up the heights of Majuba in a red coat.

At the next luncheon the company included T. S. Eliot, Laurence Binyon, Cuthbert Headlam and Geoffrey Dawson, of *The Times*. I regarded Dawson with no very friendly eye, for he had certainly inspired if not written the famous 'Stab in the back' article about Czechoslovakia. He astonished me by saying that he had never been in a public house in his life. If he *had* troubled, in 1939, to find out what the man in the street – or the man in the pub – was thinking, he might have arrived at a truer picture of the public temper. Still, these Literary Society lunches were a very pleasant reminder that civilization did go on, in spite of everything. And then one of the members, Sir Jasper Ridley, put me up for the Beefsteak Club, and as one could lunch or dine there any day, the problem of war-time loneliness was solved.

I saw a good deal of Maclagan who was just coming to the end of his time as Director of the Victoria and Albert Museum. In appearance he was extremely ecclesiastical, and his reserved manner led many people to believe he was cold and remote. He could indeed, if he wished to, freeze people more effectively than anyone I have ever known. Before we closed the Museum, I once had a rather tiresome visitor – a much bedizened middle-aged lady who brought in some rather inferior drawings for sale. When I declined to buy them she insisted on seeing the Director. I took her over to his office and remained in the outer office while he dealt with the matter. When she emerged there were, almost literally, icicles hanging from her hair. But he was always very kind to me, as was his wife Lady Maclagan. Having supper with them one night, I was touched to discover that this daughter of the House of Lascelles had herself gone out with a a jug to fetch beer from the local pub.

I had been on the road for a couple of years when a new accountant's quarrel started. The Ministry of Education, whose servant I was, did not see why they should go on paying my salary when I was working full time for the National Savings Committee, and the latter declared that they could not afford to take me on their pay-roll. In the end a compromise was arranged by which I was to return to the Museum at intervals for fire watching, spending the night in a bedroom made out of an office on the top floor. It was a curious sensation being, apart from the Warding Staff, the only person in the huge building. Fortunately, except for the most precious volumes, the Library had been left intact. I simply went along the shelves and helped myself, and, until the V-bombs started, there was nothing much to disturb my tranquillity. I had, however, one unexpected visitor.

I received a letter from Miss Birnie-Philip, Whistler's surviving sister-in-law. She said she had just read my life of Whistler (it had been out for about twelve years but she seemed to have come across it only recently) and she requested, nay, demanded, an appointment to see me. This was duly arranged and I met her at the gate. She was a rather formidable-looking old lady and I noticed that she carried an umbrella with a particularly knobbly handle. I had the uncomfortable feeling that she intended to hit me over the head with it. She declined to shake hands and when I asked why, she said it was because I had insulted her sister, Whistler's wife. When I asked how, she said I had mentioned her in the same sentence with 'bad women'. Poor Jo Heffernan! Poor Maud Franklin! This was inconsistent with her later remark that they had never been anything but models.

She gave me however a lot of information about Godwin and about her own family. Her sister Trixie had, of course, been married to Godwin before she was married to Whistler and had had a son by him. This son was once at a party where Teddy and Edie Craig (the children of Godwin and Ellen Terry) were also present. Someone said to him, 'There are your brother and sister,' but he turned away saying, 'I have no brother or sister.' Miss Birnie-Philip seemed to have a particular dislike of Ellen Terry whom she described as 'the vampire in Godwin's life. Strange how some people are whitewashed.'

I have never worked harder with anyone than I did with this relic of the past. She said she had a collection of Whistler's letters to Fantin-Latour and that she intended to burn them. By tea-time I almost thought I had persuaded her not to do so. Miss Birnie-Philip is dead now and whether she burnt them or not I have never been able to discover.

So, dividing my time between travelling and tours of duty at the Museum, I watched the war grind to its conclusion. My diary for May 8, 1945 reads: 'V-E Day. The war in Europe is over. I think I must have died some time during the last five years for I feel nothing – except a horrible conviction that Russia is going to play for her own hand. She will set up a puppet government in the border States and then absorb them into the Soviet Union . . .

'To the Savoy for the Wall-paper lunch. Rather surprisingly Ernest Bevin turned up and made an excellent speech, but he did not stay and open the exhibition. Walked to Trafalgar Square with Michael Ayrton and listened to Churchill's broadcast announcing the end of hostilities in Europe. Then to the Exhibition in Suffolk Street which is pleasantly presented. One of the displays shows how a Portal house could be decorated – with two pieces of exquisite French furniture and four Cézannes! Why don't they eat cake? Walked back to Chelsea through the thronged Park. The crowd very cheerful. There was a bonfire in our little square at night. About two o'clock a violent thunderstorm. The Walküre carrying off the soul of the Third Reich!'

215

CHAPTER 11

Familiar Spirits

Napoleon the Third was fond of remarking that he had been educated at the University of Ham – the name of the fortress where he had been imprisoned after his first, abortive *coup d'état*. I might with equal justice claim that I was educated, so far at least as one subject was concerned, at the University of Bradshaw. During my long train journeys up and down the country I had almost unlimited time for reading, and I decided to read all the books in the London Library under the rubric 'Occultism'. I carried them off ten at a time, as the generous laws of the Library permitted, and they helped me to forget the discomforts of railway travel in war-time.

I read the works of Eliphas Lévi, Papus and the 'Philosophe Inconnu', Maury's *La Magie et l'astrologie* and Jacob's *Curiosités des Sciences Occultes*. I struggled with the *Clavicula Salamonis*, the Chinese *Book of Changes* and the various editions of the Qabalah. I read Michelet's *La Sorcière* and Waite on the Rosicrucians. I glanced at the works of that astonishing sixteenth-century galaxy of occultists and mystics: Kunrath, Meister Eckhart, Boehme and Paracelsus. I made myself acquainted with the lore of the Tetramorph and the symbols of the Tarot. I read all the modern works on extra-sensory perception, and Ernest Jones on the *Nightmare*. Sylvan Muldoon told me how to project the astral body and John Mulholland warned me to *Beware Familiar Spirits*. I followed Jung as a *Modern Man in Search of a Soul*. I even read Madame Blavatsky.

There is little doubt that Madame Blavatsky had certain hypnotic and mediumistic powers; there is none whatever that

216

she was an old fraud. The temptation to play tricks on her followers was irresistible. But *Isis Unveiled* is far from being a negligible book, chiefly because she was a plagiarist on a colossal scale. Somehow she had become possessed of a whole library of occultism; she pillaged it wholesale and, as she was too lazy to paraphrase, she simply transcribed great chunks of the original texts. *Isis Unveiled*, therefore, is quite a good introduction to the literature of the subject. It is true that she did not provide a bibliography, but this has since been done for her, with malicious intent.

I think I must always have been interested in the Dark Side of Nature. At all events, the very first entry in my diary (in 1917, when I was still a schoolboy) is concerned with a visit to a Spiritualistic meeting in Liverpool, in the company of Malcolm Knox, now Principal of St Andrew's. Perhaps I had better say at once that I have no sympathy with Spiritualism. I am interested in levitation, not in uplift, and the arguments for individual survival still leave me unconvinced. Yet as we sat at the back of the hall (it was formerly a Church but had been transformed into an Ethical Societies' temple by the simple expedient of knocking the crosses off the roof), I began to make a kind of mental appeal to the Medium. 'Come on,' I kept saying under my breath. 'Come on, talk to me.' Suddenly she interrupted what she was saying and pointing her finger at me in the back row said, 'And you, friend—'

Then she described the figure she said she saw standing behind me, and the man she described was well known to me. He was not dead, but was the master at my school with whom I happened to be having some special lessons. On the rare occasions when I have attended Spiritualist meetings since I have always been able to make the medium talk to me.

I have had some curious experiences. On one occasion I was walking with my wife along a twisting, hilly Cornish road. I saw, or thought I saw, a motor-cyclist go past us, right to the top of the hill, and fall off. I had just time to say to my wife, 'Did you see that?' and she had just time to answer, 'Yes,' when the *real* motor-cyclist did go past us and did fall off on the brow of the hill. I call this 'Doing-a-Dunne'.

Also, I have been *guided* in the most curious fashion. Sometime in the 'twenties an old man brought into the Museum four large, faded drawings in pen and bistre wash. They represented theatrical scenes, and as the date was plainly towards the end of the sixteenth century, they were undoubtedly the earliest stage scenes I have ever seen. With the Director's approval they were duly purchased, and I was looking forward to an interesting if difficult piece of research to find out what they really were.

Where should I start? I half remembered having seen an article on sixteenth-century stage designs in an old volume of *La Gazette des Beaux-Arts*. This, with other periodicals, was in a room at the far end of the Museum Library, and to reach it it was necessary to go along a gallery, through what was then the Geography Section. I had no interest in this, and so far as I know had never handled any of the books. I made my way rapidly along the gallery, suddenly stopped and, for no reason at all, took down a book with a plain brown-paper back. I opened it, and there was an engraving of the drawing I had in my hand. The drawings we had just acquired were the designs by Bernardo Buontalenti delle Girandole for the *Intermezzi* at Florence in 1589: the very starting point of perspective scenery. No doubt I would have found this out sooner or later but my 'guide' had certainly saved me a lot of trouble.

Is everything known to the unconscious mind if only we could tap it when we want to? When I was writing my book on Huysmans I was stuck for an account of the Abbey of Solesmes about the time he visited it. Histories of the Benedictine Order did not give me what I wanted, and I had given up the search as hopeless. Then a French scholar of my acquaintance asked me to check a reference for him on something quite different: an incident in the life of Henri III. I went to the London Library, ascended to the Biography Section, and began to look for a biography of Henri III. Nearby was a book entitled *La Vie d'un Prêtre* by Père Houtin. I took it down, opened it, and there was an account of the Abbey of Solesmes at the very time I wanted. Coincidence? Unconscious memory? Who can say? I *know* I had never seen Père Houtin's book before, and was unaware of its existence. This kind of thing has happened to me half a dozen times.

Just before the outbreak of war I had decided to write a book on Nostradamus. The name of Nostradamus had cropped up from time to time in my reading yet I could gain no clear picture of this enigmatic figure. The *Encyclopaedia Britannica* treated with scorn his claims as a prophet but, rather inconsistently, admitting that he seemed to know a good deal about the French Revolution. As his book of *Centuries* was published in 1555 this was itself sufficiently remarkable. Fortunately the London Library had a number of editions of his works and I began to study them.

I was disappointed to find that *Centuries* meant not centuries of years but centuries of quatrains. There was no kind of chronological order, and the verses, written in crabbed French (sometimes in Latin, sometimes in Provençal) were obscure in the extreme. Yet there was one stanza (the famous 'Varennes' quatrain) which made one pause before throwing the volume aside in disgust.

It will be admitted, I think, that the little town of Varennes has only come into the limelight of history once – the famous Flight to Varennes of Louis XVI and Marie-Antoinette. And this is the quatrain:

> *De Nuict viendra par la Forest de Reines*
> *Deux pars, Valtorte, Herne la pierre blanche,*
> *Le moyne noir en gris dedans Varennes:*
> *Esleu Cap. cause tempeste, feu, sang, tranche.*

Now, whatever the obscurities of these verses, they are plainly concerned with the flight, by night, through a forest, of two persons, one of whom is compared to a white stone and one to a grey monk. Marie-Antoinette wore white on the fatal expedition, and her husband grey. 'Monk' perhaps because Louis XVI was never an ardent lover and for the first part of his married life was actually impotent; and 'Esleu Cap', because he was first Capet to be King of France not by divine right but by the will of a Constituent Assembly. And his flight certainly resulted in tempest, fire, blood and the *tranche* of the guillotine. I determined to investigate the matter further if only to clear my own mind.

I read all the commentators I could lay my hands on. Most of these were, of course, French and some were fanatical French Royalists, only too anxious to prove that the return of the Bourbons was inevitable and imminent. At best I thought I might be able to produce a commentary myself; at worst Nostradamus would provide me with a detective story and a crossword puzzle to while away the long hours in trains. I felt I was plunging into a strange world. I even began to study the advertisements in occultist magazines.

Some of these were curious enough. One of them urged its readers to 'Buy our psycholoid levitating trumpet. Medium writes: Sat for seven years. Trumpet never levitated. Yours levitated the first night in a red light.' I did not purchase a levitating trumpet, but I visited an 'Egyptian Sand Medium', and a whole variety of rather depressed fortune tellers who eked out a precarious living in the less fashionable parts of Bayswater.

I had never been to a dark séance but, seeing one advertised, I applied for a ticket and, for the modest expenditure of seven and sixpence, was admitted to the circle. We assembled in what I can only describe as the front parlour of a small house in a back street in Balham. There were fourteen others present and they seemed to me just the kind of people who might have attended, in my youth, the meetings of the Band of Hope. We were introduced to the medium, a sandy-haired young man with a foxy face and a Welsh accent, and soon adjourned to the back parlour where we were seated in a circle, or rather, a half circle, holding hands.

The medium was tied in a chair against the wall and I noticed that his left hand was very loosely secured. Within reach of this hand was a table with rattles, squeaky toys and other apparatus. At his feet lay the levitating trumpet, with a splash of luminous paint on it so that its position could be seen in the dark.

The lights were lowered and we were requested to sing. We sang, passing without any apparent sense of incongruity, from 'Abide With Me' to 'Roll out the Barrel', and from 'Angels Hovering Round' to 'Who, Who, Who's Your Lady Friend?'

The advertisement had said: 'Manifestations guaranteed', and very soon things began to happen. There were raps and strange noises. The levitating trumpet danced in the air and even seemed to bang against the wall above the medium's head. Then it became motionless at about the level of his face and a voice came through it:

'Hello! Hello!'

'Is that you, Dad?' cried one of the circle, and the trumpet immediately answered: 'Yes, this is Dad.'

'God bless you, Dad; have you any message for us tonight?'

And Dad pronounced perhaps the feeblest message that has ever come even from the Beyond: 'Go on as you're going on now.'

The medium was playing safe, as mediums will. Rebecca West once told me of her visit to a séance, in which the medium had professed to be speaking with the voice of 'Grandfather West'. It is a pity, perhaps, that the works of Ibsen are not included in the syllabus of psychic colleges. And even a glance at *Who's Who* might have told him that Rebecca's real name was Fairfield.

However, the audience at my séance seemed to be completely satisfied; and then came the medium's crowning effort: levitation. When the lights went up he was found, still tied to his chair, at the other end of the room. It seemed to me quite possible, in spite of the fact that he was tied to the chair, to tilt it forward and move on his toes.

Another thing that interested me was the arc of spittle on the wall behind where his head had been. This, no doubt, had been ejected from the levitating trumpet when it was banged against the wall. So spirits spit! The whole thing was fraudulent. I had read the literature of pseudo-Spiritualist tricks and I thought I could have put up a better show myself. The medium had earned about five guineas for the evening's work – the same rate, perhaps, as a conjurer at a children's party.

But the interesting thing is that, by the time the foolery was finished, the atmosphere of that little back parlour in Balham was so charged with *evil* that I fled from the house as quickly as I could. No doubt the Collective Unconscious – whatever that may be – contains all the devils that mankind has ever imagined, and it is only too easy to call them up. I felt that I had had enough of this particular line of enquiry.

There were, of course, others.

Browsing one day in the London Library I came across the works of William Lilly, the seventeenth-century astrologer, a man of sufficient repute in his day to be the valued friend of Elias Ashmole, founder of the Ashmolean Museum. In 1651 Lilly published *Monarchy or No Monarchy*, and this volume contained two curious woodcuts. In one of them he depicted a number of corpses in their shrouds, but without coffins, and two men hastily digging graves. In the other, *under the sign of London*, he showed a great conflagration. After the Great Fire of 1666 he was summoned to the bar of the House of Commons because (to quote Sir Robert Brooke, Chairman of the Committee) 'in a book of yours long since printed, you hinted some such thing by one of your hieroglyphics'. After his explanations he was dismissed 'with great civility'.

All this is historical, but what interested me were what Lilly calls 'Corporatures', or, as we would say, the physical characteristics of those born under the various Signs of the Zodiac. I looked myself up and found that he made quite a good show at describing my 'corporature'.

If one were writing a life of Freud one would presumably begin by having oneself psycho-analysed; and as I was writing a life of Nostradamus I thought it my duty to have my horoscope cast by a professional astrologer. I applied therefore to Mr Philip Metman, who agreed to undertake the task. When I went to see him I found a scholarly Dutchman who asked me the necessary details and promised to send me my horoscope. I asked him, for my own instruction, to put in the 'aspects' and to give me the round instead of the square map as being more easily comprehensible to a beginner.

When it came I was fascinated by the technical language and not unimpressed by it as an exercise in psychological algebra:

'The opposition between Neptune and Saturn gives a certain melancholic trend to the character which, however, may be concealed by the humorous tendencies of Uranus in the third in trine to Mercury on the cusp of the seventh house. The latter gives great capability of self-expression and easy contact with others . . . another important problem is that expressed by Venus at the cusp of the fifth house (in Aquarius) in square to Jupiter in the second and with the moon at the cusp of the eighth. This indicates a difficulty in taking woman seriously as a mystery or, to say it in other words: a conflict between the conception of woman as the bestower of pleasure and the vision of the benevolent mother. The ascendant in Libra, however, will easily veil this conflict by its capacity to be "kind and charming".'

I was interested to learn that my 'ascendant' was Venus in Libra, that is, Venus in the House of her Exaltation, Venus at her most fishy. Perhaps that explains my passion for anything edible that comes out of the sea, especially oysters. I was glad to know that my inner conflicts were decently veiled. All the same some of these remarks seemed to me to be getting uncomfortably near the truth. I regret to say that I paid for this and other astrological enquiries by writing a satirical lyric on astrology for a BBC revue:

> Let me see the paper,
> Open at page two,
> Where that kind astrologer,
> Tells me what to do.

Monday's rather trying—
Not too bad, I hope.
Tuesday's good for shopping,
For luck, wear heliotrope.
Wednesday brings a big surprise,
Health is good and spirits rise,
Thursday is a trifle black,
'Lots of talk behind your back',
But when Saturday draws near,
All your troubles disappear.
It must be true, it says so here,
It's written in the stars!

Refrain

Oh, the stars! oh, the stars!
I regulate life by the stars.
Shall I buy a new hat? Shall I go for a walk?
Shall I put half a crown on the favourite at York?
Is it twins or quadruplets I'll get from the Stork?
It's all written down in the stars.
Oh, the stars! Oh, the stars!
Those, busy preoccupied stars!
As each Sunday comes round I'm delighted to see
That they take such an interest in poor little me,
It's extremely obliging, I'm sure you'll agree,
Of the stars.

Were you born in April
Or the end of June?
Are you under Saturn
Or merely in the Moon?
Sagittarius rising,
Mars is glowing red;
Throw away your diamonds,
Wear amethyst instead.
Relatives will give offence,
Venus causes great expense,
Friends will let you down, no doubt,
But my advice will help you out.

You have nothing more to fear,
Jupiter is drawing near.
It must be true, it says so here,
It's written in the stars.

Refrain
Oh, the stars! Oh, the stars!
I regulate life by the stars.
Shall I wear blue on Thursday, on Friday wear white?
Shall I get out of bed on the left or the right?
Shall I have a sick headache on Saturday night?
It's all written down in the stars.
Oh, the stars! Oh, the stars!
Those fussy and motherly stars!
Oh, it gives me a thrill that a man such as I
Is of so much importance that the stars in the sky
Are concerned when I'm born, and disturbed when I die—
Oh, the stars!

I knew another professional astrologer, this time a personal friend named Louis de Wohl. So I went to Louis and told him that I wanted him to cast my horoscope and I wanted to see him doing it. When he had finished I said, half jokingly: 'Well, I've learnt several things about my character that I knew only too well already. Is there anything in the immediate future?'

'Yes,' said Louis, quite seriously. 'In twenty-eight days you will change your job.'

Pure coincidence if you like, but the fact remains that exactly twenty-eight days later I left the Treasury and embarked on an entirely different career, as I have related in the last chapter.

Louis's own career was astonishing enough. He afterwards became an extremely successful novelist, and the author of books on such subjects as the True Cross, but when I first knew him he was a refugee from Hitler's Germany. He was a large, jolly man, and very good company. Having lost sight of him for years I met him again in Piccadilly after the War.

'Hallo, Louis,' I said, 'what have you been doing all this time?'

'You won't believe me if I tell you.'

'Tell me anyway.'

He told me that, soon after the outbreak of war, he had become convinced that Hitler was using astrologers: that is, he was definitely influenced in his choice of days for a particular operation, and even in his choice of generals, by astrological considerations. So Louis went to MI5, put this suggestion to them and offered to do *counter-astrological espionage* for the British Government. He was taken on, given an office and a uniform. And he looked so unconvincing in the uniform that the first day he ventured abroad he was picked up three times by the agents of his own organisation. They just couldn't believe in Louis de Wohl as a British major. Fantastic as this story seems I have confirmed it since from other sources.

When my book on Nostradamus was finally published, towards the end of the War, it brought me letters from all over the world; and the writers of some of these letters were more than a little cracked. One of them offered to introduce me to Jesus Christ who, he said, lived in the next Breton village. There were letters from the United States and South America, even from India. But the letter which interested me most bore the Hastings postmark. It began:

'Do what thou wilt shall be the whole of the Law . . .' I turned to the end of the letter and read:

'Love is the Law, love under will.

Yours fraternally,

Aleister Crowley.'

The 'yours fraternally' gave me rather a turn. But Crowley said he had read my book on Nostradamus and found it most interesting. He was living in a small hotel near Hastings, and would I care to come and see him?

I went to Hastings (it was towards the end of March, 1947), took a cab about four miles into the country and was set down at a small Regency house, now a private hotel. Crowley was called and came downstairs to greet me. I was shocked by his appearance. When I had met him at Gwen Otter's in the 'twenties he was still the Crowley of John's first portrait. A large man he seemed, and rather bloated. Now he seemed to have shrunk both in height and girth and he wore a little straggly beard, like an old bonze. His face was the colour of grey mud. His clothes, a tweed coat, a double-breasted waistcoat and voluminous plus-fours of different material seemed to hang loosely about him. He greeted me with great courtesy, explained that, as he was 'on a diet', he could not lunch with me, but I was to come up to his room afterwards.

We went into a sitting-room until lunch was ready and I tried to establish contact. I asked him about the third volume of his *Confessions* and he told me it was withdrawn on the eve of publication. Only two or three copies existed; he did not possess one himself and could not tell me where to find one. The fourth and fifth volumes, he said, existed only in manuscript – 'deposited with trustworthy friends'. They carried the story 'up to Cefalu'.

After the meal I went up to Crowley's room, wondering if he had purposely chosen No. 13. I found him sitting on a divan bed with a little table before him. On another table was his luncheon – a boiled egg which he had not touched. He was drinking a glass of brandy and offered me some. It was excellent. He was in his shirt sleeves and the sleeves were marked with little spots of blood. A few books were on shelves and on the mantelpiece. Above was his self-portrait in the Chinese manner. Two of his water colours of the Himalayas were on other walls; also a reproduction of John's new portrait. On a chest of drawers stood a painted Egyptian stele and on the little table before him a pile of books, an empty tin to serve as an ashtray, a pipe, several bottles of medicine and a small box containing a hypodermic syringe.

He gave me coffee and a cigarette. He himself smoked a pipe incessantly, only pausing to give himself an injection from time to time. He asked me about my interest in occultism. I said I thought the essence of Magic was summed up in Blake's phrase: 'Push imagination to the point of vision, and the trick is done.'

227

'Ah,' he said, 'you realise that Magic is something we do to ourselves. It is *more convenient* to assume the objective existence of an Angel who gives us new knowledge than to allege that our invocation has awakened a supernatural power in ourselves.'

I went on to discuss the power of the mind over the body, and remarked that, if we added to the power of suggestion the possibility of telepathic communication, a rational approach to magical phenomena became possible. Crowley declared that his own approach to Magic was completely rationalistic.

I mentioned certain recent examples of the stigmata, and Crowley told a curious story of one of his pupils, Elfrida Tyrell, who, growing alarmed by his teaching because it was not sufficiently Christian, was told to go away and, using the meditations prescribed for her, to concentrate upon the crucifix. After a few days she implored him to go and see her and he found that she had the stigmata on her hands. They do not seem to have been actual wounds because he described them as 'rosy'.

Hardly pausing in his conversation he took up the syringe, dissolved a little scarlet pellet in the glass chamber, rolled back his sleeve and gave himself a *piqure*. The heroin injection seemed to give him new life. The muddy look in his face vanished, and the wonderful brown eyes glowed. From time to time he turned them upon me, and I began to understand the hypnotic fascination he must once have possessed.

Anxious to stimulate his memory, I brought up the names of several people known to have been interested in Magic. I mentioned MacGregor Mathers. I knew I was treading on dangerous ground. Probably we shall never know the full truth of Crowley's duel with MacGregor Mathers, Head of the Hermetic Order of the Golden Dawn, but it seems to have resulted in a complete victory for Crowley. He was admitted to the Order in 1898 when he was only an *apprenti sorcier*. 'In those days I was only bluffing,' said Crowley, and I refrained from asking him when the bluffing had stopped and the real Magic had begun.

His teacher had been the magician George Cecil Jones and he made such rapid progress that he was able to mix on terms of equality with such redoubtable occultists as Dr Woodhouse, Dr W. Wynn Westcott, Mathers, Florence Farr and the mysterious lady whose real name was Fräulein Sprengel but who called herself 'Sapiens Dominabitur Astris'. The mystery is made more opaque by Crowley's remark in his *Confessions* that there was a certain Madame Horos who *pretended* to be Fräulein Sprengel and 'deceived' Mathers. Whatever that may mean Crowley and Mathers soon became enemies, and when Crowley threatened to publish the rituals of the Order in the third number of *The Equinox*, due to appear in March, 1910, he was served with an injunction issued on behalf of Mathers. Crowley successfully appealed, and *The Equinox* duly appeared. After that, as may well be imagined, it was war. Eric Maclagan once told me that Crowley had blackmailed Mathers with such effect that the latter had to leave the country.

Crowley was also at war with the O.T.O. or Ordo Templi Orientis, and apropos of this conflict Crowley told me the following strange story. Once, he said, when he had just published a book (he would not tell me the name of the book – 'that would cost you a hundred and fifty pounds') he was visited by three men who accused him of having violated the secret of the O.T.O. He denied it, and one of them, striding across the room, pulled down a book from the shelf, opening it and pointed to a certain passage. The men threatened him with the direst penalties unless he at once took the oath and became a member of the O.T.O. He agreed. The curious thing was that years afterwards – and there could, he said, be no possible illusion about this – he realised that there was a discrepancy in the dates. The threatening visit had actually taken place two years *before* the publication of the book. I could make nothing of this and to conceal my embarrassment asked him if the O.T.O. still existed. 'Of course,' he said, 'I am the Grand Master in England'.

Now, to my surprise, he spoke of MacGregor Mathers with

respect; of Waite with contempt (he called him 'pompous').
He implied that most modern occultists had simply borrowed
from him (Crowley) without acknowledgement, but he excepted
Dion Fortune, who had always admitted her debt. I mentioned
Stanislas de Guaïta and he said he found his works incomprehensible. He told a story I couldn't understand of some woman
who had taken one of his books to Germany. Hitler had got hold
of it and had used its technique; but he had misunderstood it
and so brought himself to disaster.

Feeling that the conversation was leaving reality behind, I
asked him if he had known William Seabrooke, the author of
Magic in the Modern World. 'Yes,' he said, he had known him
and had even stayed with him in a shack somewhere in America.
Seabrooke stole all his material, particularly that used in *The
Magic Island*. He had disgusting habits, even allowing his dog
to lick his face. Crowley seemed particularly shocked by this.
Seabrooke drank himself to death. He always travelled with a
case-load of chains, being a masochist as well as a sadist.

We spoke of the Tarot and he seemed surprised that I knew
so much about it without having read his book. I replied that I
had read Papus. 'Ah,' he said, 'my opposite number in France.'
This was a bloomer; Papus has been dead for about fifty years.
He produced *The Book of Thoth*, his own work on the Tarot, and
allowed me (for a price) to take a copy away with me. It had
elaborate coloured illustration, by Lady Harris. 'I inspired them
all,' said Crowley. 'I made her do some of them five times before
I was satisfied.'

I had read enough in occultist literature to be able to talk the
language. We spoke of the Body of Light and the methods of
its projection, the 'vibration of God-names' the evocation by
deosil circumambulation, the banishing by the same process
widdershins, the consecration of the circle. At last Crowley
growled, 'It seems to me that you know more than you have any
right to know, *without being one of us*.'

Rather foolishly, I asked him if he was acquainted with the
Chinese divining rods. He produced a set from a cigar box and

spread them out on the bed. 'I must ask you not to touch them. They are full of my emanations. I use them every day.' I did not touch them. He saw me to the door with great courtesy, and I returned to London.

I still do not know what to think about Crowley. He has been called by many opprobrious names: traitor, blackmailer, fraud. I do not think he was a traitor, in spite of his activities in America during the First World War. It is true that he edited the *Fatherland*, and had staged a dramatic 'Declaration of Irish Independence', in which he publicly tore up his British passport.

Crowley himself maintained that he was all the time acting in the British interest; and indeed some of the articles in the *Fatherland* were so plainly tongue-in-cheek that it is astonishing that even the Germans accepted them. That he was a blackmailer is, I think, more than likely; that he was a fraud is certain. But was he nothing but a fraud?

He died shortly after my interview with him and the story was current (I do not vouch for it) that, shortly before his end, his doctor had said to him: 'I am going to cut off your heroin.' Crowley replied: 'If you do I shall die – and I shall take you with me.' He did die, and the doctor died a fortnight later. One could not help feeling in dealing with Crowley that there was a real touch of diabolism. Shortly after Crowley's death I was present at a conversation between Louis Umfraville Wilkinson (Louis Marlow, the novelist) and a young man with literary aspirations. They were talking about Crowley and the young man remarked: 'You know, I would like to write the Life of Crowley now he's safely dead.' 'Ah,' said Wilkinson, 'but what do you mean by *safely* dead?'

Is occultism nothing but rather sinister nonsense? I do not think so. Perhaps it is a core of knowledge protected from the curiosity of the profane by its own lunatic fringe. Perhaps true occultism and mysticism are merely two different approaches to the same goal. The path of occultism is more circuitous, but not so steep. It is possible by the use of the appropriate techniques to enlarge the borders of apprehension, to obtain a glimpse, if only a glimpse, of the mystery of Being.

I do not think I am a credulous person: quite the contrary. Yet once or twice in my life I have had what I can only describe as an illumination. During one of my war-time journeys I arrived at Scunthorpe. It was in the depths of winter and bitterly cold; snow was falling. Having spoken in a factory I made my way back to the station, only to find that there would be no train for the next two hours. Fortunately a cinema was open and I went in.

I have no memory of the title or subject of the film. But one of the scenes showed a woman in a décolleté dress standing on a terrace, by moonlight. And as I watched her I heard a voice saying, quite distinctly: 'If that is the beauty of mortal woman, what must the beauty of the Holy Wisdom be?'

I left the cinema and took my seat in the train with the prospect of many hours before me in the dark, dirty and unheated carriage. I was unconscious of any discomfort. For the past twenty-four hours I had hardly eaten anything; yet I was not hungry. In fact, I hardly seemed to inhabit my body at all. Looking out of the window I watched the snow-covered landscape gliding past. But it was like no landscape I had ever seen before. It seemed to be bathed in an unearthly light. It was so beautiful that I was moved to tears. I found myself murmuring the words of Elephas Lévi: *'Je crois à l'Inconnu que Dieu personifie'*. I passed the entire journey in this strange exalted state, trance, *samadhi*, call it what you will, and didn't come to until the train stopped at the London terminus and the crack of the anti-aircraft guns reminded me of what is called reality.

That there was a Reality beyond reality I had no doubt. Nor did I doubt its ultimate beneficence. In spite of the difficulties which have beset Mankind at every step of its way and in spite of the dangers that threaten us now, I believe that if the Universe had meant to say 'No', it would have said it at the very beginning. Somehow, beyond the compass of our minds, it means to make an affirmation; it means to say 'Yes'.

Rose of the World, oh! fruitful Vine,
Whate'er the name we call Thee by—
Truth, Beauty, Piety—or Wine;
Thou may'st not cease, Thou can'st not die.
From the dry root new virtue flows
From the dead husk the seeds escape
And o'er the ruin climbs the Rose,
And in the desert glows the Grape.

CHAPTER 12

Taste and Fashion

The War over, I said goodbye to Lord Kindersley and my colleagues on the National Savings Committee and returned to my duties at the Victoria and Albert Museum. Leigh Ashton had now succeeded Sir Eric Maclagan as Director. We were almost of the same age, had been contemporaries at Oxford and had entered the Museum on the same day. Up to the middle of the 'thirties we had been comparatively junior. Now, except for one or two older men on the point of retirement, we found ourselves the senior members of the staff. Ashton had, of course, a wonderful oportunity of rearranging the contents of the Museum according to his own ideas. This he did brilliantly. I don't think anyone else in England could have done it so well. The public image of the great Museum as it exists today is almost entirely his creation.

Most of the objects were still dispersed in various hiding places and some time elapsed before they could be brought together again. Meanwhile it was decided to hold a series of special exhibitions in the still vacant rooms, and the most important of these was an exhibition of the works of Matisse and a selection of the works of Picasso.

The works of Picasso, less familiar then than they are today, created enormous excitement. The Great British Public did not know what to make of them, but enormous numbers of people queued for admission. One Sunday afternoon, when the exhibition rooms were crowded, there was almost a riot. An elderly lady jumped on a chair and began a speech attacking Picasso. His paintings, she said, were 'ugly, angular and immoral'. The lady's name was Holman-Hunt. A few days later, leafing through an old number of *The Illustrated London News* I was amused to note that the art critic of that paper, reporting on an exhibition of Holman-Hunt's works, had described them in exactly the same terms, 'ugly, angular and immoral'. Perhaps an unconscious memory had caused them to be used again.

That the paintings of Picasso – and of Holman-Hunt – should be described as ugly and angular I could understand, even if I didn't agree. But why immoral? I suppose the anthropologists are right when they tell us that, in primitive societies – and, it would seem, in so-called civilized societies also – immoral merely means unusual, unexpected and therefore shocking. Perhaps, too, there is a carry-over from Ruskin's doctrine of 'truth to Nature'. When an artist sits down to paint some natural object and does not reproduce it on his canvas with photographic accuracy he is telling a lie. So much at least I gathered from listening to some of the visitors' comments.

Picasso himself did not come over for this exhibition, but some time afterwards he paid a visit to Sheffield where there was some kind of Left-wing congress. He was so much incensed by the official hostility to this that he refused to attend the party which had been arranged for him in London. He was however present at a party in his honour, at the studio of Feliks Topolski in 'Little Venice', and this was the only time I ever met him.

When I arrived I found only Henry Moore who had, like me, been invited for eight o'clock. All the other guests had been asked to come at ten. However, we dined together in the neighbourhood and returned to the studio to find an extraordinary collection of Left-wingers and artists, and some who were neither – or both. There was no sign of Picasso and, towards midnight, I was preparing to leave when suddenly he appeared in the doorway. I was astonished by his small size, and even more by his piercing eyes – the eyes of a child. When he learned that I was from the Victoria and Albert he expressed his gratitude for all the trouble we had taken in arranging the exhibition. Then he caught sight of Epstein, rushed up to him and kissed him. It was, of course, the French *accolade* and I was both amused and touched by this tribute of one great artist to another.

Epstein is now, I suppose, somewhat out of fashion with the *avant-garde* critics. He once complained to me that in the first part of his life he had been abused for outrageous modernity and in the second part for having fallen out of the Movement. It was interesting to note that, in spite of all the official recognition he had begun to receive he still had a chip on his shoulder. I am in two minds myself about his carving but he was surely one of the greatest *modellers* of all time. After all, carving and modelling are two very different talents.

He told me an amusing story about the days when he was carving the figures on the British Medical Association building in the Strand. Somehow the word had got about that the figures were indecent, and one day when Epstein was on the scaffolding working away, he saw a policeman climbing up the ladder. Seeing a man in a workman's blouse the policeman paid no attention to him, but gazing at the first figure, opened his notebook. Peering over his shoulder Epstein saw that he had written the one word, 'Rude'. He then passed on to the next figure, and this time wrote 'Very rude'. He then shut his note-book, climbed down the ladder, and Epstein never heard any more about it.

He was not the easiest of men to get on with. When he received his knighthood, the BBC asked me to broadcast on his work. I was so anxious to say what he wanted said that I took my script to his studio and asked him to check it. After it had been broadcast I telephoned to ask if he had heard it.

'Yes.'

'And did you like it?'

'No.'

I was at this time much involved in broadcasting. Early in the 'thirties the BBC had put a long poem of mine on the air with various voices, noises off, indeed 'the works'. Later, I had done dramatized biographies of Whistler and others. Now, immediately after the War, I was asked to join the Brains Trust. This was still the primitive, sound-radio Brains Trust, and it was still using its original members, including Professor Joad and Commander Campbell. It was fascinating to watch them both *playing themselves*. Campbell began his remarks with the inevitable 'When I was in Patagonia . . .'; and Joad, who sat on the chairman's right, just couldn't help leaning sideways to see the next question a few seconds before the rest of us knew what it was going to be. Gamesmanship!

Soon afterwards I was asked to join 'The Critics'. I was in turn art critic, literary critic and chairman. It was quite hard work as it involved seeing a play, seeing a film, reading a book, watching a radio programme and visiting an art exhibition; and the recording took the greater part of a day. I could see my annual leave being steadily eaten away. I valued the programme chiefly as an opportunity of meeting the principal professional critics: Dilys Powell, Harold Hobson, William Plomer and R. H. Wilenski. Wilenski and I became great friends and he got me to do a whole series of monographs for his 'Faber Gallery'. I was also engaged for a time in the 'Animal, Vegetable or Mineral' programme.

I was also involved once more in the world of the cinema. For years we had been striving at the Victoria and Albert Museum to convince the film people that it was in their interest to consult us (free of charge) in all matters of historical accuracy. We answered all kinds of questions. Peter Brook came one day to learn how to play faro. Then Metro-Goldwyn-Mayer asked me to help with a film about *The Young Elizabeth*, and this happened at a fortunate moment. The Museum had a large collection of electrotypes, mostly of sixteenth-century goldsmith's work; but modern purists frown upon such things and they were all about to be sold for scrap. MGM wanted to 'dress the scene' (for example, for a great dinner at Hampton Court) with plenty of glittering plate. I was able to arrange a sale of the electrotypes to Metro-Goldwyn-Mayer, thereby saving the film company several thousand pounds and benefiting the Exchequer to the tune of several hundreds.

Years had elapsed since I had had anything to do with writing for the screen but I was now asked to collaborate with Donald Wilson (an old friend from *The Amateur Gentleman* days) in the script of *Warning to Wantons*. It was a rushed job and provided the only occasion when I have ever written 13,000 words in thirteen consecutive hours. One of the main problems was the choice of a leading lady. She had to be young, pretty, small and preferably French. A young actress from the Atelier Theatre in Paris was flown over for an interview. On a telephone call from Donald I dashed to Brown's Hotel and was shown into her suite. I noted in my diary: 'Her name is Edith Vignaud (we may have to change it) her size, *petite*, her hair blonde, her figure perfect, her face, a flower. She was dressed in the new line: a longish tartan skirt with a serrated edge, a scarlet, tight-fitting jacket. Her plaid hat with a white osprey was lying on a chair. She was delighted I could speak French . . . Test tomorrow at Pinewood at 8 a.m. poor girl and then flies back to Paris. I am enchanted. She will be just right.' We *did* change her name. We re-christened her Anne Vernon and it was as Anne Vernon that she went on to triumph.

On my return to the Museum after the War, Leigh Ashton had offered me the post of Keeper of the Department of Textiles, which included our very large costume collection. I declined, as I was quite content to remain Keeper of Prints and Drawings. Nonetheless an increasing number of people seemed to have got it into their heads that I *was* connected with the costume collection and began to send me specimens of dresses – and even parcels of their great-grandmother's underwear. One huge package was found to contain eighty pairs of women's drawers, vintage 1900! Most of the dresses went to the Department of Textiles; the underwear, declined by the Museum, was sent to Mrs Doris Langley Moore for her Museum of Costume, now, after many struggles, established at Bath. People would telephone me to ask such questions as: 'What was the uniform of a surgeon's mate in a British man-of-war in 1793?' I have even picked up the telephone and heard a voice at the other end say: 'Are you the old clothes man?'

It was my own fault. I found, somewhat to my distress, that my writings, especially *Taste and Fashion*, which came out just before the War, had established me as something of an 'Authority' on costume. Yet my interest had never been in the dresses themselves. My study of Fashion had, originally, a purely technical and utilitarian purpose. I wanted to date pictures.

There was in my department what is probably the largest collection of miniatures in the world, and people were constantly bringing in their own family portraits for an opinion. A visitor would come into the Students' Room, produce a miniature and say: 'This is a portrait of my great-great aunt Augusta who danced at the Waterloo Ball.'

And I would say: 'I'm sorry, but it's a girl of about twenty, and she's wearing the clothes of 1840. So, whatever she did, she couldn't have danced at the Waterloo Ball.'

It is astonishing how often the family records are a generation out. While the sitter for a portrait is still alive no one thinks of writing the name on the back, still less the date. Fifty years later no one knows who the sitter was, and as most people are extremely vague on the subject of the history of costume, they have no means of correcting an error.

A Catholic priest once asked me to go to see him because a pious parishioner had bequeathed to him 'the blood-stained ruff of St Thomas More'. It was certainly a blood-stained ruff and might well have belonged to a Catholic martyr. But it couldn't have belonged to St Thomas More for the good and sufficient reason that ruffs had not been invented in his day.

'But,' people say, 'isn't it possible to *anticipate* a fashion?'

And the answer is, quite simply, 'NO'. If one were shown a photograph of a lady in a cloche hat and a hem-line about the knees and the owner said: 'This is my Aunt Maud, who was an intimate friend of King Edward VII,' one would know that something had gone wrong with the family records – as well as with Aunt Maud.

But having established, for this purely technical purpose, a file of Fashion, I found myself led irresistibly into some curious avenues of speculation. Having studied the What and the When, I began to wonder about the How and the Why. I am still wondering, but I began to evolve certain theories; and these theories (about the so-called 'cycles' of Fashion, the relationship between dress design and other aspects of the applied arts, about the 'gap in appreciation' and the economic and social factors controlling the evolution of Taste) began to evoke a surprising amount of public interest. The publishers of *Taste and Fashion* asked for a final chapter to bring the book up to date. The Political and Economic Planners suggested an article on 'Clothes and Class Distinction' for the first number of PEP Papers. The Oxford University Press commissioned a little book on *Style in Costume* and John Murray one on *The Shape of Things*. Nikolaus Pevsner asked me to write a King Penguin on *British Military Uniforms* and this had the curious fortune to excite the interest of the Turkish military authorities who published a translation of it in the official Army Gazette. The National Book League got me to organize an exhibition of 'The Literature of Fashion'.

With the actual designers I had, so far, had little to do, but in the summer of 1945 I was visited in my office by a courtly old gentleman whose name was Reville-Terry. He said he wanted me to collaborate with him in re-launching his fashion house. He said we must 'get together' 'lay foundations' and 'leave no stone unturned'. 'If you could give me an hour a week.' 'I was four years at the Court of Siam,' he told me. 'Ten queens have come knocking at my door.' I was touched by this revenant. It was like being visited by the ghost of Poiret or Worth, but I could not imagine what I could do to help him and I never saw him again.

My activities in this field brought me first the acquaintance and then the friendship of some of the principal costume

authorities in England, notably Dr C. Willett-Cunnington and
Captain Liddell-Hart. Doris Langley Moore I knew already.
Cunnington's remarkable collection (about a thousand dresses
and as many accessories) I used to borrow for television programmes.

It is sometimes forgotten that Alexandra Palace was in
operation before the war; my first television broadcast was in
1937. The officials used to say, with awe in their voices, 'We
have four thousand lookers-in.' It was all a kind of glorified
charade, and the most unexpected things could happen. On one
occasion, in a talk on sports clothes, we had a girl in a whole
series of bathing costumes, worn one on top of the other, the
most modern being the one nearest the skin. Her job was to take
them off one at a time at a given signal, but unfortunately she
took off the last two in a single operation. As one had no monitor
in those days, it was impossible to tell which picture was 'live'
to the general public and for two desperate minutes I had to go
on talking about nothing in particular until the poor girl
struggled back into her clothes.

After the war programmes were planned on a more ambitious
scale, and I gave a commentary on a series of presentations of
the dresses of the great French fashion houses. Dior sent over
his mannequins with his principal *vendeuse* to keep them in
order. As things were getting into rather a tangle I said to her,
'They don't seem to understand what we want.'

'What can you expect,' she said, 'they are narcissistic
nitwits.'

'That's rather hard, isn't it?'

And she answered: 'If they were not narcissistic nitwits how
could they endure to be mannequins?'

This is not quite true; I have known several intelligent girls
who were successful mannequins.

Pierre Balmain not only sent over his girls and his dresses
but appeared in person, and I had the opportunity of a long conversation with him during the interminable hold-ups which seem
inseparable from television rehearsals. The hard-boiled view is,

of course, that Fashion is completely arbitrary, being dictated by a handful of clever men in Paris whose only object is to sell their goods. I asked Balmain if he considered that he was a 'dictator' of Fashion, and he answered: 'I will tell you what I do. Some months before presenting a collection I go to my country house and make, perhaps, three hundred drawings. Thirty of these are made up in my Paris workrooms, and, if I am lucky, *one* influences the mode.'

I believe that the successful *couturier* is a kind of medium possessed by a spirit, and the spirit which possesses him is the Spirit of the Age.

One of the television shows was in the form of a dialogue with Professor J. C. Flügel of London University, who was one of the few professional psychologists to turn his attention to what is surely a most important department of psychology. His book on dress is a classic, and he was, so far as I know, the first to propound the theory of 'the shifting erogenous zone'. According to this theory the naked body has little or no erotic appeal; but if a part of it is, so to speak, shut off, it acquires erotic capital, and it then becomes possible to draw attention to it with effective results. When the body of woman is thus divided into 'zones', the function of the dress designers is to emphasise them one after the other, and this shifting of emphasis is what we know as Fashion. This seemed to me to throw a flood of light on the vagaries of the mode.

Fired by Flügel's example, I plunged into the muddy waters of psycho-analysis, read Ferenczi and Róheim and tried to use their theory of the Libido-flux as a means of explaining to myself why the body of a woman is 'eroticised' all over while that of a man is not. At Flügel's invitation I propounded these notions both to the Progressive League and the British Psychological Society. I got the impression that I scared them.

The study of clothes can certainly lead one into strange places, even into the realm of sexual aberrations. One day at the Museum we received a letter from a lady living in a remote London suburb who said that her late husband, who was a psychologist (I knew immediately what *that* meant), had left a collection of fashion material which she would be glad to sell. I found a trim little house and a trim little woman who gave me tea and left me to study her husband's collection. It consisted chiefly of photographs, and as I had expected, it was fetichist material, admirably arranged and classified. All the pictures were of excessive tight-lacing and excessively high heels.

'Well,' I said, 'the Museum would give you £10 for it, but if you could find a private collector I daresay he would give you more.'

A week later she telephoned me to say that she had found a private collector who had paid her £25. She thanked me for my good advice.

A curious moral problem arises. I had helped a poor widow, deprived the Museum of an interesting collection of material, and promoted somebody's private vice. But whether I was justified or not I was that night visited by a Great Thought, and the Great Thought was this: Fashion is the comparative of which Fetichism is the superlative. Art has been defined as exaggeration *à propos*. Fashion might be defined as exaggeration *mal à propos* – to the point where cruelty begins. This seemed to me a very exciting idea. 'Your nonsense,' Veronica called it.

This and similar notions, tentatively expressed in various journals, began to bring me a large correspondence from foreign scholars. I already knew some of them, such as Torsten Lenk of Stockholm and François Boucher of the Carnavalet Museum in Paris. It so happened that about this time (the early 50's) the wealthy Marinotti family of Milan had decided to take over the Palazzo Grassi in Venice and to make it an international cultural centre. Boucher had already arranged one or two exhibitions for them and he now suggested that in 1952 there should be held there the 'First International Congress of Costume and the Arts'. Paolo Marinotti agreed and asked Boucher to organise it. The steering committee, consisting of the representatives of fourteen European nations, met in Paris and I, in spite of my protests, was elected President. It was a remarkable assembly of the Principal European scholars in this field: Boucher, Lenk, van Thienen of Amsterdam; Rocamora of Barcelona; Mrs Pylkkaanen of Helsinki; Mrs Andersen of Copenhagen; Mrs Kielland of Oslo, Bruno Thomas of Vienna; Hugo Schneider of Zurich, and the veteran Paul Post of Berlin. These, with the Italian representatives, set about drawing up the programme and making the necessary arrangements, and after a week's rather desperate work, everything was ready. It was decided that the language of the Congress should be French, and this suited everybody but the Scandinavians, for whose benefit the proceedings had to be translated back again into English.

The first International Congress of Costume and the Arts duly took place. The official receptions were held in the Palazzo Grassi on the Grand Canal, and it certainly excited my imagination to stand at the entrance and 'receive' the Mayor of Venice arriving by gondola with liveried gondoliers. Our deliberations were held in the Palazzo Vendramin some distance away along the Grand Canal and here we listened, for a week, to a series of learned papers on all aspects of costume history. It was very hot and at times as I sat in the Presidential chair I could feel the perspiration running down the back of my neck. The *Séances* were attended by a considerable number of interested people from all over Europe. Everything went very well, although there *were* a few moments of international tension which had to be smoothed over by the President.

The value of such reunions does not reside in the papers read and listened to, for these are nearly always accessible in print afterwards, but in the personal contacts with foreign scholars. And of course in the pleasure of being in Venice for any purpose whatever. When the actual work of the Congress was over the delegates stayed on for a few days and the generous Marinotti organisation arranged a whole series of expeditions: to the villas of the Brenta, to Padua and Vicenza and, of course, to Torcello, that proto-Venice with its Cathedral older than St Mark's. We were waiting on the quay for the *vaporetto* to take us there when I noticed one of the learned ladies of the

French delegation clad in a macintosh and grasping an umbrella.

All my admiration for the French cannot conceal from me that their sense of humour is very different from our own.

I said: '*Vous êtes pessimiste, Mademoiselle X.*'

She looked at me gravely. '*Mais non, Monsieur, je ne suis pas pessimiste.*' And for the next twenty minutes she expounded to me her exact philosophical position from which it was plain that she was not, in fact, a pessimist.

It was a blazing day and when we were disembarking and I saw her again, still clad in her macintosh and holding her umbrella, I couldn't refrain from murmuring: '*Toujours pessimiste, Mademoiselle X!*' A cloud came over her eyes and I could see that she was saying to herself: 'This *stupid* man! Have I got to explain my philosophic position to him all over again?'

The Congress ended with a resolution that there should be an international bibliography of costume and, in an endeavour to implement this *voeu*, a series of meetings was held, first in Venice and then in Paris. These meetings provided an even sharper lesson than the Congress itself in the differences of national temperament. I was no longer in the chair and was able to watch the proceedings with a certain detachment and it was astonishing how completely all the delegates ran true to type. Paolo Marinotti kept intervening – as he had every right to do, for it was his organisation that was financing the project – to remind us that technicalities were a secondary consideration. '*Nous avons un flambeau à la main. C'est pour l'*uomo *que nous travaillons!*' The Frenchman, diplomatic and suave but determined to make his point, the grave and rather touchy Spaniard, the Dutchman who was the only one present who spoke *everybody's* language, the Scandinavians who spoke only their own tongue – and English, the solid German, the charming Austrian: all these provided a fascinating study.

François Boucher had co-opted a very learned lady from the *Bibliothèque Nationale* who obviously regarded us as a lot of unruly schoolchildren. She kept saying: '*Il faut être systématique.*

Une bibliographie est une bibliographie,' ending each phrase with a little frosty smile.

It had been the general opinion in Venice that all the delegates were typical of their nationality – except myself. I was now revealed in my true colours as *tout à fait britannique.* For it seemed to me that all this talk of bibliography as a kind of Platonic Idea was getting us nowhere and I intervened to say that, in my view, the object of a bibliography was to enable a student – perhaps a rather stupid student – to find the book he needed.

A violent thunderstorm was raging outside and perhaps our tempers were getting a little frayed. When I had explained the very much simplified scheme which I had suggested, the lady from the *Bibliothèque Nationale* said, *'Ce n'est pas logique, Monsieur.'*

'Je m'en fiche de la logique!' said I.

The effect was electric. The Italians shouted with laughter, the Scandinavians were delighted, the German guffawed, even the Spaniard smiled. The French were *horrified.* No *mot de Cambronne* could have shocked them more. Of course I made peace with them afterwards, but I could see that the lady from the *Bibliothèque Nationale* could not quite find it in her heart to forgive me. All the same, if the simpler scheme *had* been adopted there might now be in existence a useful international bibliography of costume. The more ambitious project came to nothing.

So much for the academic side of costume; what of the 'rag trade' itself? I was on good terms with many of the English designers. I broadcast with Hardy Amies and took part in a debate with Victor Stiebel at the Forum Club, I had a great admiration for both these men not only for their talent as dress designers but for the way in which they laid themselves out to be helpful. Both accepted invitations to lecture at the Geffrye Museum in the East End. It was part of my job to do such things but that they should do them was an act of pure benevolence.

With fashion journalists my relations were not at the beginning quite so happy. Some of them were extremely annoyed by my theories, and the publication in 1946 of *A Letter to a Girl on the Future of Clothes* was greeted with a good deal of ridicule. In this little book I had addressed a girl of ten years old and told her that when she was twenty her clothes would be straight in line and plain in colour and with the waist in the wrong place. In this I was basing myself entirely on historical analogies. It seemed to me that there were two 'post-crisis epochs' in modern history: the period following the French Revolution and the period following the First World War, and that the dresses which had finally emerged after these upheavals had had certain characteristics in common, an absence of curves, an absence of colour and a displaced waist – very high in 1800, very low in 1925. Both were 'little girl' dresses, for in post-crisis epochs it is the very young woman who calls the tune. *Our* post-crisis dress, I ventured to prophesy, would therefore have similar characteristics. As 1946 was the very year of Dior's New Look – the exact antithesis of all this – my remarks excited only incredulity. However, in 1956, Dior brought out his H-line, and fashion ever since has shown a marked tendency to return to the modes of the 'twenties.

This caused considerable interest in the fashion industry on both sides of the Atlantic and in the summer of 1958 I was invited to give a talk on the subject at the annual dinner of the International Silk Association in New York. I had never been to America before, and jumped at the chance. The first attempt to cross the Atlantic was a failure. When we were some 500 miles out something went wrong, so we threw our petrol into the sea and limped back to London. Twenty-four hours later we touched down at Idlewild and here I found a much befurred man smoking a cigar: the chauffeur who had been sent to fetch me.

'How do, old bean?' he said.

What a beautiful city New York is in the early hours of the morning when the streets are deserted and the sun is just striking the top of the Empire State Building! The car (it was a 'Cad.' the chauffeur told me proudly, and fitted with stereophonic sound) drew up at my hotel on Fifth Avenue and I was shown into a palatial suite. In the middle of the floor was a case (yes, a case!) of liquor. But everybody knows how overwhelming is American hospitality.

Three months later I was back in New York to take part in a Quiz programme with the unexpected name of 'Brains and Brawn'. This was such a curious affair, that in retrospect, I am not quite sure that it wasn't a dream. I was teamed up with a very famous man called Jackie Jensen of Boston Red Sox. We never met but he scored points for me at baseball ten miles away while I scored points for him in the Rockefeller Centre, many floors up in the heart of New York. The whole thing was very well organised, the questions being posed by the Brooklyn Museum, and there was no cheating – at least no one told *me* anything. In the end the united 'Brains and Brawn' of Jackie Jensen and myself resulted in our both being awarded a Studebaker 'station-waggon'. I never set eyes on this, the only motor-car I have ever possessed, for when I left America it was still on the assembly lines at Detroit. A friend in New York kindly took it off my hands. I reckon that it would have cost me about £1,000 to bring it to England. Shortly after this I went to America again, this time to Dallas, Texas, in order to receive the Neiman-Marcus Award for my 'services to Fashion'. A curious, if flattering, result of just trying to date pictures.

One of my last actions before retiring from the Museum was yet another fashion-foray. A letter arrived from the firm of Worth-Paquin announcing the closing of their Paris House and offering us the entire records of the combined establishments. We were given four days to make up our minds. Next day I took the early plane and by noon was in the Rue du Faubourg St Honoré and knocking at the door.

Inside was a chaos of abandoned workshops, offices and showrooms. Ancient *vendeuses* with red eyes were standing about uncertain what to do next. I saw Worth's portrait upside down in a corner. I was shown into the room where the archives were kept and stayed there until I had satisfied myself that they were worth having. Worth having! There were about 20,000 original designs for dresses, some of them going back to the 'sixties. Worth, being no draughtsman, had, I was interested to note, worked on ready-made lithographs of head and arms, filling in his designs for the crinoline dresses of the period. What an astonishing career it was, that of the Lincolnshire youth, the shop-assistant at Swan and Edgar's, who went to Paris in the 'fifties and, in ten years, was the unchallenged dictator of the mode!

Some of the account books were fascinating, in particular one huge, leather-bound volume labelled *'Debiteurs'*. I flicked over the pages and found the names of *La Belle Otéro* and other famous ladies of half a century ago; what they bought, who paid for it, and how much! I decided to accept the entire collection on behalf of the Museum and before the day was out I had arranged for its transport to South Kensington. I knew that my friend François Boucher would have liked the collection for his *Société des Amis du Costume*; but, after all, Worth *was* an Englishman and I felt justified in grabbing the lot. The House of Worth had lasted in Paris for just a hundred years. Worth-Paquin now operates entirely from London.

It would be absurd to pretend that I did not get a lot of fun out of these events, but I regarded them with mixed feelings nonetheless. I had attained some sort of position as an authority on costume. I sometimes wish I hadn't. All my gratitude to the Victoria and Albert Museum for providing me with a profession for nearly forty years cannot conceal from me that it has dictated my path in a way I would not, perhaps, have chosen. Instead of proceeding, in however pedestrian a fashion, along the highways of literature I had been diverted into the bypaths of expertise. I did not intend to become an art expert, a social historian, or even a 'philosopher of fashion'.

When a man has reached the sixties and has retired from his profession he is bound to look back and ask himself whether it has all been worth while. Has he succeeded in tracing a 'surface pattern' and, if so, what does it mean? I suppose one could call Keyserling to witness: 'Whoever profoundly understands a superficial part of Life necessarily gains metaphysical insight along with it'. Surface pattern is the cross-section of Something: the cross-section of a fourth-dimensional solid called History.

But has History itself a meaning? When I was an undergraduate it was the fashion to deny that it had any; and when one reads the works of the opposite school – the Spenglers and the Toynbees – it does sometimes seem as if the pattern they find is rather a function of their own minds than a property of external events. Men conceive the Ultimate Reality in terms of their own predilections. To the Greek philosophers God was a philosopher, to the Roman lawyers he was a lawyer – and sometimes a rather pettifogging lawyer at that. Some have conceived Him as a mathematician, some as an artist. Certainly an aesthetic pattern seems easier to believe in than a moral one.

For moral optimism has been badly shaken by the events of the last fifty years, and modern philosophers seem to take a positive delight in demonstrating the meaninglessness, the *absurdity* of the universe we live in. And, in spite of Eliot, the world *does* seem more likely to end with a bang than a whimper. If that is so, to what end was all this careful classification of objects?

Most young men with literary aspirations start by thinking of themselves as poets. Experience slowly teaches them that the heights of Parnassus are not so easily scaled. The projected Epic never takes shape. Let us turn to prose then, and write the Great Novel, or the world-shaking Play! In the end they have to content themselves with the immortality of a footnote – 'Gigadibs, *op. cit.*'. I suppose many a man of my age is discontented with the *persona* he has so laboriously built up. Is it too late to escape from it even now? Might one not begin again and start a new literary career – under another name?

I have been exceptionally fortunate in my life ('so far' one adds, to placate the jealous gods); fortunate in my family, fortunate in my friends. Fortunate also in my temperament for although, like Dr Johnson's friend, I try to be a philosopher, 'cheerfulness keeps breaking through'. The hand of the barometer points, pretty steadily, to 'Set Fair'. Perhaps this is not fortunate, after all. I have sometimes wondered if a nice, big, fat neurosis would not have helped me to write better books. But if you only want a neurosis in order to write better books, it means that you are very unlikely to develop one at all.

I am conscious of a certain hardening of the arteries. The sounding cataract no longer haunts me like a passion, although I still take pleasure in fields and woods and the far horizon. Most of the music composed since 1900, most of the poetry written since 1930 and many of the pictures painted since 1950 fail to awake in me the authentic frisson. But I have rediscovered the novel (now that I no longer have to do my writing in the evening and have time to read) and can even appreciate the anti-novel, in the hands of its best exponents. Memoirs of all kinds continue to delight me. Bertrand Russell once said that the secret of happiness was 'a friendly interest in people and things', and I think I have that. Also an inextinguishable curiosity. So long as these last I shall be in no hurry to depart.

Index

Agate, James, 115
Alexander, George, 189
Alexander, Miss, 123
Allen, Sir Hugh, 67
Allgood, Sarah, 114, 138, **141**
Alma-Tadema, Laura, 161
Amies, Hardy, 246
Andersen, Mrs, 244
Andersen, Hans, 138
Andrews, Henry, 76
Andersen, Hans, 138
Arlott, John, 208
Armstrong, John, 137
Arnold, Matthew, 12, 62
Ashton, Sir Leigh, 84, 88, 234, 238
Asquith, Earl of, and Oxford, 65, 76
Asquith, Margot, 76
Auden, W. H., 182
Austen, Lady, 83
Ayrton, Michael, 215

Baddeley, Hermione, 183
Bakst, Léon, 61, 136
Balfour, Ronald, 197, 209
Balmain, Pierre, 241, 242
Barker, Ernest, 58
Barker, Florence Mary, 16
Batten, Jean, 209
Bax, Arnold, 125
Beaton, Cecil, 152 190,
Beddington, Jack, 203
Beerbohm Max, 88, 94, 95, 96, 99
Beerbohm, Mrs, 94, 96
Bell, Clive, 111
Bell, Vanessa, 110
Bennett, Arnold, 99, 112, 127, 128
Benois, Alexander, 131, 190
Benois, Nadia, 190
Berenson, Bernard, 100, 101
Bergner, Elizabeth, 143
Betjeman, John, 28
Binyon, Laurence, 106, 213
Birkenhead, Earl of, 65, 66
Birkenhead, Lady, 128
Birnie-Philip, Miss, 214, 215
Birrell, Augustine, 128
Blake, Vernon, 110
Blanche, Jacques Émile, 123
Blunden, Edmund, 62
Boothby, Lord, 211
Borenius, Tancred, 168

Boucher, François, 243, 244, 245, 249
Boult, Sir Adrian, 31
Bowra, Sir Maurice, 60, 80, 81
Brecht, Bertholt, 132, 139, 143
Brent, Romney, 146, 147, 148, 151, 152
Brockhurst, Gerald, 109
Brook, Peter, 237
Brown, Ford Madox, 122, 123
Brown, Pamela, 194

Campbell, Commander, 237
Campbell of Airds, Col. Ian, 173
Campbell, Mrs Patrick, 187, 188, 189, 190
Campbell, R. J., 26
Campbell, Stella Patrick, 189
Cape, Jonathan, 187, 189
Carpenter, Dr Estlin, 36
Carrick, Edward, see Craig, Edward
Chamberlain, Sir Neville, 197
Charteris, Sir Evan, 128
Chesterton, G. K., 112
Christie, Father S. V., 66, 67
Church, Richard, 113
Churchill, Lord Ivor, 195
Churchill, Sir Winston, 203, 215
Clark, Sir Kenneth, 212, 213
Clausen, Sir George, 110, 111
Cochran, Sir Charles, 145, 146, 147, 149, 150, 151, 152, 169, 175
Cocteau, Jean, 129, 139
Codrington, Prof K. de B., 84
Cohen, Harriet, 125
Colefax, Lady, 128
Collingridge, Alan, 65
Collins, Frank, 151
Colson, Percy, 169, 170
Condamine, Robin de la, see Farquharson
Connolly, Cyril 211
Coward, Noël, 211
Courtenay, Lady, 37
Craig, Edie, 215
Craig, Edward, 96, 131, 155
Craig, Gordon, 95, 96, 131, 132, 155, 215
Craig, Mrs, 96
Cripps, Sir Stafford, 37
Crowley, Aleister, 116, 117, 118, 119, 226, 227, 228, 229, 230, 231
Cunnington, Dr C. Willet, 241
Curtis-Bennett, Sir Noel, 208

Darwin, Bernard, 212
Davies, Fanny, 31
Dawkins, Professor, 166, 168
Dawson, Geoffrey, 213
Dean, Basil, 141, 142
Dean-Paul, Brenda, 119
de la Condamine, Robin, *see* Farquhar-
    son
de la Mare, Walter, 112, 113
Delysia, 121
Demant, Canon, 37
de Margerie, Raymond, 194
de Mille, Agnes, 149
de Wohl, Louis, 225, 226
Dicksee, Sir Frank, 111
Dietrich, Marlene, 156
Dior, Christian, 241, 247
Dobson, Frank, 111
Dolin, Anton, 169
Douglas, Lord Alfred, 168, 169, 199
Douglas, Sholto, 168
Drinkwater, John, 95, 113, 124
Duff, Lady Juliet, 109
Dukes, Ashley, 115, 144

Easton, J. Murray, 175
Eliot, T. S., 39, 213
Ellis, Mary, 146
Elton, Lord, 62
Enthoven, Mrs Gabrielle, 132, 133,
    189
Epstein, Sir Jacob, 111, 199, 236
Evans, Dame Edith, 115, 150

Fagan, J. B., 136
Fairbanks, Douglas Jnr, 153, 154, 155,
    156, 193
Fairbanks, The, 152
Farjeon, Herbert, 183, 184
Farnol, Geoffrey, 153
Farquharson, Robert, 119, 120, 121
Ffrangcon-Davies, Gwen, 139
Flügel, Prof J. C., 242
Fougasse, 113
Foyle, Christina, 157
Foyle, William, 157
Franklin, Ellis, 107
Fraser, Claud Lovat, 131
Freedman, Barnett, 108, 109
Freeman, John, 90
Fry, Roger, 110

Galsworthy, John, 80
Gantillon, Simon, 139
Gazelee, Sir Stephen, 212

George, W. L., 100
Gertler, Mark, 115
Gielgud, Sir John, 132, 133, 134, 136,
    211
Gill, Eric, 111
Godfrey, Peter, 139, 140
Golding, Louis, 62
Goldring, Douglas, 123
Gooden, Stephen, 127
Goss, John, 115
Gosse, Edmund, 28, 90, 91, 92, 93, 100
Gosse, Mrs, 91
Gosse, Sylvia, 93
Gould, Gerald, 110
Grant, Duncan, 110, 111
Graves, Robert, 62
Green, Julien, 174
Gregory, Maundy, 168
Grigg, Sir Edward, 212
Guedalla, Philip, 112, 124, 125

Haden, Annie, 123
Haden, Sir Seymore, 106
Haggard, Stephen, 182
Haire, Norman, 121
Haldane, J.B.S., 59
Haldane, Lord, 65
Hamilton, General, Sir Ian, 212, 213
Hammill, Katherine, 184
Hammond, Aubrey, 141, 142
Harcourt-Smith, Sir Cecil, 88
Hardie, Martin, 86, 87, 94, 106, 109,
    112
Hardwicke, Sir Cedric, 139
Harris, Lady, 230
Harris, Robert, 136
Harrod, Sir Roy, 80, 81
Hartley, L. P., 61
Hawkins, Sir Anthony, *see* Hope,
    Anthony
Headlam, Cuthbert, 213
Heal, Ambrose, 168
Healy, Maurice, 168, 173, 175, 176,
    177
Heffernan, Jo, 124, 214
Hervey, Lilian, 162
Herz, Frank, 125, 136, 144
Hickinbotham, Edward, 31, 32
Hill, Stuart, 121
Hinton, Mary, 194
Hoare, Eustace, 177
Hobson, Harold, 237
Hogarth, Mary, 90, 93
Holland, Vyvyan, 164, 165, 166, 169,
    173, 174, 175, 178, 204
Hollis, Christopher, 61
Honey, G. F., 14
Hope, Anthony, 112

Index

Hore-Belisha, Lord, 65, 66
Horton, Percy, 108
Hügel, Baron von, 36, 69
Hughes, Richard, 62, 209
Hunt, Violet, 121, 122, 123
'Hutch', 121
Hutchinson, Mrs Mary, 211
Huxley, Aldous, 62, 113
Huxley, Julian, 59, 60

Iddesleigh, Lord, 158
Irving, Ernest, 141
Isham, Sir Gyles, 182

Jacks, L. P., 36, 56, 69
Jacks, Maurice, 36
Jackson, Sir Barry, 133, 136, 185, 186
Jacob, Prof E. F., 80, 81
Jacobs, W. W., 21, 112
Jensen, Jackie, 248
Joad, Professor, 237
John, Augustus, 94, 99, 111, 116, 123, 210, 227
Johnston, see Layton
Jones, Robert Edmond, 131
Joseph, H. W. B., 58, 59

Kelly, Grace, 117
Kelly, Sir Gerald, 117
Kennedy, Daisy, 124
Keynes, Lord, 211
Kielland, Mrs, 244
Kimmins, Anthony, 154
Kindersley, Lord, 203, 234
King, William, 88
Knoblock, Edward, 194
Knopf, Alfred, 144
Knox, E. V., 113, 212
Knox, Sir Malcolm, 217

L. D. H., 32, 33, 34, 35, 37, 38, 39, 40, 41, 42, 46, 55, 56, 70, 71, 73, 74, 75, 77, 78, 100, 164
Lamb, Henry, 111
Lancaster, Osbert, 113
Lanchester, Elsa, 137, 138, 193
Lankaster, Ray, 98
Landi, Elissa, 136, 155
Lane, John, 91
Lang, Matheson, 120
Larraldi, Romolo, see Brent, Romney
Lascelles, Sir Alan, 212
Laughton, Charles, 138, 196
Laver, Arthur James, 15
Laver, George, 14
Laver, Henry, 13, 14, 15
Laver, James, 15
Laver, Lucy, 20
Laver, Robert, 15

Lavery, Lady, 154
Lawrence, D. H., 89, 140
Lawrence, Gertrude, 146, 148, 149, 152, 153
Layton and Johnstone, 121
Lehmann, Beatrix, 139
Leigh, Vivien, 144
Lenk, Torsten, 243, 244
Leslie, Sir Shane, 166, 167, 168
Lewis, D. B. Wyndham, 113
Lewis, Wyndham, 89, 111, 168
Liddell-Hart, Capt B. H., 241
Livingstone, Sir R. W., 80
Lock, W. J., 112
Loraine, Robert, 115
Low, David, 112
Lucas, E. V., 112

McBey, James, 109
MacCarthy, Desmond, 128, 129, 130
MacCarthy, Mrs, 128
McEvan, Ambrose, 111
Mackenzie, Compton, 22, 57
Maclagan, Lady, 214
Maclagan, Sir Eric, 88, 127, 212, 213, 229, 234
Mac Liammóir, Michaéal, 169
McQuilland, Louis, 113, 115
Macy, George, 199
Mair, George, 114
Malcolm, Sir Dugald, 212
Mansfield, Katherine, 118, 119
Marinotti, Paolo, 24, 244
Marlow, Louis, see Wilkinson, L. U.
Marsh, Sir Edward, 109, 128
Marshall, Herbert, 115
Marshall, Norman, 192, 194
Martin, Jane, 15
Martin, Sarah, 19
Martindale, Father, S.J., 70
Masefield, John, 62, 65
Mason, James, 194
Maughan, Somerset, 152, 183
Mauriac, François, 194, 195
Maurice, Gen Sir Frederick, 107
Maxwell, Elsa, 152
May, Phil, 210
Mayer, Dorothy Moulton, 125, 127
Mayer, Ernest, 136, 141
Mayer, Sir Robert, 125
Messell, Oliver, 149, 150
Metman, Philip, 223
Meynell, Sir Francis, 127, 168
Millay, Edna St Vincent, 199
Miller, Gilbert, 184
Mills, Florence, 121
Moiseiwitch, Tanya, 124
Monckton, Sir Walter, 212

Index

Moore, Doris Langley, 238, 241
Moore, George, 93, 94, 99, 130
Moore, Henry, 235
Moore, Sturge, 168, 199
Morgan, Campbell, 26
Morgan, Charles, 62, 194
Mortimer, Raymond, 128
Mottram, R. H., 113
Muggeridge, Malcolm, 113
Murray, Basil, 61
Murray, John, 240
Murray, Sir Gilbert, 61
Murry, Middleton, 181

Nash, Paul, 111, 131
Neame, Barry, 171
Neuburg, Victor, 117
Newbolt, Sir Henry, 112
Ney, Marie, 144
Nichols, Beverley, 57, 61, 179
Nichols, Robert, 62
Nicholson, Sir William, 111, 210
Nicolson, Sir Harold, 112

O'Brien, Kate, 138
O'Casey, Sean, 138
Oke, Richard, 132
Olivier, Laurence, 142
Oman, Charles, 82
O'Neill, Maire, 14, 138, 141
Orpen, Sir William, 95, 100, 111
Otter, Gwen, 115, 116, 117, 118, 119, 121, 129
Owen, Will, 21, 112

Palmer, A. H., 106
Palmer, George, 88
Partington, Wilfred, 109, 110, 111
Patch, Wally, 154
Pemberton, Max, 112
Percy, Esmé, 120
Pevsner, Nikolaus, 240
Pinto, V. de S., 62
Pirie, Gordon, 168
Piscator, Erwin, 143
Playfair, Sir Nigel, 115
Plomer, William, 237
Poel, William, 110
Pollitt, Harry, 180
Porter, Alan, 62
Porter, Cole, 146, 147, 148
Porter, Mrs, 147
Powell, Dilys, 237
Price, Prof H. H., 68
Pryce-Jones, Alan, 28
Pryde, James, 111, 210

Queensberry, Cathleen, 169
Queensberry, Marquess of, 169

Radcliffe, Viscount, 60, 80, 81
Rambert, Marie, 115
Ranevsky, Boris, 114
Rau, Arthur, 76
Rawlings, Margaret, 141
Rawnsley, Canon, 33
Ray, Cyril, 113
Read, Sir Herbert, 88, 89
Reinhardt, Max, 134
Reville-Terry, 240
Reynolds, Alfred, 185, 186
Reynolds, Quentin, 213
Rhoades, Geoffrey, 108
Richards, Grant, 166, 168
Richthofen, Frieda von, 88
Ricketts, Charles, 131
Ridley, Sir Jasper, 213
Robeson, Paul, 121
Robins, W. P., 109
Robinson, Cayley, 110
Rocamora, 244
Romains, Jules, 138, 196
Ross, Marita, 162, 163
Rosse, Countess of, 150
Rothenstein, Mrs, 100
Rothenstein, Sir John, 99
Rothenstein, Sir William, 89, 90, 91, 93, 94, 95, 96, 97, 98, 99, 102, 108, 111, 123
Rothschild, Lady, 211
Ruskin, John, 21, 102, 122
Russell, Lord, 211, 251

Sadleir, Michael, 110, 160
Saintsbury, Prof George, 164, 170
Samuel, Lord, 107
Sandeman, Christopher, 194
Sargent, John, 110
Sargent, Sir Malcolm, 126
Sauer, Emil, 125
Sayers, Dorothy, 183
Schneider, Dr Hugo, 244
Scott, Geoffrey, 102
Scott, Harold, 137
Scott, Lady Sybil, 102
Seabrooke, William, 230
Searle, Ronald, 113
Shaw, George Bernard, 76, 95, 99, 185, 188
Shaw, Mrs, 185
Shaw, Reeves, 126, 127
Sheringham, George, 131
Sickert, Walter R., 90, 93, 99, 110
Simon, André, 165, 170, 173, 174, 175, 177

Index

Simon, Lady, 76
Simon, Lord, 26, 76
Simon, Rev Mark, 25
Sitwell, Sacheverell, 102
Sitwells, The, 62, 91
Smith, A. H., 80, 81
Smith, Bosworth, 200
Smith, Gipsy, 26
Smith, Logan Pearsall, 28
Souter, John B., 163
Spender, Stephen, 180
Spooner, Warden, 58, 68
Squire, Sir John, 62, 90, 100, 112, 170,
    199
Steel, A. B., 80, 81
Steen, Marguerite, 210
Sternheim, Carl, 144
Stewart-Liberty, Ivor, 171
Stiebel, Victor, 246
Stone, William, 161, 213
Stopes, Dr Marie, 66, 67
Strachey, John, 62
Straus, Ralph, 112, 166
Strauss, Dr Eric, 80, 81
Struther, Jan, 130
Symons, Arthur, 110, 199
Symons, A. J. A., 165, 166, 168, 170,
    171, 172

Thesiger, Ernest, 119, 139
Thienen, Prof F. van, 244
Thomas, Dr Bruno, 244
Thomas, Anne, 14
Tod, Quentin, 141
Toller, Ernst, 134, 139
Tonks, Henry, 111
Topolski, Feliks, 235
Tovey, Donald, 31
Trappes-Lomax, Michael, 80, 81
Turleigh, Veronica, 136, 137, 139, 140,
    169, 182, 194, 209, 210, 211, 243
Turner, J. M. W.,

Urquhart, 'Sligger', 70
Ustinov, Peter, 190
Ustinow, Vladimir, 190

Valentine, Alexander B. B., 61
Van der Poel, A., 171
Vernon, Anne, 238
Vignaud, Edith, *see* Vernon, Anne
Villars, Paul, 130

Waddell, Lela, 117
Waldman, Milton, 209
Walpole, Hugh, 128
Walter, Bruno, 125
Warren, Dorothy, 140
Waugh, Alec, 119, 174
Waugh, Evelyn, 57, 70, 119
Webb, Mrs Sydney, 37
Weekley, Montague, 88
Weingartner, Felix, 125
Weisse, Henry Victor, 31
Welby, Earle, 168
Welch, Elizabeth, 148
Wells, H. G., 22, 94, 144, 174
West, Rebecca, 124
Wheen, Arthur, 89
Wilenski, R. H., 237
Wilkinson, Louis Umfraville, 231
Williams-Ellis, Clough, 138, 209
Wilson, Sir Arnold, 181
Wilson, Donald, 238
Wimperis, Arthur, 112, 113
Winston, Bruce, 143
Wise, Thomas J., 110
Wolfe, Edward, 194
Wolfe, Sir Humbert, 112, 199
Wong, Anna May, 142, 143
Woodruff, Douglas, 66, 80, 81
Woodward, Prof, 80, 81
Woolcott, Alexander, 184
Wright, Thomas, 92
Wyndham, Richard, 172, 173

Yeats, W. B., 31, 62, 66, 93, 94
Yeats-Brown, Francis, 181

Zinkeisen, Doris, 150